A Short History
of Rudeness

Also by Mark Caldwell

The Last Crusade

A Short History
of Rudeness

*Manners, Morals, and
Misbehavior in Modern America*

Mark Caldwell

Picador USA / New York

p. 13—Reprinted with the permission of Simon & Schuster from *The Poems of W. B. Yeats: A New Edition*, edited by Richard J. Finnernan. Copyright © 1924 by Macmillan Publishing Company, renewed 1952 by Bertha Georgie Yeats.
pp. 82–83—Reprinted with the permission of IBM Corporation.

Picador® is a U.S. registered trademark and is used by St. Martin's Press under license from Pan Books Limited.

Production Editor: David Stanford Burr

Book Design: James Sinclair

Library of Congress Cataloging-in-Publication Data

Caldwell, Mark.
　　A short history of rudeness : manners, morals, and misbehavior in modern America / Mark Caldwell.—1st Picador USA ed.
　　　　p.　　cm.
　　Includes bibliographical references.
　　ISBN 0-312-20432-9
　　1. Etiquette—United States—History.　2. United States—Social life and customs.　I. Title.
BJ1853.C23　　1999
395'.0973—dc21

99-22051
CIP

10　9　8　7　6　5　4

For

James O'Shea
and
Agnes Ball O'Shea

contents

acknowledgments

I would like to thank Ann Rittenberg, my agent, without whose time, encouragement, and criticism this book could never have been undertaken, and George Witte, my editor at Picador USA, without whose genial, sensible, and shrewd advice it would never have been completed.

Thanks are also due to Robert Godfrey, Doug Golde, David Kaye, Walter Kendrick, Kit Kreilick, Jim McCabe, Doyle McCarthy, Carrie McGinnis, James O'Shea, Agnes O'Shea, Daniel Papernik, M.D., Ralph Sassone, Lois Schwartz, Polly Shulman, and Fred Wegener.

Nor could the book have been written without generous help and cooperation from the IBM Corporation and the IBM Archives, the New York Public Library, the New-York Historical Society, the Bard College Library, and the Fordham University School of Law.

Finally, I owe a debt of gratitude to Fordham University for its generous support.

. . . Arrogance and hatred are the wares
Peddled in the thoroughfares.
How but in custom and in ceremony
Are innocence and beauty born?
Ceremony's a name for the rich horn,
And custom for the spreading laurel tree.
  —William Butler Yeats (1865–1939)

Hey, kid, pass the fuckin' mustard.
—Attributed to George Herman "Babe"
        Ruth (1895–1948)

A Short History
of Rudeness

introduction

What *are* manners, anyway?

Elizabeth L. Post—Emily's granddaughter-in-law—is *Good Housekeeping*'s resident specialist on this thorny subject. In her January 1994 column, "Etiquette for Every Day," she fielded a dozen questions. They run a formidable and wholly typical gamut; Heloise, Ann Landers, Dr. Ruth, and the Pet Doctor combined could hardly face a more challenging fusillade.

One reader asks: if somebody holds two doors for you in a row, do you thank him/her twice? (Up to you.) Another: how do you handle a foil-clad baked potato? (Peel the foil off, but don't crumple it into a ball.) On the morning of their departure, is it rude for the hostess to bowl into her guests' bedroom, rip the sheets off the mattress, and suggest they leave early in order not to miss their plane? (Er, yes.) Is it permissible for the store where you've set up your bridal registry to send ads to your wedding invitees? (No.) What do you do with the sorbet sometimes served between courses at formal dinners? (Eat it.) What should you say at a restaurant if your sister-in-law starts shoveling the condiment packets into her purse? ("You know, you could get into trouble doing that.")[1]

Almost any problem, it seems, can pose as a question of etiquette, and few etiquette questions resolve to a single universally acknowledged answer. Most of *Good Housekeeping*'s readers' queries, for example, might have elicited replies completely different from Elizabeth Post's, yet equally plausible (tactfully ignore the pilfering in-law; use a fork to denude your wrapped potato; doing up the beds is an acceptably diplomatic way to rouse your guests and ensure they make their flight). Manners, good and bad, pervade so much of daily life that at times they seem to embrace everything—considerateness and selfishness, freedom and anarchy, birth and death, cooking and upholstery, crime and punishment, linens and sex. Manners are trivial, profound, and amorphous beyond compassing. Manners are what is left when serious issues of human relations are removed from consideration; yet without manners serious human relations are impossible. And everybody cares about them, from Castel Gandolfo and the White House to San Quentin (especially the latter; society's outcasts are understandably alert to slights, and so beware above all perils the drug dealer who thinks he's met with disrespect).

Indeed, in recent years civility and the perceived trashing thereof have become an American obsession, from cultural critics to politicians. In 1998, even New York's mayor, the notably abrasive and snappish Rudolph W. Giuliani, embarked on a quixotic crusade to improve the manners of the city's civil servants, pedestrians, motorists, taxi drivers, and deliverymen. Politician or pundit, the reformer's theme is usually the same: a rude culture of self-indulgence has trampled good manners and public virtue; oafishness and riot abound; the tide of vulgarity must be stemmed. Yet this is hardly a novel obsession. Americans have undergone periodic anxiety attacks over their manners since the dawn of the republic. There was, for instance, a flurry of concern during the first few decades of the nineteenth century, and another at the dawn of the twentieth. Indeed, the cyclical character of this worry—its tendency to recur amidst the stocktaking natural as one era fades and another prospectively looms—suggests that whatever its merits our current preoccupation with civility may be part of a general syndrome of premillennial jitters.

It's difficult to pinpoint the earliest tremor of this latest, thousand-year manners panic, but Allan Bloom's surprise best-seller *The Closing of the American Mind* (1987) is a likely candidate. On the surface a denunciation of contemporary American higher education—which (Bloom thought) had abandoned rigor in favor of moral and intellectual fads—the book was at bottom a long howl of despair over lost civility. Instead of guarding and perpetuating the refined culture of a classically trained elite, Bloom argued, the American university, beginning in the despised 1960s, had become a rubber stamp of mindless approval for vulgar cant and rude prejudice. The result was not so much an intellectual loss as a moral and cultural one, a fatal lowering of the nation's civic tone, a wholesale abandonment of the elite values that once led the nation, even if they never wholly dominated it. "Our desire becomes an oracle we consult," Bloom wrote. "It is now the last word, while in the past it was the questionable and dangerous part of us."[2]

The Closing of the American Mind quickly became more than a manifesto against a cheapened education: it heralded a still-ongoing wrangle over the perceived decline of manners, the loss of a once dominant culture of elegance, morality, taste, and restraint. This debate ultimately engaged participants of all political stripes and from all backgrounds. In 1997 the chief justice of New York's Court of Appeals promulgated a civility code for combative attorneys and supercilious judges (a lawyer quickly shot back in a *New York Times* Op-Ed piece that attorneys were, after all, *trained* to be ferocious). On CNN, a Virginia traffic cop blamed the worsening accident rate on a meltdown in driver manners; the National Highway Traffic Safety Administration recently estimated that uncontrolled rage was a factor in twenty-eight thousand highway deaths every year.[3] Businesses, like Manhattan's Etiquette International, have sprung up to grind the spikes off your interpersonal interface for a price; the Connecticut-based (and incomparably named) Academie for Instruction in the Social Graces offers daylong manners seminars for children at flossy hotels.

Even foundations have found the problem grave enough to address. Perhaps prompted by examples of eloquence like a recent U.S. representative's demand, on the floor of the House, "for Congress to tell the President to shove his veto pen up his deficit,"[4] the Pew Charitable Trust recently bankrolled a $700,000 weekend retreat in Hershey, Pennsylvania, in an effort to cure Congress's addiction to invective and personal abuse; 220 U.S. representatives attended. Of course it did little good: within weeks Tom DeLay (R-Tex.) and David Obey (D-Wis.) were in the headlines for a shoving match and a volley of obscenities on the House floor.[5]

As I prepared to undertake this book, I was first encouraged, then not a little nonplussed, by the intensity of interest the subject provoked among friends, colleagues, acquaintances. Everyone—whether notably fastidious or a confirmed and unapologetic slob—leaped upon it with a firm opinion and multiple examples of noteworthy tact or (oftener) ill-breeding. But something about manners, in theory such a fussy subject, quickly arouses passions and *idées fixes*. People think the deepest essence of rudeness epitomized in their last brush with it, and brusquely dismiss competing definitions. An editor friend reported outrage when a deli clerk playfully announced he wouldn't hand her bagel over unless she told him her first name. Didn't this mixture of overfamiliarity and coercion combine the two most basic—indeed, the only real—forms of boorishness? An academic colleague slipped into a lecture on blue jeans, which, he insisted, were a skeleton key to the mysteries of manners. Designer jeans—tacky to the Levis-clad bourgeoisie, stylish to the working class—embodied, he insisted, a collision of values that struck to the root of why people disagree about matters of etiquette. An attorney, thinking still more abstractly, dwelt on the currently powerful urge to criminalize behavior such as sexual harassment that might once have been thought merely rude if reprehensible at all. Didn't this portend a dangerous shift in our understanding of civility, a tendency to inflate conflicts once resolved informally into wounding gladiatorial combat?

None of these questions is irrelevant. Any or all might provoke an appeal to Miss Manners, Mary Mitchell (King Features Syndicate's Ms. Demeanor and author of *The Complete Idiot's Guide to Etiquette*), Elizabeth L. or Peggy Post. Each would respond with a common-sense ruling on the problem at hand. Yet none really explores at length the underlying dynamics of civility and rudeness, and none attempts to explain why, as the millennium approaches, we seem so suddenly and perhaps disproportionately exercised about the subject.

This book aims to address some of these systemic questions. It doesn't compete with Judith Martin or Letitia Baldrige, offers no advice, won't answer questions, and won't settle quarrels. In fact, I rather hope it will start a few. And it won't treat etiquette as a bottomless well of amusing absurdities, like the well-established tradition of humor books that send up the inexplicable customs of ages past. It will, on the other hand, explore what makes manners so compelling a concern, yet at the same time so elusive. It will try to map out the difference between civility and rudeness by plumbing their hidden social, psychological, and even biological undercurrents.

And it will address a nagging contemporary conundrum. If on the one hand America is convinced good manners are important, why did 89 percent of the respondents to a 1996 *U.S. News & World Report* survey feel that the nation was basically uncivil? Were the millions who flocked to *Beavis and Butt-head Do America* in the early weeks of its 1996 release all members of the remaining 11 percent? In a society ostensibly worried about the threat of barbarism, why are Howard Stern and Dennis Rodman culture heroes; why are gut-tersnipe talk shows and tabloid TV offal like *Cops*—ready-to-hand signs of imminent apocalypse—nonetheless enduringly popular?

To answer such questions requires a close look at the history of politeness and rudeness in America since the turn of the twentieth century. But useful though I hope this will prove, it's also a task to make the historian blanch. Etiquette is everywhere, rudeness ubiq-uitous. Yet both dwell oftenest in the daily goings-on of unofficial life and thus elude "serious" annals. When George Bush vomited into Prime Minister Miyazawa's lap in Tokyo in 1992, he wrecked a state dinner and ruffled Japanese-American relations, but the in-cident found its natural forum in grapevine jokes, late-night TV, political cartoons, and humor columns. Our manners appear in the sharpest relief in ephemera—movies, broadcast media, popular fic-tion, mass-market magazines, filler news items, business backwaters such as the wedding and funeral industries—enterprises that don't affect the macroeconomic picture but touch us at critical junctures in our personal lives.

Authorities like Miss Manners and Letitia Baldrige are, for all their influence, very much voices of popular culture. Their attitudes, being influential and widely shared, are significant, but also often half-formulated or even self-contradictory, shriveling under close scrutiny. No accredited university offers a degree in etiquette, and few of the great modern doyennes of manners had any measurable qualifications for the trade. Letitia Baldrige, at least, served as Jackie Kennedy's chief of staff and social secretary to the U.S. ambassador at Rome. But Emily Post, though socially well connected, began her writing career as a novelist. Amy Vanderbilt started out as a beat reporter on Staten Island. Viola Tree (1844–1938), a British eti-quette columnist in the 1930s for Lord Northcliffe's *Sunday Dis-patch*, who came to the trade with experience as an actress and opera singer, was disarmingly frank about her lack of training. "The in-formation given to my readers," she once wrote, "is either from memory, mimicry, or instinct."[6] Civility and rudeness play themselves out just where the academic hesitates to go, among the un-measurables of daily life, in anecdotes, in random events and imperfectly recorded human exchanges that may often seem un-readable, too eccentric and evanescent for systematic analysis.

And insofar as they *can* be analyzed, they demand multiple ap-proaches, resisting subjection to any one discipline. History, soci-ology, anthropology, psychology, communications theory, language, and linguistics—all offer resources. Nor can the hard sciences be ignored: one of the bedrock principles of sociobiology (the still-nascent and controversial field pioneered by Edward O. Wilson) is that manners, whatever their moral content, are products of biolog-ical evolution with significant echoes in the lives of other animals. Wilson cites a delightfully apposite old German fable, according to which a group of porcupines, massed together against the cold, freeze when too far apart and prick each other when too close to-gether. When they finally work out the exact degree of proximity that keeps them both warm and unstabbed, they call it good man-ners.[7]

This book owes a great deal to the research of scholars in a number of disciplines, as the following pages will demonstrate. But my own perspective is that of the literary and cultural critic most interested in reading a layered text of words, actions, and images for meanings both manifest and covert. This is a useful way of telling the story of twentieth-century American manners, weaving together multiple narrative threads, many characters (admirable and not), shifts and nuances of tone, and a wealth of hidden or unconscious themes. In pursuing and elucidating such themes, I have co-opted—and I hope sufficiently credited—the work of dozens of writers and investigators from a wide range of fields. But gossip, media buzz, and anecdote are the richest archives for a study of modern civility, and though often suspect to the historian or scientist, they are in-dispensable to the student of culture, replete with veins of meaning that mustn't be ignored, even when slender and prone to break off without warning.

A history of civility and rudeness is also necessarily thematic rather than chronological. Manners don't evolve along a time line, like fashion or automobile design. Rather, tectonic pressures build slowly, then erupt: the social landscape tends to realign itself in shocks. The best way to track such changes is to examine the fault lines—the places where civility breaks down and reconfigures itself. Movement, for example: a master theme in the national narrative is mobility—which, in common with all kinds of change, challenges social comity. Working life; marriage and death; the vital but troubled bonds between parents and children, between men and women, among people of different race; all will serve as touchstones for analysis. And no chronicle of modern manners can afford to ignore the representational realm that rose to echo the real world but now threatens, like the shadows of the statues in Plato's cave, to replace it in our minds: press, film, TV, cyberspace.

As we range among such topics, several themes will recur so persistently as to warrant raising them briefly here as a guide to what follows.

Perhaps most germane is a reminder of how treacherous the subject can be, how deftly it eludes efforts to pin it down; how one's strenuous attempt to placate can offend or enrage the intended recipient; how, in the right circumstances, the crudest remark, rightly phrased, can restore a group's fraying social temper. Indeed, manners are so consistently confusing that one comes to suspect this is essential to their proper functioning. Civility in one context may be barbarism in another; what's superficially polite can be covertly rude, and vice versa. The etiquette columnist's simple answer to a manners question may settle a dispute, but usually skates over vexing ethical and interpersonal issues that a more ruminative consideration would address and perhaps resolve.

Consider a case on which I was asked, as tyro etiquette authority, to hand down a ruling. A friend (thirtyish, male, on his way to the dentist) heads for an empty subway seat on which a truculent-looking lady has placed a carpetbag. The friend, deciding from her mien not to risk a spoken request, just sits down. She hisses out, "Can't you even say 'Excuse me'?" What, the friend asks, was the proper response? Silence? A probably unmerited and certainly insincere but soothing apology? Or a gratifying off-with-her-head retort?

A pragmatic solution is easily devised: Utter the apology, think the retort. This calms the woman, saves the friend's self-respect, and prevents the incident from escalating into a brawl. But it also evades some real dilemmas. Perhaps it was rude to nudge the carpetbag out of the way; but it was also rude to commandeer two seats. Who was ruder? Or who politer, since both parties might plausibly claim they were only trying to advance the cause of good manners? The friend's silence was meant not to provoke an already riled-looking woman; her protest a plea for considerateness. And isn't such casuistry beside the point anyway? The deepest beauty of "Excuse me" is exactly that it's not a true apology, indeed implies no real emotion at all. Its rote vacuity is just what makes it so useful. It helps us steer daily among countless social reefs, without effort or even thought, much less a crisis of conscience.

There was, as an alert reader would surely have divined, a troublesome intimation of class strife in this subway contretemps. The friend was a Manhattan yuppie, the woman wore the blue uniform of a home health-care aide or food service worker. Did she bristle because she'd detected something patronizing in his attitude? Would a shopping bag from Henri Bendel have transformed the whole situation from the outset, by signaling to the friend that he was dealing with an equal—a like-minded and like-privileged person, in one's relations with whom suspicion and conflict are simply not an expected part of the picture?

Class is to the discussion of civility what the ghost of the murdered king is to *Hamlet*—a ubiquitous exhalation poisoning the atmosphere, elusive, intimidating, but impossible to lay to rest. Emily Post was a solidly entrenched member of New York's social elite (her father, Bruce Price, developed Tuxedo Park, New York, perhaps the most exclusive gated enclave of the early twentieth century); Amy Vanderbilt bore a name that, while it would have rung as hopelessly upstart in a blue-blooded Astor's or a Rhinelander's ear, sounded nearly royal to the public at large. "Polite" and "classy" are at least semisynonymous: an 1879 British etiquette manual frankly defined manners as "the barrier which society draws around itself as a shield."[8] Rarely is it conscience or even aesthetics that determines good social form, but rather our sense of what "the best" people do. Yet "best" is a slippery adjective, masking a treacherous confusion. Are the cynosures of civility the best people morally, or merely members of a widely (and perhaps foolishly) envied status group? Our national values and our moment in history conspire to make us suspicious of such invidious modes of distinction.

Thus, as egalitarian and democratic Americans, we often wax vague or self-contradictory about what we mean by "classy." This problem bedeviled Emily Post through several successive editions of her *Etiquette: The Blue Book of Social Usage*. If class means style and elegance, an adroit beggar might exemplify it as fully as a duke. Yet, of course, such "class" is not in practice quite as independent as a strict moralist might hope from money, social position, or the arrogant self-confidence that comes from belonging to a privileged coterie. Good manners, so appealing when they seem to rise from kindliness, become repellent when they abet the cause of snobbery, envy, or social injustice.

And snobbery, be it noted, is a thoroughly bidirectional vice. If the bourgeoisie condescends to the lower ranks, the blue-collar classes are equally capable of what might be termed con*a*scending— branding social higher-ups as snotty, trend crazed, vulgar, and immoral. This is neatly illustrated in an incident recorded by the British anthropologist Viola Klein, when a working-class woman visited Buckingham Palace and was scandalized by its window draperies. Proper housekeeping in the woman's native Lancashire meant hanging curtains with their patterns facing outward to the street, matching each other and the color scheme of the house exterior. But "the front curtains at the Palace did not match, and it was a sign of pretty sluttish housekeeping in her opinion."[9]

The ready entry of anger and resentment into questions of etiquette reveals another problem: the propensity of manners to get themselves hopelessly entangled with ethics. Rudeness rarely kills and politeness will not by itself earn one sainthood: in theory, therefore, they ought to lend themselves to even-toned discussion, with the discriminating detachment of connoisseurship. Instead, they tend provoke a moral passion utterly out of proportion, one might think, to their significance. Books on civility, from the late Christopher Lasch's *The Culture of Narcissism* (1979) to Robert Hughes's *Culture of Complaint* (1994) and Gertrude Himmelfarb's *The De-Moralization of Society* (1995) are all jeremiads and united, however different their political perspectives, by the tone of high dudgeon they take at the perceived coarsening of American manners.

In one sense, this is reassuring: those who express outrage or alarm over the state of civility are at least affirming its importance, either because they see etiquette as a seismograph, recording shifts and disruptions in deep-lying morals, or because actively practicing it improves those morals. Such sentiments ennoble good manners, surely, yet don't necessarily afford a basis for enforcing them. In fact, they may accomplish the very reverse, by overburdening a system of semi-instinctual customs that collapses if scrutinized too closely. Does an insistence on their ethical importance strengthen the delicate machinery of manners or merely throw a spanner into the works? This is a crucial question, and I will return to it repeatedly in the following pages.

A final point: the focus of this book is largely urban, with New York oftener than not supplying the examples analyzed. John Kasson, in his indispensable *Rudeness and Civility* (1990), a study of American etiquette in the nineteenth century, remarked that rural and suburban manners are subjects yet to attract the attention they surely deserve. But that, in part, is because sources are fewer and harder to track down. Since the decline and ultimate demise of late medieval and Renaissance court life, cities have become the chief factories of manners making in the West. In the United States, New York has maintained, at least since the mid-1800s, its dominance, from early etiquette experts like Mary Sherwood to the best known modern names in the field, Emily Post and Amy Vanderbilt.

There's much to study. New York nourishes a deep narcissistic interest in itself, and abounds in scholarly and popular chroniclers, from Jacob Riis to Sidney Lumet, from Washington Irving to Jay McInerney and Tama Janowitz. It was and remains a destination for the most ambitious of the nation's elite, a magnet for those seeking to emulate the privileged, a cauldron of mixing and colliding cultures, and a hothouse for the cultivation of manners new and old. Other metropolises rival it—Boston and Philadelphia in the Victorian era; today, with a culture electronically globalized and decentralized, Los Angeles, Washington, D.C., Chicago, and perhaps other cities compete as engines of cultural change. But New York remains the largest and most compulsively observed American metropolis, and it's thus perhaps the best imaginable human game preserve for the researcher interested in etiquette.

And also, of course, the reverse. To be urbane in the full New York sense has always implied pugnaciousness as well as suavity. And the city has, at least since the middle of the nineteenth century, brooked no competitor as the national (perhaps the world) capital of rudeness.

PART ONE

Public Life

chapter one

Colonel Mann and Mrs. Post: Manners, Morals, and Class in Modern America

The rudest man of the twentieth century was a master of every social grace.

A paradox? Not entirely: as Amy Vanderbilt wrote in the first edition of her enduringly popular etiquette guide, "some of the rudest and most objectionable people I have ever known have been technically the most 'correct'."[1] And Colonel William d'Alton Mann might have been born to prove her point. He appeared in New York in the 1890s, at the dawn of a turbulent era of world war, boom, and depression. Yet if one could believe his *Who's Who* entry, Mann was everything turn-of-the-century Americans most admired: Civil War hero, entrepreneur, business tycoon, millionaire, inventor, editor, publisher. He presided daily over his own table at Delmonico's, the grand restaurant at the corner of Fifth Avenue and 26th Street. Like most real and would-be metropolitan aristocrats, he kept several residences—a Manhattan brownstone, a country house in Morristown, and a private island retreat on Lake George in the Adirondacks, where he dispensed seigniorial hospitality to friends and employees alike. He was a family man, with a faithful, dowdy wife and a daughter on whom he doted.

Yet by 1905 he was being roundly vilified by every respectable newspaper in the city and several national magazines as a social menace, a coarse criminal mocker of every bond that united the privileged world of New York's elite. And for this hurricane of civic outrage, Mann, if he had to trace the blame to a single person, might well have pointed to a then obscure and deeply unhappy young society matron—the thirty-three-year-old Emily Post, a decade and a half before she launched her public career as the century's leading doyenne of manners and protectress of etiquette.

Mann's origins were shadowy and probably humble (his life was thoroughly and entertainingly chronicled in 1965 by *New Yorker* writer Andy Logan).[2] Born in Sandusky, Ohio, on September 27, 1839, to a family of thirteen children, he studied engineering for a while, then earned first a captain's and finally a colonel's commission in the Civil War, ultimately distinguishing himself at Gettysburg. He also raked in a fortune in royalties by inventing an equipment-toting rig for infantry troops, then licensing it to the U.S. and Austrian armies. After the war he settled in Mobile, Alabama, where he manufactured cottonseed oil, dabbled in railroads and oil swindles, founded the *Mobile Register* (which still publishes today), ran for Congress, and invented a luxury railroad car, the "Mann Boudoir Car" (the prototype design for the *Wagons-Lits* still in use on Continental European railroads). In appearance portly, white-haired, snowy-bearded, he might, depending on his mood and the state of your relations with him, appear as either a beaming Santa, thunder-voiced Jehovah, or swaggering Falstaff.

In 1891, his brother, E. D. Mann, vanished in the aftermath of an obscenity conviction and left his business—a soon to be notorious New York weekly named *Town Topics*—leaderless. The magazine had begun life some years earlier as *The American Queen*, edited by Louis Keller, the founder of the *Social Register*, and "dedicated to art, music, literature, and society."[3] Under E. D. Mann, however, while preserving a tone of strict propriety, it ripened into a scandal sheet, faithfully reporting high-society peccadilloes and often identifying perpetrators by name.

With his brother now incommunicado at a location unknown, Colonel Mann came to New York, assumed the editorship, and gradually raised *Town Topics* to a hitherto unmatched mastery in the art of scandal. The gossip was personal, vicious, salacious. But the sophistication with which Mann served it up was a world above that of latter-day tabloids like the *National Enquirer* or the *Globe*. Mann himself rewrote and edited the magazine's opening "Saunterings" feature. The prose was refined, funny, elegant, and razor-sharp, a clear precursor of *The New Yorker*'s "Talk of the Town" in its *soigné* tone, but with a hidden payload of brutal satire underneath the polish. As the Saunterer, Mann became a celebrity in his own right, and apparently an intimate of the very elite he took delight in savaging. "When mature spinsters take it into their heads to indulge themselves in a little souse party," a typical item commenced,

> they should do it in the privacy of their house. I thought this at the *reveillon* at a certain hotel on New Year's Eve, when I saw the hennaed head of a fair but fat and fully forty maiden vainly striving to direct her uncertain feet on a zigzag course around the tables. Ordinarily she is a very handsome lady, but youth—sweet, sweet youth—is the only period at which one may be drunk and still retain some degree of attractiveness.[4]

Nor were all Mann's targets left thus mercifully nameless. When her 1915 charity ball at Sherry's slid into rigor mortis at the intended height of the festivities, and an exasperated Mrs. Alexander Blair Thaw, the Pennsylvania Railroad heiress, hurled herself in a tantrum upon the balalaika orchestra (which had donated its services free of charge), "Saunterings" gleefully identified her.

In 1904, the Saunterer unleashed a scathing attack on the twenty-year-old Alice Roosevelt, just beginning her controversial social career:

> From wearing costly lingerie to indulging in fancy dances for the edification of men was only a step. And then came—second step—indulging freely in stimulants. Flying all around Newport without a chaperon was another thing that greatly concerned Mother Grundy. There may have been no reason for the old lady making such a fuss about it, but if the young woman knew some of the tales that are told at the clubs at Newport she would be more careful in the future about what she does and how she does it. They are given to saying almost anything at the Reading Room, but I was really surprised to hear her name mentioned openly there in connection with that of a certain multi-millionaire of the colony and with certain doings that gentle people are not supposed to discuss. They also said that she should not have listened to the risqué jokes told her by the son of one of her Newport hostesses.[5]

Mann typically wrote "Saunterings" items up from notes supplied by eavesdropping servants or hired spies disguised as ball musicians. But the unsavory side of this information-gathering system hardly fazed him. "There is no feature of my paper of which I am more proud," he wrote, trumpeting Saunterings' "reformative and regenerative influence. To save the sinner by rebuking the sin is an achievement over which the angels rejoice."[6] Mann ducked lawsuits by a clever device: describing the scandal without naming names in one item, then following it with an apparently innocuous social note that just happened to identify the miscreants. Readers quickly cracked the code; *Town Topics* was never successfully sued for libel.

The colonel stoutly maintained—and from all the evidence really seems to have believed—that he was performing a public service. Taunting the errant to purge incivility, however, was not his sole aim. For behind its satiric commentary on the manners of the rich, *Town Topics* was actually the front for a blackmail operation perhaps unique in history. Having nosed out a lapse, Mann would dispatch a henchman, who would threaten to publish in "Saunterings" unless the culprit either bought advertising in the magazine or a block of its essentially worthless stock.

If the victim balked, a damaging item duly appeared (to be followed by as many more as the magazine's considerable ingenuity could gather). But—fiendishly enough—the outcome was just as bad if the blackmailer cooperated, because Mann, in mock gratitude, would then plant not one but a whole series of flattering—indeed, suspiciously unctuous—notices in "Saunterings." This merely had the effect of revealing to the ever-growing number of those who knew how *Town Topics* worked that the subject had either paid (out of vanity) for favorable coverage, or (out of fear) to hide a shameful secret. And, of course, when the payoff took the form of an advertisement in the magazine, its appearance blazoned not only the advertiser's business but the probability that he'd forked over liberally to conceal a blackmailable secret. By paying, in other words, one simply purchased a different, more ironic kind of exposure; to anyone well attuned to the magazine, it became completely impossible to distinguish between florid compliment and corrosive insult.

Mann enjoyed the double if paradoxical rewards of crime and sanctimony until 1905, when he miscalculated by making an ill-judged attempt to blackmail Emily Post's husband, Edwin. A Wall Street stockbroker mired in a financial bad patch, and on strained and distant terms with his wife, Post had been supporting a Broadway chorine in what the euphemism of the day called a "white apartment" in Stamford, Connecticut. Unable to disgorge the $500 demanded by Mann, Post confessed to Emily. From the very beginning, her sense of propriety differed sharply from the false modesty that would have counseled hushing the matter up at all costs. Instead, she advised him to contact the district attorney and set up a sting operation. He did. Mann's agent, Charles P. Ahle, was arrested in Post's Wall Street office on July 11, 1905,[7] triggering a public sensation, which was to fill the columns of newspapers and titillate readers for nearly a year. *Collier's* magazine, prompted (its publisher claimed) by the scabrousness of the attack on Alice Roosevelt, launched a series of sharply worded articles, disclosing that Mann had been paying a city juvenile court judge, Joseph Deuel, to vet *Town Topics* for actionable items. This was bait laid for Mann, but Deuel hotheadedly seized it, suing *Collier's* editor, Norman Hapgood, for libel. A jury took exactly seven minutes to declare Hapgood innocent, and the district attorney, sifting through Mann's testimony, promptly charged him with perjury, and subjected him to a criminal prosecution that kept the fires of scandal burning well into the spring of 1906.

In the midst of all this, another, even more titillating scam came to light: a keepsake folio, bound in green morocco, profusely embossed in gold leaf, printed on the heaviest and crispest vellum, and floridly titled *Fads and Fancies of Representative Americans at the Beginning of the Twentieth Century, Being a Portrayal of Their Tastes, Diversions and Achievements*. It too was a front for blackmail and extortion, but here the stakes were higher. Inside were short and apparently flattering biographical tributes to eighty-one eminent Americans, including a past president, Grover Cleveland, and the chief executive then sitting, Theodore Roosevelt (whom Mann must have thought above holding any grudges over Alice). To gain an ironically flattering mention in *Fads and Fancies* (and avoid a public sniffing of one's dirty linen in *Town Topics*), one paid a minimum of $1,500, but some subscribers—presumably those with the biggest bank accounts and the most explosive secrets—forked over as much as $9,000, essentially to immortalize themselves as victims (and hence as guilty provokers) of blackmail.

In its singularly insolent way, *Fads and Fancies* is a masterpiece of double entendre. It opens with a declaration that "the plates from which the impressions were made have been destroyed." Reassurance to the bibliophile? Or a derisive echo of the blackmailer's promise to destroy incriminating material? The introduction teeters delicately between gushing with appreciative wonderment and throwing down a gauntlet: "American society! What is it? Who gives it the right of being? Whence is it derived? What influences have borne upon it and shaped it?" This pointed question gets no answer, but there is an explanation of high society's usefulness to the less privileged onlooker. "It is the touch of romance in their workaday world," it dryly continues, "to read in the papers of how such a one, who has risen from their ranks by his own energy and ability, is now disporting himself among the world's greatest on equal terms."[8]

With all Mann's schemes exploding to a chorus of scorn, it looked, to the relief of polite society, as if fashionable New York was about to rid itself of its most dauntless and pernicious pest. But they'd underestimated their enemy. Mann ultimately beat his perjury rap, and while it's not clear that he ever fully reassembled his blackmail apparatus, *Town Topics* lost little of its bite, declining only after his death in 1920. It lingered on into the 1930s, when, to the relief of the sinning elite and the chagrin of everybody else, it folded.

Are Manners Moral?

Colonel Mann's saga was a juicy scandal in its own right. But it also betokened a sense of crisis about manners that marked the early years of this century. Between 1900 and 1920, the nation's popular magazines were full of articles assessing the state of American social behavior and carrying titles like "Has the American Bad Manners?" (*Ladies' Home Journal*, 1900), "Decay of American Manners" (*Harper's Weekly*, 1903), and "Are We Ashamed of Good Manners?" (*Century Magazine*, 1909). Interest in the subject peaked in 1922 with the runaway success of Emily Post's *Etiquette*. Though it echoed popular late Victorian etiquette authorities like Mary Elizabeth Wilson Sherwood (1826–1903), Post's book soon overshadowed them, in part because it acknowledged the treacherous and shifting ground under the subject, and addressed frankly a widening conviction among Americans that good conduct and morality were becoming unglued from each other.

Fated enemies though they were, Mann and Post, had they ever met, could nonetheless have seen eye to eye on one key point. Both took manners seriously; neither thought them a trivial study; both saw them as indissolubly linked to the gravest issues of morality. Blackmailer and extortionist he may have been, but a genuine moral indignation fueled Mann's attack on the hypocrisy of the gilded class he'd stealthily invaded. He despised the perverse misuse of social polish as a cover for vice. Manners, he thought, ought to reflect morals and reinforce them, not cover up for their absence. And Post, though she belonged to that class by unassailable birthright, agreed emphatically as to the moral importance of manners and the extent to which her compatriots often casually betrayed them. "The code of ethics," Emily Post wrote, "is an immutable law of etiquette." True good manners were therefore the reverse of vacuous rituals. "The code of a thoroughbred," she continued, ". . . is the code of instinctive decency, ethical integrity, self-respect and loyalty."[9]

As the twentieth century closes, Americans seem troubled anew by the state of their manners and seem also to agree that the problem is serious, even momentous. But is civility really on a par with more obviously fateful ethical issues—war, murder, euthanasia? Philosophy, in fact, has traditionally been very much of two minds about the moral significance of manners. Thomas Hobbes (1588–1679), the great seventeenth-century English social theorist, disparaged etiquette, defining it in his best known work, *Leviathan*, as "how one should salute another, or how a man should wash his mouth, or pick his teeth before company and such other points of the *small morals*."[10] Hobbes meant the latter phrase pejoratively, ranking good manners far beneath issues of real moral moment.

Immanuel Kant (1724–1804), the hugely influential eighteenth-century German ethicist and metaphysician, characteristically took a more nuanced and convoluted position. On the whole he seems to have thought etiquette ("accessibility, affability, politeness, refinement, propriety, courtesy, and ingratiating and captivating behavior," as he defined it in an early lecture at the University of Königsberg) a concern separate from and inferior to morals. Manners, he argued, "call for no large measure of moral determination and cannot, therefore, be reckoned as virtues." Yet he didn't finally dismiss them, for "even though [manners] are no virtues, they are a means of developing virtue. . . . The more we refine the crude elements in our nature, the more we improve our humanity and the more capable it grows of feeling the driving force of virtuous principles."[11]

Advocates of manners often repeat this idea forcefully—none more so than Edmund Burke (1729–1797):

> Manners are of more importance than laws. Upon them, in a great measure the laws depend. The law touches us but here and there, and now and then. Manners are what vex or soothe, corrupt or purify, exalt or debase, barbarize or refine us, by a constant, steady, uniform, insensible operation, like that of the air we breathe in. They give their whole form and colour to our lives. According to their quality, they aid morals, they supply them, or they totally destroy them.[12]

Elsewhere, Burke accorded even more importance to manners, asserting—in the brief and tantalizing way so characteristic of him—that they actually help to form laws. "Whilst *manners* remain entire," he wrote in 1777, "they will correct the vices of law and soften it at length to their own temper."[13]

Conservative such convictions may be, but they are also common, and not merely theoretical. Judith Martin, for example, sometimes makes tongue-in-cheek assertions to the effect that "Miss Manners does not mess around in that morass known as morality."[14] Yet many of the problems she confronts, even where they start with protocol, escalate into questions of right and wrong. In the summer of 1996 she advised the relatives, friends, and recoverers of the victims of the just-crashed TWA Flight 800. "The more horrendous the situation, the more you need etiquette," she was quoted as saying in *Newsday*. "This is why etiquette is so extremely strict in situations where the issues you are debating are of major importance—the courtroom, the government legislature, diplomacy."[15] Indeed, a breakdown in manners can deteriorate into a confrontation where both morals and laws are violated, and what ought to be an easily settled interpersonal ruction flashes into violence. On the Fourth of July in 1995,[16] a group of teenagers riding in an old Chevrolet on Interstate 17 near Phoenix accidentally sideswiped a pickup truck during a maneuver to avoid another car. But when they exited the freeway and tried to talk to the driver of the truck, a passenger leaped from it and shot a sixteen-year-old sitting in the Chevrolet's back seat, leaving him a quadriplegic—probably for life. Small morals aren't really small if they can tame the passions that lead to this kind of tragedy.

In her book *The De-Moralization of Society: From Victorian Virtues to Modern Values*, Gertrude Himmelfarb deplores what she sees as a perverse modern urge to wall custom and convention off from morality, reducing right and wrong to questions of personal taste and preference. "Virtue" (as opposed to the contemporary "value," a term Himmelfarb despises as indicative of moral relativism) is her word for an organic normative blend of manners and morals that she views as characteristic of a now lost time and place of grace: Victorian England. According to Himmelfarb, Edmund Burke foreshadowed a widespread middle-class Victorian conviction that manners are "the harbingers of morals writ large, the civilities of private life that were the corollaries of civilized social life."[17] By observing superficial civilities punctiliously, Himmelfarb thinks, Victorian society affirmed in everyday life its allegiance to deeper ethical values as well. The benefit, she argues, was double. Normal existence was more graceful and pleasant than now; catastrophic breaches were rarer.

In this moralistic model, even hypocrisy has its uses, becoming, as Rochefoucauld put it, "the homage vice thinks it should render to virtue,"[18] rather than the monstrous gap between superficial propriety and deep-down rottenness that Colonel Mann both deplored and illustrated. Himmelfarb cites the diaries of Queen Victoria's four-time prime minister, William Gladstone, which harrowingly record the chasm between his unvaryingly circumspect public utterances and his compulsive secret interest in pornography and nubile prostitutes. Gladstone's need to appear respectable, however ill it matched his real thoughts, may (by serving as a constant and painful reminder of the virtues he wasn't practicing) have kept him aspiring to goodness.

The urge to re-moralize public behavior, upgrading optional niceties into duties in the hope that this will stiffen our moral spines, has been sounding more and more insistently among a wide spectrum of cultural critics, political theorists, and philosophers. Their ranks predictably include conservatives like Himmelfarb, William Bennett, James Q. Wilson, and the late Christopher Lasch, but they include too a surprising number of voices from the center and the left: Richard Sennett, for example, makes an analogous case in *The Fall of Public Man* (1976), as does Nicolaus Mills in *The Triumph of Meanness* (1997). Jürgen Habermas, the contemporary German philosopher, has spent a long career attempting to assemble a metaphysics of civility, a system designed to guarantee individual freedom yet at the same time subject it to reasonable government by moral principles: " 'Moral consciousness' signifies the ability to make use of interactive competence for *consciously* processing morally relevant conflicts of action. . . . Competent agents will—independently of accidental communities of social origin, tradition, basic attitude, and so on—be in agreement about such a fundamental point of view only if it arises from the very structures of possible interaction."[19]

Simplified, this rather abstract formulation means that productive communication is impossible without support from a bedrock of morals—a shared belief (for example) that any useful social interaction depends on reciprocity. And while Habermas is far more concerned with the politics of deliberative democracy than he is with etiquette, his point is nevertheless relevant for our discussion. If social interactions do indeed collapse for want of a firm moral underpinning, then manners—which form, after all, a key part of social interaction—are vital.

Michael Sandel's widely discussed *Democracy's Discontent* (1996) contends that American politics, once ruled by a consensus that government should create a climate friendly to the practice of public virtue, has degenerated into what he calls the "procedural republic," a society obsessed at all costs with preserving as absolute the autonomy of the individual. Sandel quotes Benjamin Rush's 1786 *Plan for the Establishment of Public Schools* approvingly as supplying a moral compass we've since abandoned in favor of moral relativism: "Let our pupil be taught that he does not belong to himself, but that he is public property."[20]

Miss Manners would surely agree, as would her predecessors, Emily Post and Amy Vanderbilt. Behavior that ignores the proximity and the sensitivity of others may fall short of crime, but remains wrong. The diner sitting next you at a lunch counter who mops her face with a paper napkin, crumples it, then tosses it onto the Formica inches from your plate, commits an antisocial and thus immoral act as well as a rude and unsanitary one. The risk of disease, while small, is real enough to constitute a moral assault if not a legal one. And even discounting the possibility of physical harm, city dwellers in the developed world like to keep their distance from others, instinctively avoiding unwanted contact: observe, the next time you board a jammed train, bus, or subway car, how deftly even oblivious-looking people contort themselves into unnatural postures simply to avoid unseemly closeness to fellow commuters.

Yet every instance where manners are morally momentous coun-

terbalances another where they're trivial—situations where wrong-
ness is plainly a matter not of ethics but taste, and where
miscalculations signal only that one hasn't mastered the ways of
whatever class or clique one wants to join. In 1922, the year of
Emily Post's debut as a manners expert, Doubleday placed a series
of advertisements in *Redbook* magazine for a competing guide (the
author, not cited, was Lillian Eichler, and the guide her two-volume
Book of Etiquette). Though Eichler, like Post, often stressed the
moral dimension of manners, the ads appealed to readers on far
different grounds. They were a month-to-month soap opera, re-
counting the social misadventures of a well-meaning and ambitious
but instructively gauche young couple, Ted and Violet Creighton.[21]

In the February 1922 installment, they've been invited by
Mr. and Mrs. Brandon to an elegant dinner party. "They were to
dine at the Brandon home—actually be the guests of William
Brandon! . . . But were they ready for it?" Mr. Brandon is consid-
ering Ted for an executive job, and since Ted's rival Roberts and
his wife are also guests, the dinner is a test.

"The first two courses of the dinner passed rather pleasantly,"
the narrative begins.

> But then, something happened. Violet noticed that Mrs. Rob-
> erts had glanced at her husband and frowned ever so slightly.
> She wondered what was wrong. Perhaps it was incorrect to
> cut lettuce with a knife. Perhaps Ted should not have used his
> fork that way. In her embarrassment she dropped her knife
> and bent down to pick it up at the same time that the butler
> did. Oh, it was humiliating, unbearable! They didn't know
> what to do, how to act!

In the evening's crowning abasement, Ted mistakenly follows the
ladies when they adjourn to the drawing room, provoking the
"amused glances of the others." Hence he's not surprised when Mr.
Brandon—politely waiting until Violet is out of earshot, retrieving

her coat—tells him they've failed the exam. "I'm sorry, Creighton, but I've decided to consider Roberts for the vacancy. I need a man whose social position is assured."

Ludicrous as the vignette appears at this remove, it raises a serious issue. The Creightons and the Brandons obviously agree on the importance of etiquette, and the ad confidently expected readers would do likewise. But the actual customs described are in themselves empty of moral meaning, indifferent conventions whose only possible use is to denote social class at its snobbiest. And every use made of them by the characters is flagrantly *im*moral. Even the Creightons, however hapless, are not without guilt. They hope, after all, to use etiquette as a forged passport to worlds they don't belong in. Roberts is worse, wielding social rituals as stealth weapons against an unarmed rival. Mr. Brandon is worse yet: he treats manners as tools of triage for an exercise in social Darwinism. And the ad itself outdoes all of its characters in cynicism, by trading on etiquette to wheedle the reader into buying the volume out of *mauvaise honte*.

For every instance, in other words, where manners are morals writ in miniature, there's an opposing instance where they either lack moral significance entirely or (worse) serve as vehicles for pretense, fakery, and greed. And if manners aren't always good, rudeness isn't always bad. History's truly immortal louts tend to be conscious opponents of the codes they violate, mockers of pretension, satirists who rarely view their acts of rudeness as immoral. Quite the reverse. Rudeness, they seem to be telling us, can supply the good swift kick a besotted society deserves and needs. Plato's Athens, conventionally the apotheosis of civilized Western urbanity, endured Diogenes the Cynic, who (according to tradition) dwelt in contented filth under an overturned bathtub outside the city gates, heaping ribald scorn on philosophers and citizens alike. A characteristic high point in his career occurred when he wandered into a lecture at which Plato was pontificating on human nature before the cream of Athenian youth. "Plato had defined man as an animal, biped and featherless, and was applauded. Diogenes plucked a fowl and brought it into the lecture-room with the words, 'Here is Plato's man.' "[22] Yet Diogenes figured to his fellow Athenians not as a nuisance but a valuable gadfly (as even Plato conceded, red-facedly adding "having broad nails" to his definition of man).

Nor did the impulse to use rudeness as a moral corrective expire with Diogenes. In early 1996, at a Washington meeting of city officials, Sandi Webb (a councilwoman from Simi Valley, California) leaped to her feet, gave U.S. senator Diane Feinstein the finger, then stomped out. "I blew it," Webb later conceded, in a characteristically mid-nineties version of public apology. "I was so pissed at her, I got up and left."[23] Called to account for such outbursts, the perpetrators typically invoke just such a defense: they know it was unmannerly, but thought an insult just the right note, a needed stink bomb thrown at smug and immoral convention. Colonel William Mann, after all, proved a thorn in society's side because he claimed to understand its mores, to have found out just how his presumed betters were violating the code that should have governed them, and then rebuked them by wielding it not only more expertly than they did but more lethally.

Manners and Class

Another, perhaps even more vexing problem complicates the urge to accord etiquette the moral dignity of ethics: the close and troublesome linkage between manners and class. In fact, the two are embarrassingly inseparable. Manners almost always function as tokens of solidarity in a distinct human social group, which—if its status is high enough—can decree anything polite by fiat. A sixteenth-century German chronicle reports an old aristocratic Christmas tradition in which dinner companions festively pelted each other with dog turds.[24] The Aztecs cannibalized their enemies, but rigid class observance controlled the carnage, and as far as they were concerned rendered it civil: Montezuma got one thigh from each corpse, the priests the blood, and the rib cage went to the commoners.[25] However one defines the group—as members of a social stratum, an economic cohort, a family, even a federation of outcasts—a mannerly custom's real function is to bond the group together. As such, it needs only to be recognizable and distinctive; its moral content is irrelevant.

Etymologically, "etiquette" means "ticket." Manners—especially when they constitute acquired rituals rather than instinctive considerateness—have immemorially served both as a badge of entry into an elite class and a barrier against encroachments by the déclassé. In the Renaissance, while the strictures of civility seem to have been simpler than they were later to become, the classes who claimed them defended them fiercely. Laws patrolled class frontiers, regulating what we'd now regard purely as issues of taste and manners. "None," Queen Elizabeth I proclaimed in 1597 in a typical edict, "shall wear . . . silk of color purple under the degree of an earl, except Knights of the Garter in their purple mantles only."[26] A clumsy attempt to sneak across class lines branded one not just as a boor but as a criminal.

This strict ordering of human relations extended well beyond dress. A map of any premodern Western city instantly reveals that social class located people as well as clothing them and regulating deportment. Note, for example, these street names from a sixteenth-century plan of Paris: the rue des Tainturiers, the rue des Menestriers, the rue des Estuves (Dyers' Street, Fiddlers' Street, Bathhouse Street)—a street for every group and every group relegated to its proper street.[27] Any pedestrian knew instantly what sort of people lived behind each facade, what they were at least supposed to be doing there, hence what sort of demeanor to expect and to display in response. If an outsider materialized, one might plausibly guess why she was there (a double-edged convenience: bathhouses were the preferred resort for commercial sex in medieval Paris).

Groups might shift neighborhoods over time, as John Stow

(1525?–1605) noted in his 1598 *Survey of London*, but they remained firmly wedded to recognized locales:

> The goldsmiths of Gutheron's lane and Old Exchange are now for the most part removed into the south side of West Cheape, the pep[p]erers and grocers of Soper's lane are now in Bucklesberrie.... The skinners from St. Marie Pellipers or at the Axe, into Budge row and Walbrooke; the stock [i.e., dried] fishmongers in Thames Street; wet fishmongers in Knightriders street and Bridge Street.[28]

Classes can shrink or expand in number; the lines between them may blur or shift (and most historians and sociologists would agree that class has been changing dynamically since the Renaissance if not before). But if class distinctions vanish altogether, etiquette necessarily vanishes with them. The civil virtues Gertrude Himmelfarb praises were both the property and the distinguishing badge of the British Victorian bourgeoisie. In a society that believes in stratification, this would not be troubling. But in America, values if not realities are egalitarian, and the persistence of sharp class distinctions is therefore a source of discomfort. This presents a formidable problem. If manners are moral, and a rigid class system is immoral, then how can good manners not only coexist with but depend upon class?

Throughout the long publishing history of *Etiquette*, Emily Post wrestled with this difficulty. She repeatedly insisted that those who practiced good manners were indeed members of a genuine class. Yet she also argued, rather contradictorily, that this group couldn't be identified with any particular social stratum; for, in another conviction she shared with Colonel Mann, Post believed that what passed for patrician in early twentieth-century Manhattan hardly deserved to stand as a reliable guide for either etiquette or ethics. In her 1945 edition, Post confronted the problem squarely, quoting a letter from a disgruntled reader who bridled at the prospect of imitating New York "Café Society," a group less mannerly than "pretentious and vulgar." Just who, the reader demands, are these "Best People" whose example Post commends? The answer is thoughtful but also a bit irresolute:

> There is nowhere to go to see Best Society on parade, because parading is one thing that Best Society does not intentionally do. And yet it is true (and this is one of the things hardest to make clear) that in the forefront of the public parade are to be found a certain few who are really best. But they are best in spite of, and not because of, the publicity they attract.
>
> When I say that "people of taste do this or think that," I naturally have in mind definite people whose taste is the most nearly perfect among all those whom I know. Or on occasion, perhaps, I go back in memory to the precepts of those whose excellence has remained an ideal.
>
> In other words, when I write of people of quality or fashion or taste, I always select the individual people who ideally serve as models. . . .
>
> In other words . . . Best Society, Best People, or People of Quality can all be defined as people of cultivation, courtesy, taste, and kindness—people, moreover, who are very rarely dissociated from their backgrounds.[29]

On the one hand, Post insists that good manners are inseparable from a class: the Best Society, the Best People, People of Quality. But who *are* they? The Four Hundred; the few thousand socialites just outside that charmed circle; the hundreds of thousands who make up the multitudinous yet cultivated upper bourgeoisie? Whoever they are, these Best People frustrate would-be imitators by staying invisible most of the time (which seems, in part, just what makes them "Best"). And to complicate matters yet further, Post often identifies the Best People less as a social class than a moral cult: those few charmed and charming individuals who seamlessly

integrate ethics with the skills of graceful life. She believed mean-
ingful civility depended upon a model elite. And she couldn't, despite her own lofty pedigree, quite bring herself to accept that such
an elite should rise upon naked social privilege. Yet at the same time
it seemed implausible to look for models of etiquette among para-
gons of pure disinterested virtue. Gandhi and Mother Teresa may
be ethical cynosures, but offer at best vague guidance in the milieu
of multi-course dinners, wedding customs, or forms of address.

Harriet Martineau (1802–1876), an astute British observer of the
American scene, had put the problem succinctly almost a century
before Post, in her book *Society in America* (1837). "There will be
rank, and tenacity of rank, wherever there is society. As this is natural, inevitable, it is of course right. The question must be what is
to entitle to rank."[30] For Martineau, the America of the 1830s
evinced a disturbing a tendency to make wealth the sole touchstone
of status. As a staunch democrat, Martineau found this troubling,
and it might have upset an admirer of hereditary aristocracy quite
as much. Whatever the determining hallmark of class, and despite
our national suspicion of it, historians tend to agree that from
roughly 1850 onward, class distinctions in America were becoming
both more numerous and sharper. Yet a growing and ramifying class
system is inherently a less stable one, harder to read, hence easier
for the shrewd to manipulate. Class ferment enabled Colonel Mann,
so obscure as to his social origins, to infiltrate the early twentieth-
century Manhattan elite—an ambition that would have been nearly
unrealizable two or three generations before, when the landscape of
status was both simpler and more rigid. But by 1900, class had become confusing and unreliable as a predictor of social behavior, and
thus far more permeable to the aspiring interloper.

That a feverish multiplication of class distinctions conceals a
breakdown, a new ferment in what (back in the Middle Ages) must
have seemed an eternal social division of the world was a key insight
developed in perhaps the greatest twentieth-century history of manners, Norbert Elias's *The Civilizing Process* (1939). "Diminishing

contrasts, increasing varieties"[31] was Elias's evocative phrase for the phenomenon. As the once-yawning medieval gulf between aristocrat and peasant first narrowed, then began to be bridged, the opportunity arose for smaller and less broadly delineated social groups to emerge, each nervously establishing its own distinguishing customs and taboos. On the one hand, as social hierarchy broke down, sharp behavioral contrasts between peasant and aristocrat naturally diminished. But that, just as naturally, spurred social anxiety, prompting people both to revive old distinctions and to invent new ones. Both stratagems, however, are driven by the panic that naturally attends a destabilized and (in the long run) decomposing class system.

To Americans in the first few decades after the revolution, class seemed moribund if not dead and the quest for civility thus appeared to pose a very different problem: "republican" manners. How might America build a system of etiquette in a society free of invidious social distinctions? Who—to use Emily Post's formulation—were the Best People in a polity where there supposedly weren't even any Better ones? By the middle of the nineteenth century, the United States was generating wealth at an unprecedented rate. But the benefits of prosperity spread themselves unevenly, and the country began to fragment into sharply differentiated economic strata, which quickly acquired a sense of relative status with distinguishing customs to match. Republican manners became a quaint vestige of the past. The social historian Stuart Blumin quotes an 1877 letter from Lydia Maria Child, the Boston editor of a children's magazine and an astute social observer:

No living person can help being aware of an increasing tendency toward a strong *demarcation of classes* in this country. The genteel classes do not inter-marry with the middle classes; the middle classes do not intermarry with the laboring class; nothing is *said* about it, but there is a systematic avoidance of it. Moreover, they don't mix socially, they are as much strangers to each other, as if they lived in different countries.[32]

John Kasson, in his authoritative study of manners in nineteenth-century America, *Rudeness and Civility* (1990), also shows how an increasing awareness of stratification heightened Americans' interest in class-based etiquette, with the privileged upper strata naturally enough supplying the model everybody else strove to emulate. But this was a veneer. In fact, those multiplying distinctions meant the system was becoming more fluid, affording more opportunities for the ambitious to rise into once exclusive ranks. Growth here was really a sign of underlying fragility. The more ranks there were, the less any one could maintain its clout as society's Supreme Court of manners.

In his classic 1940s study of social stratification in "Elmtown," a small Illinois city, August Hollingshead delineated five distinct social castes. Predictably, the stratum most preoccupied with etiquette and precedence was Class 3—the one perched agonizingly in the middle, unsure whether it belonged with the elite or the anonymous mass. Unlike the town's true aristocrats, who ignored the society column in the local paper, Class 3 hostesses strove mightily to have their parties written up: "when and where the party occurred, who was there, the entertainment offered, the refreshments served, and a detailed description of the decorations." The hostess who failed to get coverage in the *Bugle* lost face. "The obvious search for publicity," Hollingshead suggested, "may be a symbol of the strain inherent in this class's pivotal position between two conspicuous layers of the social structure."[33]

Perhaps the surest sign that class distinctions are blurring, however, is the disagreement they've provoked among modern historians, sociologists, and philosophers. "Class" has been a fighting word among specialists at least since the turn of the twentieth century. To Karl Marx (1818–1883), the only real classes were economic; the social proprieties any given class might observe were at best accidental. But Max Weber (1864–1920), the early twentieth-century sociologist and critic of Marx, disagreed, accepting the existence of economic classes but contrasting them with what he called *Stände*, or "status groups"—collections of people far more confused and shifting as to their boundaries, and defining themselves, necessarily approximately, according to the degree of social esteem they command:

> In contrast to the purely economically determined "class situation," we wish to designate as *status situation* every typical component of the life of men that is determined by a specific, positive or negative, social estimation of *honor*. This honor may be connected with any quality shared by a plurality. . . . But status honor need not necessarily be linked with a class [i.e., economic] situation. On the contrary, it normally stands in sharp opposition to the pretensions of sheer property.[34]

Yet even concepts of class as flexible and open-ended as Weber's have come under attack from contemporary commentators such as Jean Baudrillard, for whom the very idea of social class is an illusion—who thinks, in fact, that all social analysis is a self-generating and meaningless intellectual exercise based on no underlying reality. The social, Baudrillard has asserted, "which serves as a universal alibi for every discourse, no longer analyses anything, no longer designates anything. Not only is it useless—wherever it appears it conceals something else . . . it is only abstraction and residue . . . a simulation and an illusion"[35]

With cultural historians laboring in such a dither about class, it shouldn't be in the least surprising that Emily Post found it a challenge to locate those Best People whose manners we ought to be imitating. As classes crumble around their members, and come to seem ever more abstract and unreal even to historians, rules of social behavior, so dependent on perceptions of class, inevitably become loose and vague. Thus etiquette loses its sure moorings in the clear relation of superior to inferior.

The contrast between Emily Post's and William Mann's confusing new twentieth-century social world and the stabler order it replaced emerges sharply in the memoirs of a New Yorker who entered old age a generation before Mann's assault on the bastions of social New York. Abram Child Dayton (?–1877) could proudly trace his ancestry back to Ralph Dayton (the founder of Long Island's East Hampton) and Elias Dayton (a Revolutionary War hero and member of the Continental Congress).[36] In 1871, Abram Dayton wrote a memoir called *Last Days of Knickerbocker Life in New York*, a backward glance into the Gotham of Dayton's youth in the 1830s, to him an era of defunct graciousness. It was in effect a world where class was much more firmly fixed, yet far simpler and less of an obsession than it was soon to become. Sentiment, of course, may have prettified Dayton's recollections; but many late American Victorians shared his nostalgia for a bygone era he saw as simple, stable, and reassuring.

In 1830 there was no "Seclusion Coterie," as Dayton scornfully termed the self-appointed crème de la crème of the Gilded Age. His description of the city's pre–Civil War social hierarchy, curiously and significantly, reverses the ambiguity we've seen above. Republican or not, early nineteenth-century New York did have a social hierarchy, but with fewer layers and far easier interclass relations. People observed codes of behavior more punctiliously, Dayton thought, but worried about them less, being largely content to stay in the class they belonged to and whose mores they had already mastered. "Comfortable independence assumed cordial welcome by one class to the other, and really no aristocracy existed or was claimed, save where the distinction was cheerfully awarded to the cultivated and refined."[37]

The upper echelon, as Dayton pictured it, was chiefly professional: clergy, lawyers, doctors, "men who were looked up to with that deferential respect which always has and ever will be awarded to those [whose] lives and talents are devoted to the study of social progress." Just below this aristocracy (of merit rather than birth) ranked the merchant class, "but the dividing line between *store* and *shop* was not so distinctly drawn as now; the status of employer and employee was less closely defined, the latter not infrequently being an inmate, and ever a welcome guest at the home of his employer." The most numerous group in the New York of Dayton's youth was that era's version of the working class: "that large class known as mechanics, who with their journeymen, apprentices and laborers, has always formed so formidable a proportion of every city." And finally the underclass, a predictable lightning rod for reproach: "Loungers or non-producers were marked persons at a time when 'Early to bed and early to rise' was a ruling motto, and 'to work while daylight lasts,' was the governing habit from the learned professional man to the humblest artizan."[38]

Propriety was nonetheless an obsession, and rules, Dayton recalls, were simple but strictly observed. Nobody seemed to wallow in doubt about what was permissible; ease of social relations coexisted with, indeed depended on, a certain rigidity of behavior.

As late as 1835 James Thompson, a confectioner, opened a store at 171 Broadway, for the sale of cakes and other dainties, to accommodate ladies who were engaged in shopping; but for a long time this embryo Delmonico languished in neglect, even though the sisters of the proprietor, middle-aged women, were the sole attendants, and it was situated on the most frequented portion of the promenade. Tempting *morceaux* were displayed in the windows, but all in vain, sideway glances were the only recognition vouchsafed them by dame or miss; society ruled that it was not proper to enter and partake.[39]

Instead of oppressing, Dayton insists, the rules reassured, offering a notable example in the Lime Kiln Man.[40] A key figure in his memoir, this formidable-looking tramp stalked the streets during the 1830s, clad in rags and bespattered with lime from the abandoned kiln where he slept (and eventually died). By the turn of the twentieth century, the tramp had become a figure of popular terror, a barometer of the nation's social instability, occasioning anguished warnings in pamphlets like Orlando F. Lewis's *Vagrancy in the United States* (1907). Yet the Lime Kiln Man struck Dayton and his contemporaries not as the threat he'd seem in today's peril-strewn urban wilderness, but rather as a fascinating—even oddly reassuring—curiosity. "This tall gaunt cadaverous figure," Dayton wrote, "was usually clad in the loose cotton garb of a laborer, bespattered with lime, his uncut, uncombed locks were matted by constant contact with the same material, which also besmeared his long attenuated face."

The Lime Kiln Man aroused fascinated sympathy rather than fear or annoyance because, outlandish though he was, the New Yorkers of the 1830s inherited their Renaissance forebears' assurance about how to read social behavior. The Lime Kiln Man's laborer's dress, Dayton writes, identified him as "the personification of abject poverty," hence someone to pity. Yet his manner suggested a loftier class. "He was never known to solicit alms . . . and he even gave no heed to the gaze of those who with pitying eye looked upon him as a fit object for succor"—a nobility of mien that led to frequent "speculations about his being some distinguished exile, etc." The repertory of social signs an early Victorian Gothamite read in this cracked vagabond was thus a comfortably small one; each observable detail placed him firmly and clearly at one or another level in a stable hierarchy of class. So solid was the system that a show of contradictory signs—like the Lime Kiln Man's—sparked not confusion and anxiety but rather fascination and eager guesswork.

Compare the homeless Manhattanite of the 1980s and '90s, panhandling on the subway, muttering or raving along the sidewalk. In our social milieu, the simple signs of poverty and even of nobility still survive, of course. But now, in a thronged and maddeningly complex social marketplace, they compete with a hundred other signaling mannerisms as well. A bag lady may be a Wellesley alumna, cash lacing the rags in her granny cart; goodfellas wear Armani and Agnès B. Jarred into alertness by media crazes and the complexities of our own experience, we troll, uneasily, at times only half-consciously, for hundreds of signs, trying nervously to sort them out. Cut adrift from its stabilizing anchor in a once rigid class system, human comportment has floated into a world where the iconography of civility can conceal assaults ranging from vulgarity to barbarism, even to mortal danger. It's scarcely surprising that the increasing preoccupation with manners, etiquette, and civility America evinced in the nineteenth century has turned in the twentieth into anxiety, even panic.

Manners and Entropy

We should not, then, be surprised that manners—particularly American manners in the twentieth century—are problematic. But does that signify, as Himmelfarb and others warn, that they are in fact collapsing?

History offers useful cautions against apocalypticism. Complaints about the death of deportment are hardly novel—writing in 1405, Christine de Pizan, an early arbitress of etiquette, was already whining about the lost elegance of what, in her *Treasury of the City of Ladies*, she called the "good old days."[41] In *The Civilizing Process*, Norbert Elias (focusing on Germany and France from the feudal and medieval periods through the eighteenth and nineteenth centuries) discerned over that period not a falling off but a strong growth in civility, a tightening of restrictions on proper behavior, and an intensifying obsession with bodily propriety. As a bellwether, Elias cites Erasmus's 1530 treatise, *On Civility in Children*, so popular it passed through 130 editions by the eighteenth century.[42] This little book's fascination for the modern reader lies in the fact that it hints not at a stuffy and tyrannically laced-up past, but rather the reverse: a freer, less self-conscious, less puritanical code of manners, and a frank acceptance of the animal in all of us.

Erasmus wanted to encourage good deportment, but still took it for granted that at meals diners would seize food in their bare hands from a common dish, cutting off bite-sized chunks with their own knives. Eating with one's hands, Erasmus thought, wasn't disgusting. Nor was coating one's fingers in the process with a layer of rich grease. What *is* rude, he says, is wiping those fingers on one's coat: "it is better," he counsels, "to use the tablecloth or the serviette."[43] Similarly, "it is not vomiting," he says, "but holding the vomit in your throat that is foul."[44] Farting, a social problem that even the notably uninhibited latest edition of the *Amy Vanderbilt Complete Book of Etiquette* doesn't index, is disposed of efficiently in a note to the text: "replace [i.e., drown out] farts with coughs."

Indeed, in the Middle Ages and early Renaissance, fastidiousness in such matters was sometimes viewed not as civilized but as vain, even immoral. In the eleventh century, a Venetian doge sparked condemnation when his Greek-born wife insisted on eating with forks, at the time an unheard-of innovation. This brought the wrath of the church down on her head, and when she was later afflicted with a disfiguring disease, no less a figure than St. Bonaventure pronounced it a divine punishment for the worldly arrogance evinced by her tableware.[45]

But by the mid- to late Renaissance, it had become easier to arouse disgust, and coarsenesses that might once have passed unnoticed were beginning to cause embarrassment and even shame. People were getting nervous about the body, with its repertory of ripe effluents, stinks, and noises, and devising stratagems to tame or hide it. For example: despite a widespread modern belief, our medieval forebears *did* bathe, typically in neighborhood public baths. But so unconcerned were they about bodily privacy that in some cases bathers (male and female, child and adult) undressed at home and walked through the streets to the bathhouse naked, without occasioning any censorious comment. It was, apparently, only in the 1500s that nudity began to embarrass its practitioners and offend (at least some of) its beholders.[46]

In the Middle Ages, carving up an animal carcass felled during a hunt (as surviving literature, like the fourteenth-century poem *Ga-*

wain and the Green Knight, attests) struck people not as brutal but rather as an impeccably aristocratic ritual. Only later did etiquette come to demand that people suppress, as Elias phrased it, "every characteristic that they feel to be 'animal.' "[47] Then the eating of meat acquired new customs, both in preparation and consumption, that tried to obliterate its link with a dead animal. The fork, when it reappeared in the West toward the end of the seventeenth century, quickly won acceptance. Its era had come: another sign, perhaps, that more and more layers of ritual were interposing themselves between human culture and the "animal." The latter term was gradually becoming an insult.

Perhaps, though, the United States is an exception to this upward march of civility? Americans, having broken both politically and geographically with Europe, might be expected to dispense as well with the parent culture's sharpening hunger for ever more elaborate rituals of civility. And, at least in the early days of the republic, such seems to have been the case. Arthur Schlesinger, Sr., in a brief but entertaining history of American etiquette written in 1946, first noted the early nineteenth-century American with "republican" manners: how might a culture that had dispensed with invidious social distinctions nonetheless preserve some degree of interpersonal obligation and public decorum? John Kasson also notes—in the earlier years of the century—a widespread expectation among Americans that social rank was soon to become a vestige.[48]

Thus one might have expected a ruder and cruder standard of public behavior from pre- and early postrevolutionary America, and to some degree that expectation would have matched the facts. In eighteenth-century Virginia, the sixteen-year-old George Washington painstakingly inscribed a set of *Rules of Civility* in a neat schoolboy's copperplate hand (he'd copied these maxims from a sixteenth-century French Jesuit etiquette manual,[49] itself influenced by Erasmus). That the young Washington found them still needful in 1747 hints at what, even among the well-bred agriculturists of colonial Virginia, the aspiring gentleman was up against: "Cleanse not your teeth with the Table Cloth Napkin Fork or Knife but if Others do it let it be done w[ith] a Pick Tooth."[50]

Or consider Andrew Jackson's 1829 presidential inauguration, at which a proletarian throng stormed the White House and descended on the cake, ice cream, and orange punch, shoving invited dignitaries aside. "One hundred and fifty dollar chairs," a scandalized witness reported, "were profaned by the feet of clod-hoppers," who clambered up on them to get a better view of the man of the hour. A pair of Georgia congressmen, George Gilmer and John Floyd, aided by Floyd's two burly sons, managed to push their way into this semi-riot, but their wives were overcome by the scene, and to escape, Gilmer had to wrangle the three hundred–pound Mrs. Floyd out through a window. Jackson sneaked out the back door; officials finally lured the horde outside by placing tubs of punch on the front lawn.[51]

A couple of decades later yet, Charles Dickens, who had taken an American tour in 1842, described his fictional hero Martin Chuzzlewit's first encounter with New York on an average day.

An alderman had been elected the day before; and Party Feeling naturally running rather high on such an exciting occasion, the friends of the disappointed candidate had found it necessary to assert the great principles of Purity of Election and Freedom of Opinion by breaking a few legs and arms, and furthermore pursuing one obnoxious gentleman through the streets with the design of slitting his nose. These good-humoured little outbursts of the popular fancy were not in themselves sufficiently remarkable to create any great stir after the lapse of a whole night; but they found fresh life and notoriety in the breath of the newsboys. . . .

"Here's this morning's New York Sewer!" cried one. "Here's this morning's New York Stabber! Here's the New York Family Spy! Here's the New York Private Listener! Here's the New York Peeper! Here's the New York Plunderer! Here's the New York Keyhole Reporter! Here's the New York Rowdy Journal! Here's all the New York papers! Here's full particulars of the patriotic loco-foco movement yesterday in which the whigs was so chawed up, and the last Alabama gouging case, and the interesting Arkansas dooel with Bowie Knives, and all the Political, Commercial, and Fashionable News."[52]

Nonetheless, despite frequent scenes of republican mayhem, in the United States as in Europe, the long-term momentum of history appears to have been against, Yahooism. Kasson, like many historians of nineteenth-century America, discerns a powerful upsurge in class distinctions from the Civil War onward—an era of increasingly dramatic economic stratification, leading to the emergence of distinct and stubbornly permanent working, middle, and upper classes.

In the United States at least, mobility among these classes was possible, even frequent; upward mobility, of course, quickly became an article of national faith. That applied a powerful thrust to etiquette. Anyone hoping to rise from the working to the middle class—and then on to the American social summit—would naturally emulate the behavior of the group he or she aspired to. "Though the path to the summit rose precipitously," Kasson writes,

and was guarded by jealous watchdogs of the upper class, middle-class members might emulate some of its forms and manners.

The result was to make gentility increasingly available as a social desire and a purchasable style and commodity.[53]

Thus the curve of manners, despite an old tradition of complaints, isn't always, everywhere, and inevitably downward.

But what about the twentieth century, the age of Mike Tyson,

Linda Tripp, the Fox Television Network, the Internet flame, and outrages yet to appear above the horizon? Have a ferment in our morals, an accelerating speed in our way of life, and mounting chaos in our class relations stalled, or even reversed, five centuries of progress in the art of civility?

chapter two

Manners in Motion: The Rise of Mobility and the Breakdown of Public Behavior

For Edith Wharton (1862–1937), probably the bluest-blooded of major American writers, and approaching a pinnacle of fame and wealth at the turn of the twentieth century, mobility was liberating—a sure escape from the vulgar and commonplace. Hailing the dawn of the automobile age with unmixed enthusiasm, in 1904 she bought herself a 10-horsepower, brass-trimmed Pope-Hartford[1] and began roaring exultantly through the Berkshire Hills in it. "The motor car," she was to write in 1908, "has restored the romance of travel. Freeing us from all the compulsions and contacts of the railway, the bondage to fixed hours and the beaten track, the approach to each town through the area of ugliness and desolation created by the railway itself, it has given us back the wonder, the adventure and the novelty which enlivened the way of our posting grandparents."[2]

Yet Wharton was also—in novels like *The Custom of the Country* (1913)—a scourge of social-climbing presumption, and appreciated the drawbacks of movement as well as its attractions. In midlife she grew disillusioned with the chaotic social changes overtaking America, and forsook it for France, where, she believed, people had the good sense to stay physically and socially put—a skill, in her view, essential to the preservation of real civility. Indeed, to Wharton France uniquely maintained the well-defined, amicable, and mutually supportive class relations that Abram Dayton thought already moribund in the United States by the 1840s. French citizens, in the countryside at least,

> each had their established niche in life, the frankly avowed interests of their order, their pride in the smartness of the canal-boat, the seductions of the show-window, the glaze of the *brioches*, the crispness of the lettuce. And this admirable *fitting into the pattern*, which seems almost as if it were a moral outcome of the universal French sense of form, has led the race to the happy, the momentous discovery that good manners are a short cut to one's goal, that they lubricate the wheels of life instead of obstructing them.[3]

From the dawn of the American republic, mobility—whether from place to place or class to class—has been a national credo. We tend to echo Wharton the auto enthusiast: movement is good, a broadener of horizons, a civilizer, likelier to improve than worsen our lot. The more, therefore, the better. Only the instruments of oppression, like dictators and standing armies, try to stamp it out.

Yet ceaseless, mercurial change can also be hell on manners. The United States, from its very origins, had struck observers not just as frenziedly but self-destructively on the move. "We are a bivouac rather than a nation," D. A. Richardson wrote in 1867, "a grand Army moving from the Atlantic to the Pacific, and pitching tents by the way."[4] The migratory urge, even to early observers of the American scene, often seemed to undermine civility. Hector de Crèvecoeur (1735–1813), generally enthusiastic about movement and change, decried the neo-barbarism of citizens who'd fled to set up housekeeping on a raw frontier, always a day's, week's, or month's journey away from a stable social environment:

> They grow up a mongrel breed, half civilised, half savage. . . . You cannot imagine what an effect on manners the great distance they live from each other has! Consider one of the last settlements in its first view: of what is it composed? Europeans who have not that sufficient share of knowledge they ought to have, in order to prosper; people who have suddenly passed from oppression, dread of government, and fear of laws, into the unlimited freedom of the woods. . . . Having no place of worship to resort to, what little society this might afford is denied them. The Sunday meetings, exclusive of religious benefits, were the only social bonds that might have inspired them with some degree of emulation in neatness. Is it then surprising to see men thus situated, immersed in great and heavy labours, degenerate a little?[5]

Which Wharton was right, then, the confident futurist who celebrated mobility in her 1904 Pope-Hartford, or the social conservative who ridiculed it in her fiction?

. As she penned her encomium, England (then Europe's wealthiest major nation)[6] boasted a grand total of forty-one passenger cars.[7] To own one was a coup of high snobbery, to drive it an art requiring skill, endurance, leisure, and money. To encounter another driver was rare to begin with, and no social conundrum: the automobile tourist was by definition well off and probably prominent. But that was in 1908. In 1993, there were 194 million motor vehicles on the road in the United States;[8] between 1990 and 1996, a study by the American Automobile Association's Foundation for Traffic Safety recorded over 10,000 injuries and 218 deaths resulting from outbursts by motorists who—irked at each other's driving—attacked one another with weapons ranging from their fists to (in one instance) a crossbow.[9]

Yet the automobile represents only the most prominent visible symptom of a general American infatuation with movement. First came the inflowing surge of European, Asian, and African immigrants; then the West-surging tide of frontier settlers; then, almost simultaneously, an internal shift from the countryside into the burgeoning cities of the East and Midwest. In the twentieth century, the westward push continued, at first alongside a migration from the poverty-stricken rural South into the urban Northeast, then (after World War II) from the cities to the suburbs, from the Northeast back into a resurgent South, and finally (more recently still) from cities and suburbs out to exurbs and rural areas.

Early in our history, such restless demographics appeared to some observers a temporary and natural result of the nation's newness. So, at least, thought Joseph Kennedy, superintendent of the 1850 census. "The roving tendency of our people," he wrote, "is incident to the peculiar condition of their country and each succeeding census will prove that it is diminishing."[10] In the short run he was right: the 1850 and 1870 censuses showed 24 percent of the native population living in states other than those they were born in. That proportion had dropped to 20.6 percent by 1900. But by 1930, mobility was on the rise again, with 24 percent of the people once again reporting they'd moved from the states of their birth. And the trend has continued upward ever since, to 26.5 percent in 1950, 29.6 percent in 1960, and about 31 percent by 1990.[11]

Nor, of course, is American restlessness confined to geography: the migrant from Europe or the Atlantic seaboard hoped to move upward in class as well as westward by the compass. An impoverished immigrant scrabbling at the margins of life in Boston could mutate into a prosperous western landowner (or, if the weather was fierce and the land hostile, from a homesteader into an underclass drifter). Coast-to-coast mobility repeated itself with innumerable variations in every American region, state, city, town. In a study of residential and social patterns in turn-of-the century Omaha, the social historian Howard Chudacoff tracked a population churning incessantly from neighborhood to neighborhood. By 1900, fewer than one in twenty of Omaha's citizens appeared to be living in the same house or apartment they'd occupied in 1880; by 1920, fewer than one in thirty occupied the same residence as in 1900.[12] And as a rule, Chudacoff found movement from residence to residence accompanied social mobility, more often than not upward in a boom that—with a couple of sharp interruptions—propelled Omaha's population from 30,000 in 1880 to near 200,000 by 1920.[13]

In his study *The Moving American* (1973), the Yale historian George W. Pierson argued that such multilayered restlessness led inevitably to a breakdown in civility. "In common experience the misfits and failures, the petty gangsters and confidence men, all follow a wandering star, . . . a lodestone whose influence is baleful and destructive. It draws men away from society and civilization; it sets experience and authority at defiance; it evades the law and disintegrates convention."[14] Other historians have typically found little demographic correlation between frequent moves and hard-line antisocial patterns of behavior like crime, delinquency, or serious mental illness.[15] But there's plenty of evidence that movement can confuse and undermine the interpersonal amenities, which are less easily measurable. Pierson contended that rootlessness might well foster a superficial conviviality, but only as a mask over underlying coldness. A nation of transient strangers is a nation without a real system of social bonds, and any civility thus shallowly planted is bound to be fragile. "American social relations . . . [are] essentially those of friendly strangers. . . . Living in an unstable community, with new faces appearing continuously and old faces disappearing before one had really come to know them, a smile"—ingratiating but essentially meaningless—"had come to seem the required greeting."[16]

The apparent ease that attends a milieu of adventure and transience can all too easily explode. Air travel offers an instructive example. As recently as the 1960s, passengers were still mostly affluent, with the cachet of jet flight outweighing the temptation to rowdiness offered by speed, excitement, alcohol, and the brevity of one's contact with fellow passengers and airline personnel. But things have changed, according to the Association of Flight Attendants (AFA): rude, even criminal behavior is sharply on the rise. "There's just not the same level of civility," one Delta flight attendant, a twenty-year veteran of the airways, observed in a 1996 interview. "Everyone used to dress up when they flew. Now they're in blue jeans, cutoffs and tank tops."[17] The most extreme incident the AFA reported was the case of a first-class passenger, a fifty-two-year-old investment banker from Greenwich, Connecticut, who—angered when the flight attendant refused him a glass of wine—went berserk on a United Airlines flight from Buenos Aires to New York, climbed up and defecated on the food cart, then swabbed himself off with a wad of linen napkins. The culprit ultimately pleaded guilty to threatening the attendant and agreed to pay $49,029 in damages and cleanup costs, blandly explaining to the judge that he'd gotten angry at what he considered a rudeness: being refused service.

Why Movement Mangles Manners

Wild extremes of misbehavior can happen anywhere, of course, particularly with alcohol as a lubricant, but the confusion, tension, and alienation of travel make mayhem more likely. The Greenwich banker became national news because of the contrast between his airborne shenanigans and the sedate reputation of the affluent Connecticut suburb he hailed from. Travel seems to loosen, for good and ill, the social restraints class places on people at home. And among historians of manners there seems to be a broad consensus that etiquette was both simpler and more consistently observed in the rooted, immobile, and rigidly stratified societies of feudal Europe than in what the German sociologist Gerhard Vowinckel calls "the fundamental erosion of social structure, and hence of moral consensus"[18] that followed it with the dawn of the modern era.

Medieval mobility was limited to the aristocracy. And it was virtually synonymous with horsemanship, which excluded the lower orders because—like the earliest motorcars of the twentieth century—it demanded know-how, free time, and money (the horse has to be fed, stabled, accoutered). The rider on horseback physically dominates anyone walking along on foot. As late as the fourteenth century, equestrian accomplishment was synonymous with high breeding: the word "chivalry" indicated skilled horsemanship (etymologically it's identical with "cavalry"), and it was chiefly from such skills that the word acquired its wider and more familiar meaning of gentlemanly superiority. A new mode of mobility, as Wharton illustrated, thus begins as a hallmark of aristocratic manners. But snob appeal is not intrinsic: the experience loses its patina the moment poorer people with dimmer pedigrees get into the act.

According to a legend with at least some historical basis, the downscaling of mobility began in southern France on September 14, 1178, during a total eclipse of the sun, when a terrified mob gathered to hear their bishop preach in the market square of Avignon. An illiterate shepherd named Benoît interrupted the sermon to announce that God had commanded him to build a bridge across the Rhône. Initially the populace was incredulous, but Benoît completed the multi-span Pont d'Avignon by 1188, and was ultimately canonized for the achievement under the name of St. Bénézet.

Whatever it may have owed to miracle, this feat commemorated symbolically the dawn of an era of ever easier and more frequent travel in Europe. Thanks in part to engineering skills developed in building the great European Gothic cathedrals, roads were being improved and bridges built. Commerce and its necessarily attendant travel were increasing. The church, having established a wide-flung but centrally controlled network of monasteries and shrines,[19] began to demand travel of its functionaries and to encourage it in believers. Technological advances began to accumulate: the swivel axle[20]

(which transformed the wagon from a rigid and inflexible convey-
ance to one that could turn sharp corners and adjust to irregularities
in the roadbed), and an ingenious leather-strap suspension system,
probably invented in the 1400s in the Hungarian village of Kocs,
which turned a wagon trip from a sequence of bone-shattering jolts
into a relatively smooth ride (the village lent its name to the result:
the coach).[21]

In England, the first scheduled public coach service opened in
1637. The earliest long-distance services seem to have begun in the
1650s;[22] throughout the eighteenth century road transit became easier, faster, and cheaper, hence available to people of ever more modest means and ever less commanding social affinities. Between about
1700 and 1800, the maximum capacity of a typical stagecoach grew
from six passengers to twelve. Speed increased dramatically: the
170-mile stagecoach trip from London to York that lasted four days
in 1754 took only twenty hours by the 1800s.[23] This revolution in
transport, quietly underway for centuries before the invention of the
railroad, the car, and the plane, had profound human consequences:
in the Middle Ages, common people were more or less cemented
to the land they worked; consequently all their business and social
relations were necessarily local, with all the reliable monotony that
implies. But coaches made the world at once more accessible and
more socially confusing. No longer was your physical universe confined by the horizon you could see from your doorstep, and social
opportunities grew commensurately. As people began moving en
masse, a whole new legal system—called piepowder law in English—
evolved, with its own new courts, to deal with the problems generated by traveling natives, visiting foreigners, and their sometimes
unpredictable interactions. Mobility, for those well off enough to
achieve it, could be a sign of high class; but at the same time it had
begun to dismantle the class barriers by throwing ranks together in
rich demotic confusion, and a whole new order of misbehavior followed.

Blaise Pascal (1623–1662), the French philosopher and mathematician, started a commercial coach service in Paris in 1662, but—as if aware of social risks—restricted it to the superior orders. Commoners, "les gens du peuple," weren't permitted to ride. Yet in his *Pensées*, perversely enough, he'd recorded one of history's more trenchant aphorisms against travel: "j'ai découvert que tout le malheur des hommes vient d'une seule chose, qui est de ne savoir pas demeurer au repos, dans une chambre" ("I have discovered that all human misery comes from a single thing, which is not knowing enough to stay quietly in your own room").[24]

That ambiguity about the seductive adventure of travel versus its confusions, irritations, and jarring confrontations animated a whole tradition in eighteenth- and early nineteenth-century English literature. Tobias Smollett's comic masterpiece, *The Expedition of Humphry Clinker* (1771), amusingly records a coach journey through England by the gouty curmudgeon-hero Matthew Bramble, his quarrelsome family, and a hapless servant picked up along the way, Humphry Clinker. In the course of the adventures Clinker is mistaken for and imprisoned as a highway robber; a notorious (and real) highway robber accosts the Bramble coach-and-four, only to reveal himself as a natural gentleman eager to reform; Clinker finally turns out to be Bramble's long-lost son. Bramble's bemusement at this nation in hectic transit is summed up in his dyspeptic evaluation of the manners of its burgeoning capital, London:

> There is no distinction or subordination left. The different departments of life are jumbled together—the hod-carrier, the low mechanic, the tapster, the publican, the shopkeeper, the pettifogger, the citizen, the courtier, all tread upon the kibes of one another; actuated by the demons of profligacy and licentiousness, they are seen everywhere, rambling, riding, rolling, rushing, jostling, mixing, bouncing, cracking, and crashing in one vile ferment of stupidity and corruption—all is tumult and hurry.—One would imagine they were impelled by some disorder of the brain, that will not suffer them to be at rest.

The foot passengers run along as if they were pursued by bailiffs. The porters and chairmen trot with their burdens. People, who keep their own equipages, drive through the streets at full speed. Even citizens, physicians, apothecaries glide in their chariots like lightning. The hackney coachmen make their horses smoke, and the pavement shakes under them; and I have actually seen a waggon pass through Piccadilly at the hand-gallop. In a word, the whole nation seems to be running out of their wits.[25]

American Motion

American history began with the confusions of mobility already in worldwide ascendance. Road transport was a given, and in any case indispensable on a continent whose distances forced travel even upon those who hated it. Economic change, usually for the better, was easy and here seemed almost natural; social movement, given the nation's early republicanism, more natural yet. From the very beginning Americans seemed to take for granted the clash of types and classes that Smollett found so new and so disconcerting in 1771; it was a natural companion to the nation's commitment to equality and the banishment of caste distinctions.

Nineteenth-century foreign observers found the panorama either exhilarating or repugnant, depending on their sympathies. Frances Trollope (1780–1863) arrived from England in 1827 and spent three years in America engaged on her husband's monumentally misconceived plan to open a fancy department store in Cincinnati—then a raw frontier town of twenty thousand whose only sanitation system was a roving herd of wild pigs that swilled down refuse from the streets. In her report to Britain on the experience, the wildly successful *Domestic Manners of the Americans* (1832), Trollope characterizes American social mobility as the inevitable graveyard of manners: "Any man's son may become the equal of any other man's son; and the consciousness of this is certainly a spur to exertion: on the other hand, it is also a spur to that coarse familiarity, untempered by any shadow of respect, which is assumed by the grossest and the lowest in their intercourse with the highest and most refined."[26] Yet she also catches (it appears unconsciously) another, more perversely pleasing note: egalitarianism sometimes fosters exaggerated respectfulness toward the humble, pleasingly spiced by surliness toward superiors:

> My general appellation amongst my neighbours was "the English old woman," but in mentioning each other they constantly employed the term "lady"; and they evidently had a pleasure in using it, for I repeatedly observed, that in speaking of a neighbour, instead of saying Mrs. Such-a-one, they described her as "the lady over the way what takes in washing," or as "that there lady, out by the gully, what is making dip-candles." Mr. Trollope was as constantly called "the old man," while draymen, butchers' boys, and the labourers on the canal, were invariably denominated "them gentlemen."[27]

Harriet Martineau, a more deliberate, even-tempered, and even-handed English observer, and far more sympathetic to democracy, began her long visit to the new nation in 1834. She too observed, and remarked as noteworthy, the same impulse to maintain civility not only apart from class but in defiance of it: "After leaving the men's wards of the prison at Nashville, Tennessee, I asked the warden whether he would not let me see the women. 'We have no ladies here, at present, madam. We have never had but two ladies, who were convicted for stealing a steak; but, as it appeared that they were deserted by their husbands, and in want, they were pardoned.' "[28]

Analogously, if tact and delicacy can bloom in jail, weeds can spring up from what at first looks like aristocracy: in a world on the move, appearances afford no guide to behavior. In Mark Twain's *Roughing It* (1872), the narrator, jouncing along in an overland coach somewhere between St. Joe and Fort Kearney, is joined by a Sphinx-like woman passenger, who spends an hour or so in grim and apparently aloof silence—until a casual remark by the narrator about mosquitoes opens her conversational floodgates. "Folks'll tell you I've always ben kind o' offish and partic'lar for a gal that's raised in the woods," she allows, "and I *am*, with the rag-tag and bob-tail, and a gal *has* to be, if she wants to *be* anything, but when people comes along which is my equals, I reckon I'm a pretty sociable heifer after all."[29] In the in-between and nowhere of travel, what looks like cool reserve can spin on a dime into overfamiliarity; one person's backwoods crudity is another's natural civility.

What the nineteenth century created in the way of mobility the twentieth perfected and extended. The settlement of both coasts and the great vacant in-between did not, apparently, deplete the migratory urge. Technology invented new and ever faster modes of transport. Thanks to economic growth, local and long-distance travel came within the reach of more and more people. And this, inevitably, sparked a dawning concern over problems of civility created by constant flux.

In the few short decades between 1831 and 1904, New York City flourished, graduating from its first horse-drawn omnibuses and tramways to streetcars, railways, and ultimately the city's great early twentieth-century civic pride, the subway, whose first line opened in 1904. At first (and in spite of a mob that thronged underground to ride it on opening day) the system sparked an outpouring of civic exhilaration. The intricate mosaics in the stations, the glass tiles that lit them from the streets above, the relative quiet and cleanliness of the trains, made them attractive and even romantic: there was a brief fad for celebratory popular songs like "The Subway Express Two-Step."[30]

Within a decade reality set in, bringing a disillusionment far more comprehensible to the latter-twentieth-century subway rider. By 1905, riding it began to seem an assault on one's dignity; the *Tribune* opined in an editorial on the subway that it was actually dangerous. "Human bodies constantly give off poisonous exhalations that are extremely harmful—far more than carbon dioxide," the paper announced, attributing this conviction to "one of the leading physicians of the Health Department."[31] Colonel Mann, in his self-appointed role as watchdog of public civility, repeatedly railed in the pages of *Town Topics* at the management of the subway, denouncing its crowds, the long waits for trains, and the mercenary greed of the management.

His outrage wasn't isolated; in fact, it became near universal in January 1915, when the line suffered its first major accident. A short circuit in the system near Broadway and 55th Street produced thick clouds of black smoke; trains stalled; passengers panicked and began herding toward the nearest exits at 59th Street. There were more than two hundred injuries, but only one person died in the melee[32] (unlike the infamous Malbone Street subway crash three years later, which killed over a hundred). But there ensued a massive breakdown in manners that, however predictable it might seem now, shocked the relatively innocent New York of 1915. The *New York Sun* reported the incident thus:

> As the passengers jumped to the tracks and ran shrieking toward Fifty-ninth Street those in other trains took alarm and became wild with fear. One woman who kept her head as well as she could said she wondered that a sane member of her sex survived. There may have been some incidents of chivalry, but she saw none.
>
> The strong overran the weak. Men climbed over the prostrate bodies of women and children, and women fought with one another.[33]

The effect of the 55th Street mishap quickly snowballed through Manhattan's entire transit system, causing what the *Sun*'s headline called the "WORST TRAFFIC DAY IN HISTORY OF CITY." Tie-ups were nothing new to the metropolis; they'd been marked by observers as a noteworthy feature of urban life since the eighteenth century. What seemed new to the city's newspapers in the aftermath of this first major breakdown in the subway system was the scale of the chaos it caused, and even more important, the apparently unprecedented collapse, below ground and above, of a standard of behavior everyone had hitherto taken for granted. The "procession of human beings that daily moves from here to there in orderly, businesslike fashion," the *Sun* editorialized, "was suddenly transformed into a riot of excited, pushing, shoving men and women who seemed to forget that the world would still go on."[34]

In the following weeks, the incident percolated through the city's newspapers and magazines, surfacing in editorials, letters, and news stories, all of which seemed to record, as if for the first time, a dawning and widespread awareness that crowding and speed had thrown an unforeseen challenge to the city's sense of comity and well-being. In its Sunday edition on January 10, 1915, the *Sun* devoted considerable space to the accident, arguing that it had focused attention not just on safety but "decency." "Daily patrons of the road [i.e., the subway] are mauled and hauled about, pressed against pillars, shoved against trains and generally subjected to treatment that imperils their bodies, racks their nerves and violates every instinct of decency."[35]

Passengers, like "Miss T. H.," wrote in with complaints of their own:

—*Sir:* Why is it that a young woman of refinement and breeding cannot use the subway trains as means of travel, especially between Manhattan and Brooklyn during a "rush" hour, without being accosted or annoyed by men, usually past middle age? I think, as do many other women in my position, it is high time we receive more protection.

The kerfuffle over transit manners led to a publicity grab by the city coroner, who had the Interboro Rapid Transit Company's directors (including Cornelius Vanderbilt) arrested on a charge of culpable negligence in the incident; Colonel Mann, in *Town Topics*, embarked on a weeks-long series of diatribes against the company's iniquities: "Manager Hedley [Frank M. Hedley, the first general manager of the system], as is his habit, adds insult to injury by impudently asserting . . . that the horrors of the subway 'accident' were entirely the fault of the passengers, who rushed about in a panic, instead of hanging quietly on their straps while being suffocated."[36]

Physical mobility presents a jarring visible challenge to manners. Social movement, whether upward or downward, while less obvious in its effects, can be even more destabilizing—though scholars disagree about how easy Americans have found it to move from class to class during the twentieth century (in fact, we seem no more socially mobile than any typical industrial democracy, and some historians think the United States today is more rigidly stratified than it was in the 1800s).[37] Nonetheless, we labor under a widespread *perception* that we live in a state of tumultuous flux, both physical and social, a world in which behavior demands constant readjustment in answer to ceaseless disruptions in the constellation of friends, neighbors, relations surrounding us. And with a thing as subjective as manners, perceptions count as much as (perhaps more than) facts.

The etiquette books of the Victorian era and even the early twentieth century implied that, however tricky it was to master them, the principles underlying good manners were unchanging. Even *Vogue's Book of Etiquette: Present-day Customs of Social Intercourse, with the Rules for Their Correct Observance*, a 1929 guide, geared as its title suggests to a self-consciously modern milieu, asserted that modern civility rested on a firm, clear, universal, ancient basis—the rigid class hierarchy of the royal court, where, as the *Vogue* editors who compiled the book put it, good manners "were intended to exalt the office and enhance the romantic and dramatic dignity of the ruler."[38] Yet, *Vogue* argued, even though the hypersophisticated autocratic rituals of Louis XIV's Versailles had long vanished, etiquette might still claim a rooting in eternal verities. "The best manners in the world come from kind-heartedness and a sense of justice."[39]

Emily Post agreed, believing that while a ferment in class relations might well complicate it, civility nonetheless rested on universal and unchanging moral principles. But later twentieth-century etiquette writers often assert that manners are no exception to a general rule of confused instability, and warn that we should be ready to remake them as circumstances demand. Consider the opening of a book that billed itself as the definitive etiquette manual for a dawning decade, *Letitia Baldrige's Complete Guide to the New Manners for the '90s:*

> *Another* book on manners?
>
> Yes, another one—but this time full of help in healing the woes of the previous tumultuous decade of the eighties and full of hope for the promising nineties ahead. Does our society need a change in its manners? A resounding "yes" is the answer.[40]

The belief that a changing world demands a continuous reinvention of etiquette becomes Baldrige's theme in segments like "Answers to Questions About Manners that No One Had to Ask Before"—mostly issues arising from romantic and sexual relationships outside marriage. Baldrige returns again and again to the social sea changes that, she believes, necessitate a revolution in etiquette:

> Since the early 1960s, it's as if some Superman-like character has been hurling us through time. The Youth Rebellion of the sixties and seventies, the impact of drugs, the proliferation of sexually transmitted diseases, the increase in divorce and single-parent families, the restless mobility of modern Amer-

icans and our increasingly time-pressured lives have all splintered many traditional family formations and altered our lifestyles.[41]

Beginning in the 1980s, such perceptions fostered a brand-new genre, the intercultural manners guide. Initially, such books appealed to business people trying to overleap cultural gaps in an increasingly global economy, but it quickly became apparent that interethnic miscues weren't exclusively a problem for the jet-lagged executive. Norine Dresser's *Multicultural Manners: New Rules of Etiquette for a Changing Society* (1996), for example, emphasizes the collision of mismatched expectations in increasingly polyglot American neighborhoods. An Armenian American affectionately gives a bunch of yellow flowers to her Iranian-American friend, and sparks outrage (in Armenian folkways, as Dresser explains it, yellow says, "I miss you," but in Iran it connotes hostility).[42] To Middle Easterners, an American thumbs-up is the obscene equivalent of the raised middle finger.[43]

Of course America has always been a crucible of many, sometimes ill-matched cultures, their collisions a perennial source of stress and misunderstanding. Nor is it a novelty to suggest that restless mobility challenges our social skills and offers shocks to received notions of taste and sensibility. Baldrige on the dislocations of the American 1980s eerily echoes Tobias Smollett's perplexity at the social turmoil of eighteenth-century London. New to the twentieth century is that this perception has become commonplace, backed by the increasing speed, frequency, and scale of American physical (if not social) movement, and fed by an aggressive and ubiquitous press, eager (like *Town Topics*) to tattle in salacious detail on the lapses of the prominent, and competing (like the *Sun*, the *Herald*, the *World*, and the *Times*) to report disasters like the 1915 subway accident and its consequent snarling citywide fracas. Radio, film, television, and the multiplication of channels by which these media reach us have increased the exposure still further. Groups with customs and habits

Americans saw as obnoxious could once be ghettoized and thereby ignored, but the modern and postmodern deluge of image and information makes it hard for the majority to preserve such self-regarding insularity intact.

A certain motion sickness in etiquette and manners has thus become a hallmark of the twentieth century. The first, 1922 edition of Emily Post's *Etiquette* was in essence a backward glance, a conscious echo of the self-assured etiquette guides of earlier generations, including Helen L. Roberts's *Cyclopedia of Social Usage* or Mrs. John Sherwood's *Manners and Social Usages*, which offered their eager clientele a glimpse into the hidebound mores of a perhaps mythical but nonetheless avidly emulated "best" class. But to Post's own amazement, her book became a gigantic best-seller (it quickly overshadowed its chief nonfiction rival, Papini's *Life of Christ*, and equaled the year's top fiction title, Sinclair Lewis's *Babbitt*).[44] She found herself flooded with mail from readers with anxious questions about everything from whether or not wearing of mourning dress was obligatory ("there are some who believe, as do the races of the East, that great love should be expressed in rejoicing in the rebirth of a beloved spirit instead of selfishly mourning their own earthly loss")[45] to what's the best garnish for a lettuce salad ("about one small cheese straw apiece)."[46] Readers' queries quickly led her onto ground no socialite could easily imagine, let alone tread—like the plight of the first-time-ever hotel patron who doesn't know how to order from room service. Post soon realized that her audience was vast, polyglot, and nervous about a boggling range of concerns. As she revised *Etiquette* through successive editions, she steadily refocused it away from the hermetic world of the New York rich and onto the problems of the roiling multi-classed masses, as personified in the imaginary reader her son later dubbed "the American wonder woman, Mrs. Three-in-One" (cook, waitress, and "charming hostess").[47]

The emphasis had shifted, in other words, from a world in which one class, however vaguely defined, served as a universal model, into a frank acknowledgment of complexity and messiness, in which a hundred different kinds of social aspiration were possible and no single custom, however time-honored and apparently unexceptionable, was right for every circumstance. Perhaps it was this that rocketed Post onto a pedestal of fame no Victorian etiquette writer had ever occupied: the intractability of the subject somehow demanded a last resort authority on manners, whose personal prestige settled questions too vexed to answer by democratic debate.

Indeed, that is a distinctive contribution of the twentieth century to the history of etiquette, the spontaneous anointing of the trademarked authority, the bulwark whose stability anchors her readers in the restless social surge surrounding them. Post was well suited to the conflicting demands of this role. Over her entire career, no matter how flexibly she adapted her advice to changing social conditions, she never gave up her conviction that universal moral principles formed a permanent bedrock for etiquette. Yet in other ways Post was very much a product of the century's ferment. Her mother-in-law, for example, reacted with indignation when informed that Emily had violated the unwritten code of her class by writing for publication as a contributor to *Ainslie's Magazine* and as the author of a novel, *The Flight of the Moth*:

> "Well, lots of women write books nowadays," Edwin said. "It's getting to be quite the thing. Look at Mrs. Edith Wharton."
>
> "Exactly." Mrs. Post's mouth shut tight on the word. Then she added significantly, "A divorcée."[48]

Within a few years Post was to confirm her mother-in-law's worst fears by joining Edith Wharton among the divorced (and also in the ranks of the auto crazed, writing in 1916 of her own cross-country auto journey in a book called *By Motor to the Golden Gate*).

Post's name remains synonymous with manners, and her example set a curious pattern in later American etiquette writing by combining a resonant name with sturdy good sense to create a durable trademark. Amy Vanderbilt followed her example, albeit with a more freewheeling and informal spirit suited to the cultural earthquakes of the 1960s and 1970s. Vanderbilt began her career as a beat reporter for a Staten Island newspaper. And though she ended tragically— overweight, three times married, a workaholic, she jumped to her death from the second floor of her East 87th Street town house on Friday, December 27, 1974—like Post she too lives on as a franchise, most recently in 1995 with *The Amy Vanderbilt Complete Book of Etiquette, Entirely Rewritten and Updated.* Postmodern recruits to the trade have followed the trend as well: Miss Manners is Judith Martin's proprietary sobriquet, Ms. Demeanor is Mary Mitchell's. Martin and Mitchell problematize their subject by maintaining a certain detachment, Mitchell with broad humor, Martin with irony, satirizing the demands of etiquette even as she upholds them.

A Study in Blue: The Case of the Classless Jeans

Americans do, without doubt, move restlessly from place to place. And while social historians disagree about how frequently we shift from class to class, we nonetheless experience the sensation of social movement, because the system of classes itself is unstable, perpetually realigning itself beneath us. Most Americans believe themselves nested in a vast social middle. Yet—as the sociologist Daniel W. Rossides has pointed out—what middle class means has itself changed radically over the last century. In 1900, it meant a self-employed professional, the owner of a sizable business, or someone who lived off the income from property.[49] By midcentury, an economic boom had created a more numerous yet very differently configured middle class: professionals employed by businesses, well-paid semiprofessionals, and skilled blue-collar workers, united—despite the differences in their work—by the fact that all received salaries for jobs ultimately controlled by others. Rossides also argues that the twentieth-century American economy belched out a flood of cheap consumables that deluded even the relatively dispossessed into thinking they were rising through the social hierarchy. "And," Rossides adds, "labor segmentation, the creation of meaningless gradations among occupations, also misled Americans into thinking that things were getting better."[50]

Americans can, in other words, remain mired in place, both socially and geographically, yet experience all the dislocation, anxiety, and vertigo of headlong movement, as long as the world is in flux around them. A married couple maintaining roughly the same standard it reached in 1980 will nonetheless feel its status slipping if the formerly stay-at-home wife went to work in the mid-eighties to preserve its middle-income perks. And yet if the salary she earns is high enough, the illusion reverses into one of upward mobility. Even as people move restlessly through it, the status system itself is changing ceaselessly. Small wonder, then, if people are confused and anxious about what manners are appropriate for the status group to which they think they belong.

The great American cultural markers, the universal talismans of what is socially acceptable and what courts ostracism, invariably reflect the volatility of ideas about propriety. Denim blue jeans supply perhaps the most ubiquitous contemporary example. In the catalogue to a singularly pretentious 1994 French exhibition on the cultural history of denim, Federica Di Castro wrote an essay announcing that "jeans are a reflection of a society with no differences, or a society which is about to become so."[51] Indeed, in *The Greening of America* (1970), Charles Reich lauded them as profoundly democratic, breakers down of pernicious class barriers. Everybody wears jeans, surely, but what kind and how varies in quite distinct ways, depending on one's class and status; denim is by no means incompatible with high snobbery.

Quite the contrary: as Fred Davis remarks in his study *Fashion, Culture and Identity*, jeans are in fact an ideal "vehicle for the expression of status identity"[52] (in 1992, for example, one could spend

$960 on a Karl Lagerfeld denim outfit). Yet a history of jeans also reveals a complex series of shifts in meaning. They seemed to have originated as an outfit worn by Genoese sailors, and before the 1950s, were unambiguously work clothes, designed, advertised, and worn for heavy physical labor. In the early fifties, they were only beginning their shift from work to middle-class play clothes, a change promoted by a series of advertising campaigns;[53] it was the early seventies before they colonized schools and became common classroom wear. By the eighties, they had become not only acceptable but a near uniform in suburban American schools.

Penelope Eckert, a cultural anthropologist, studied blue jean manners at a suburban Detroit high school in the early 1980s, and found much of the student body wearing them on any given day. By this time, however, jeans had acquired a boggling array of fashion attachments like flared- and bell-bottoms of various widths, which lent them a new dimension as potential identifiers for the school's two defining and mutually hostile social groups. There was an elite caste, the "jocks," heavily invested in the school's culture, and generally high in socioeconomic status. Then there were the conscious misfits, the "burnouts," bored with school and prone to illicit pursuits like drug use. Neither group was particularly numerous, but between them they defined the extremes of possible status and social identity at the school. A far larger group, representatives of the vast American middle, self-described as "the in-between" kids, wavered between the jock and burnout alternatives.

In Eckert's study, burnouts wore bell-bottoms. Jocks preferred straight legs, and were vocal in their contempt for bell-bottoms as passé and tokens of hopeless social ignorance. But the burnouts, perfectly aware that bell-bottoms were sliding out of fashion, wore them out of conscious antimodishness, jeering at the jocks as trend slaves. To wear the wrong kind among either group earned instant derision. Caught in the throes of social panic were the in-betweens, who wavered between the jocks and the burnouts, and whose jeans—typically flared, and therefore midway between bell-bottom and straight-legged—seemed, in Eckert's interviews, to reflect their uncertainty about where they belonged.[54]

If only the patterns held steady, jeans manners might easily be mastered. It would be plain which style would win the approval of what group; one could dress accordingly, to pass as belonging among the friends one wanted and signify indifference or hostility to the tastes of the group one strove to avoid. But fashion kept changing the system, thus infinitely complicating the task of adjustment. By the mid- to late 1980s, bell-bottoms had fallen so far off the fashion map that they ceased to serve as hallmarks of countertrendiness. For males, at least, the zone of social significance in jeans had shifted (under the influence of hip-hop and ghetto culture) from the legs to where on the hips the wearer secured the waist. And now, in the 1990s, a trip to The Gap in search of jeans exposes one to a choice of styles greater (and far more freighted with significance) than the range of exotic mushrooms beckoning the gourmand at Dean & DeLuca.

Learning manners and living with their consequences would be easy if people and their social systems would only stay put. But group relations are never stable anywhere; America is and always has been more volatile than the world average. Edith Wharton, imperially touring France with her chauffeur and friends like Henry James in an expensive car safely unaffordable to the masses, pioneered an activity that at the time must have seemed a safely permanent adornment of the civilized life. But within twenty years, Henry Ford had put it into the hands of the masses. Within thirty years after that it had begun destroying the peaceful and orderly countryside Wharton could never have enjoyed without it. The mobility it (among other technologies) made so universal heightened civilization in one way, but put the skids to it in others.

chapter three

Manners from Nine to Five: Etiquette and Power in the American Workplace

Cicero, Illinois, in the 1920s may seem an unlikely site for a watershed event in the history of American business etiquette. It was, after all, Al Capone's designated capital. In 1923, he commandeered the Hawthorne Inn on 22nd Street, established headquarters in a flat on the second floor, and quickly imparted to this once dull suburb a lasting roughneck image. In 1926 his gang, on a sortie from Cicero into downtown Chicago, blew the carved name "Jesus" off the facade of the Holy Name Cathedral while gunning down two rivals ("They had the swell head and thought they were bigger than we were," Capone explained).[1] Cicero became a town the civilized classes avoided, or sped through in taxis, crouched below window level as a precaution against random gunfire.

Nevertheless, in 1924, a sprawling industrial complex on Cicero's Cermak Road became the site of a series of pathbreaking studies of worker behavior: the Hawthorne experiments, still legendary among business historians. For nearly a decade, a phalanx of investigators from the Harvard Business School, led by George Elton Mayo

(1880–1949), an Australian-born psychologist and professor of industrial research, scrutinized AT&T's Hawthorne plant, a two-hundred-acre unit of the company's equipment-manufacturing Western Electric division, employing some twelve thousand people. Though the Hawthorne experiments studied a wide range of problems in management and in workplace social behavior, when they came to an end in 1933, they'd brought the experimenters to a single conclusion, which they christened "the great *éclaircissement*,"[2] the revelation (as it seemed to them) that worker attitudes and interpersonal dynamics had more impact on the factory's output than physical conditions, job design, or management planning.

They weren't alone in bringing change about, but the Hawthorne experiments marked a watershed in how American bosses treated workers, and portended the dawn of a uniquely American and peculiarly twentieth-century business dogma: that management's key responsibility lay not in engineering workers into an efficient physical relationship with their tasks and their machines but rather in molding their mental attitudes and modifying their social behavior. The boss, once a simple overseer, now became (at least to some management theorists) a social facilitator, a suited Amy Vanderbilt, charged with maximizing efficiency by setting the company tone and building a civil community in office and factory. The idea first rose to prominence in the 1930s, but its influence is still very much alive in business manners today—not only in popular guides like Letitia Baldrige's *New Complete Guide to Executive Manners*, but also in academic and quasi-academic management theories.

Propriety, Soldering, and Soldiering: The Lesson of the Bank Wiring Room

The Bank Wiring Room Experiment took place late in the Hawthorne series, beginning in 1931. Among business historians, it's perhaps the least well known of the major studies. But it delved more deeply than any of the others into the intricacies of human relations in the workplace, and the interplay between official and informal systems of behavior. It was designed, significantly, by an investigator well schooled in the meticulous observation of human behavior: William Lloyd Warner (1898–1970), a Harvard anthropologist whose earliest professional project had been a survey of aborigine culture in Australia's Arnhem Land.[3]

There were fourteen Bank Wiring workers, all male and working in three teams to assemble the mechanical switching consoles then used in central telephone offices. Each team included three wirers and a solderer; two inspectors cycled among the three teams looking for mistakes. The wirers threaded electric cable through a labyrinth of hundreds of metal terminals on preassembled switching banks. The solderers followed, anchoring the wires permanently to the terminals. It was tedious and physically taxing work: wirers and solderers worked on their feet, bent over the consoles in an awkward and fatiguing stance. It also demanded close attention: mistakes were easy to make.

Warner's modus operandi was simple: he moved the fourteen participating workers into a room of their own, isolated from the rest of the plant. He or his associates thereafter observed everything the workers did on the job, transcribing much of their conversation verbatim, and supplementing the data with extensive interviews. There was no genius in Warner's method, save to convince the workers that unreserved cooperation would do them no harm with management. His original aim was to explain a vexing tradition of worker recalcitrance that had long plagued the Bank Wiring unit at Hawthorne, and many another assembly system in early modern industrial America.

Western Electric, using what it thought were reliable scientific methods, had worked out a program of instructions for the performance of each job, then set quotas for minimum expected output. If a team exceeded its quota, it won a financial bonus worked out according to a complicated scheme. This system was supposed to keep the workers diligent and raise output. Yet it failed to do so: though clearly capable of meeting the quota, staff stubbornly and consistently underproduced. This was called "soldiering," a practice that had become endemic among industrial pieceworkers. Early twentieth-century scientific management experts became obsessed with soldiering, but workers proved resourceful in foiling every management strategy to stamp it out.

Warner discovered the reason for soldiering, and it turned out to be cultural rather than economic. Workers distrusted management; as they explained to the interviewers, they feared that if output sank too far below the "bogey" (as the group quota was called), or rose too high above, "something might happen." If they underproduced, they'd be bawled out; if they exceeded their quotas, management would be tempted either to cut piecework rates or raise the bogey.[4] The wirers and solderers saw themselves as a cohesive interest group, and worked out a tacit agreement to limit output to a mutually acceptable level, sharply lower than management's target, but nonetheless deemed fair by the workers, and just high enough to prevent recriminations from the bosses.

The unofficial workers' standard formed the centerpiece of an unwritten code of behavior designed to support and enforce it. Anyone who inadvertently overproduced was expected to hide the excess output overnight, then loaf discreetly the following day, in order to keep to the unofficial group quota. Those who cooperated earned a reward: acceptance by the group and invitations to join in the gold-bricking activities workers pursued on company time: pooling money to buy candy from the company store, shooting craps, placing collective bets on a racehorse always dubbed the "Test Room Horse" (Phar Lap was the name of a favorite). Failure to follow the unwritten rules provoked a standard response: "binging." Either as a game, a rebuke, or a combination of both, one worker sharply punched a coworker's upper arm. The coworker was then allowed one return bing, which ended the game and settled the conflict. When on one occasion two wirers and a solderer squabbled over whether or not the shop windows should be open, a fourth wirer, exasperated, finally cut them off: "Why don't you bing each other and then shut up?"[5] Anybody who consistently overworked became fair game for a binging: one worker, for example, a twenty-two-year-old German American, to another, a twenty-one-year-old Polish American: "If you don't quit work I'll bing you" (whereupon the twenty-two-year-old struck the twenty-one-year-old and chased him around the room).[6]

Management had never caught on to the subversive system thriving under its very eyes. All the workers' unofficial activities ceased abruptly if a foreman came into the room: the workers, believing in their own code as the strongest guarantee of their own welfare, took pains to assure it remained both undetected and the governing ethos of the Bank Wiring Room. "The employees," the observers wrote,

> had their own rules and their own "logic" which, more frequently than not, were opposed to those which were imposed upon them. . . . Orders, in the narrow sense, were carried out. But if orders include the way in which a person is supposed to execute them and the way he is supposed to conduct himself, the actuality fell far short of the ideal. Those rules and regulations which related specifically to conduct were, on the whole, disregarded by employees.[7]

Unbeknownst (until Warner told them) to any of its executives, the Hawthorne plant was a quiet battleground of colliding value systems. Bosses promulgated a formal canon of proper workplace conduct, based on the official output quotas and—obviously—forbidding on-the-job diversions like craps and horse handicapping, though it did strongly support after-hours recreation; the plant offered athletic facilities that included an indoor gym, thirteen tennis courts, six baseball diamonds, and a running track, as well as a social club that organized evening classes, beauty contests, and trips.[8]

Codes of workplace manners at Hawthorne were, in other words, rooted in a factory class system, with each successive step upward in the plant hierarchy bringing a change. The wirers and solderers, for example, dressed informally, with open-necked shirts. Their immediate superiors, called section and group chiefs, wore vests, but no suitcoats. The foreman wore a full business suit with coat and vest. He preached (and seemed sincerely to accept) company policy, doggedly urging his men to attend after-hours safety meetings that the company officially encouraged but workers strove to avoid. If he found the test room untidy, or caught men either socializing or helping each other with work (both infractions of company policy), he intervened.[9] The section and group chiefs were caught between the foreman and the rank and file—inclined to endorse official company policies, but closer to the workers in status, hence more aware of the unofficial system and more sympathetic to it.

The microcosm of the Wiring Room illustrates how a formal hierarchy of status can clarify good manners in one way and confuse them in another. If only one group made the rules, just one set of norms could apply: everyone who conformed would clearly belong, anyone who rebelled could be pushed out beyond the margins. But with even two interacting social groups of differing status, the rules become exponentially more complicated. Predictably, the high-status group—in this case the executive ranks at Hawthorne—establishes the official and (to a casual observer) only guide to "best" behavior. But in practice manners are rarely if ever the exclusive preserve of one group; all ranks compete to establish them. When it suits, the lowest status group may pretend to follow the code promulgated by the elite, but in reality devise—as the Wiring Room workers did—a tacit shadow system, not just different from authorized policy but quietly contemptuous of it.

As interclass relations become complex, manners become exponentially more complex.

Business Manners and Class Hierarchy

Business is the realm of American life that perhaps most assiduously preserves vestiges of rigid class distinction. The divide between boss and worker remains significant; indeed, the sensitive question of what befits one's rank in the company arises in most contemporary guides to business manners, sounding a status-obsessed note that has more or less vanished from general guides to etiquette. Here, for example, are Barbara Pachter and Marjorie Brody, authors of *The Prentice-Hall Complete Business Etiquette Handbook* (1995):

> Your actions should acknowledge your position in the hierarchy. Failure to follow the chain of command, for instance, is a faux pas that could cost you advancement. You are demonstrating respect for the position as much as for the person. Your boss is your boss—whether your boss is younger than you are, of a different gender or from a different background. Being surly or uncooperative shows bad manners.[10]

Yet in practice such distinctions in rank become troublesome: Pachter and Brody are somewhat vague about how to deal with them in real-life situations. They advise, for instance, that "lower-ranking younger executives" should rise if "higher-ranking older executives" enter the conference room. But which takes precedence, rank or age? Nor do they specify how one should greet a higher-ranking younger—or lower-ranking older—executive. They advocate acknowledging an equal who walks into a meeting; but does that imply a superior should be met with downcast eyes and demure silence?

Thus even in business, where hierarchy (elsewhere an American anathema) remains an accepted fact, class is a troublesome and ever-shifting thing. To begin with, the executive's exalted rank, despite its aura of tradition, was in fact a relatively late and quite controversial arrival on the American business scene. According to the business historian Thomas C. Cochran,[11] the characteristic American entrepreneur of the eighteenth or early nineteenth century was an unspecialized small-time merchant. He (for business in this era was predictably a masculine domain) employed one or two bookkeeper-clerks, one or two porters for heavy physical work, perhaps an agent in a distant city. Relations between employer and employee seem to have taken their cue from the egalitarianism of the early republic—somewhat formal, as suiting the dignity of citizenship, but resolutely antihierarchical. "Proprietors showed a high degree of impersonality in their dealing with both employees and customers. Paternalism was perhaps unnecessary in this land of opportunity; at any rate its practice was limited and loyalty beyond self-interest was less expected than in cultures like those of Latin America or Japan."[12]

Workplace democracy changed markedly around the time of the Civil War, as the momentum of growth and mechanization made businesses ever bigger, more geographically dispersed yet more specialized, involved in activities that required complex organization—all innovations that seemed to demand more active oversight and control by management. The railroads, growing explosively and dependent for both safety and economic success on precisely coordinated activities, seem to have been the first American industry to evolve a fully regimented, top-to-bottom management model. The pioneer in this enterprise was a Scots-born civil engineer, Daniel C. McCallum (1815–1878), who worked for the New York and Erie Railroad; his ideas spread through the influence of Henry Varnum Poor (1812–1905), editor of the industry's premier organ, the *American Railroad Journal*.

McCallum thought efficiency demanded a firm and unrelenting control of workers; to achieve this, he advocated arranging the workforce into a minutely calibrated and rigidly controlled hierarchy of autocratic bosses and dependent inferiors. Whatever its actual effect on efficiency, the company manual McCallum wrote for the Erie became the industry standard, and summarily disposed of old-fashioned republican business egalitarianism. Every worker, Mc-

Callum insisted, owed complete obedience to his immediate superior, and must therefore enjoy little access to, much less familiarity
with, anyone higher up on the management ladder: "All subordinates should be accountable to and be directed by their immediate
superiors; as obedience cannot be enforced where the foreman in
immediate charge is interfered with by a superior officer giving orders directly to his subordinates."[13]

In McCallum's model, American business, once informal, now
came to insist on rigid class distinctions—albeit in job definition
rather than social status. McCallum's system, to the considerable
extent that it still influences American business management, is an
abiding subterranean influence on workplace manners. It was perhaps the earliest example of what management-studies jargon calls
the "U-Form" of business organization ("U" standing for "uni-
fied"),[14] in which orders emanate from a single source atop the company, then flow downward rank by rank.

This system never quite achieved what its pioneers envisioned.
By the turn of the twentieth century, the pure U-Form was already
being revised by a new generation of management specialists who,
while thinking it desirable to manipulate workers, sought means of
control other than rank and authority. The first wave of reform,
most famously represented by Frederick W. Taylor (1856–1915),[15]
ushered in what the business historian Daniel Wren has dubbed the
"Era of Scientific Management," in which bosses tried to micro-
analyze jobs and micro-manage workers, as if personnel were machines who could, through a system of rewards, be refitted and
adjusted until they reached a mechanical standard of desired efficiency. Scientific management quickly alienated many workers and
some managers, however, and by the 1920s had ushered in what
Wren calls the "Social Person" era, dominated by a belief that pro-
ductivity ultimately depended on the nuances of social interactions,
both among workers and between workers and their superiors, and
that the true key to efficient work therefore lay in amicable and
supportive human relations.

The Hawthorne experiments marked a milestone in this way of thinking, since they at least appeared to produce hard scientific data in support of it. Categorical orders about tasks on the factory floor, Social Person theorists thought, were doomed to backfire. Rather, bosses should influence workers by discovering and meeting their human needs, smoothing their relations with each other, and helping them work out their own ways of accomplishing tasks. Improving job performance thus became a matter of making life at the plant as dignified, even as pleasant as possible.

This fundamental debate over what's the right social model for the workplace, never fully resolved and probably not resolvable, remains with us, the source of a confusion about roles that has haunted employee relations ever since. Is the boss a taskmaster, laying down laws from a remote height, concerned only with extracting a maximum of labor from subordinates for the minimum possible compensation? A father figure, issuing orders and advice, but in the hope of making the worker's life better as well as improving efficiency? Or is he a friend and equal, cooperating with the rank and file to render the business mutually rewarding for manager and worker alike?

During its corporate heyday, from the 1920s until the 1990s, AT&T dramatized the contradictions of the Social Person approach. As Warner's portrait of the Bank Wiring Room showed, it was in practical organization a hierarchy, with a bold line drawn between managers with authority and manual workers subordinate to them. But in the 1920s—and even as the Depression began to bite in the 1930s—AT&T went to considerable lengths to improve workers' welfare and bolster morale. In addition to its extensive recreational facilities, the Hawthorne plant boasted a plant magazine, the *Hawthorne Microphone*, an on-site hospital for workers, a company-sponsored savings and loan association, and a stock option plan open to all employees.[16]

Such fringe benefits, in part no doubt aimed at fending off labor unrest, but also surely arising from a real concern with worker welfare, sent an oddly mixed signal. To the degree that they gave workers a feeling of privilege, they tended to suggest an egalitarian workplace, and that was certainly the feeling AT&T wanted to perpetuate, at least in its public relations. Featured in 1930 in David Lawrence's adulatory on-again off-again *Saturday Evening Post* column, "American Business and Business Men," Walter Gifford, the company president, stressed the point:

> The old master-and-servant idea, which almost necessarily existed when the owner was the manager, is giving place to a system based more on the spirit of cooperation than of conflict.
>
> There is much less bunk about business than there used to be. The pretentious conference, the domineering executive, the incompetent figurehead, are all going or gone. We don't shout at people nowadays and hammer the desk. We really hardly give orders. We suggest certain courses of action and the man who carries them out does his work better because he contributed something to the decision.[17]

Of course the elaborate network of perks and benefits, combined with top management's painstakingly expressed concern for the sensibilities of the employees, could have an antiegalitarian effect. The executive may want the best for his staff; may represent himself as a colleague, an equal, even a servant. But is this the courtesy of real deference, or only the lulling sensitive side of a disciplinarian father: benevolent, at pains not to trample the self-esteem of his offspring, but nonetheless a superior whose authority the children know better than to ignore, no matter how tactfully he exercises it? Certainly the Bank Wiring Room workers, despite AT&T's egalitarian blandishments, regarded even their foreman and his assistant with respectful awe. The horseplay that normally accompanied work stopped abruptly the instant either walked into the room. Often casually rude with each other, the workers never contradicted even a suggestion by the foreman, let alone an order or an iteration of plant policy. Yet as soon as he left, the wirers and solderers instantly reverted to their antiestablishment folkways, and set about subverting the company rules as far as (in their view) doing so served their own best interests.

AT&T was far from the first twentieth-century American business, laboring under the ideology of the Social Person era, to confuse workplace manners by remodeling the executive into a schizophrenic and (to workers) hard-to-swallow mixture of chief and chum, slapping wrists one moment and backs the next. The real pioneers of this philosophy were two influential giants of modern American business: the National Cash Register Company's John H. Patterson (1844–1922) and his even better known protégé, IBM's Thomas J. Watson (1874–1956).

Patterson, attempting to transform the cash register (then a technological and commercial white elephant called "Ritty's Incorruptible Cashier") into a staple necessity of American retailing, hit upon the idea that a successful entrepreneur should be less concerned with the product he was manufacturing than with the behavior of his employees. In practice this boiled down to a mercurial and unsettling mixture of signals. As self-esteem-building Dr. Jekyll, Patterson encouraged his sales force to think of themselves as worldly, entitled, prosperous, sophisticated, assured, at ease with anyone. But in the midst of such ego-boosting exercises, Patterson could quickly morph into an authoritarian Mr. Hyde, the tyrannical boss whose demise Gifford was prematurely to celebrate in 1930.

Patterson's system didn't hold together logically, but he seems to have carried it off anyway through sheer force of character, honing his ideas in a document fated to become legendary, the *NCR Primer*, whose lessons all National Cash Register salesmen imbibed. "When you go to a town," it counseled, "stop at the best hotel and get the best room you can. . . . You are representing a first-class concern—do it from the shine on your shoes to the room you occupy. Look it. Have the virtue, but assume the virtue if you have it not."[18] Personnel were repeatedly exhorted to worry more about maintaining the appearance and demeanor of gentlemen than mastering the use or innards of the cash register. "Put your trust in earnestness, candor and facts," the company exhorted. "There is nothing that denotes the gentleman more than earnestness and politeness."[19] At national and regional meetings, Patterson treated his employees like visiting celebrities: an honor guard escorted participants from the railroad station; they took VIP plant tours and sat down to formal banquets.

Yet even as it raised morale and self-esteem, the *Primer* slapped down presumption by prescribing a minutely choreographed canned sales pitch. This included a line-by-line script (which all salesmen were ordered to memorize and then recite verbatim to customers), and a rather patronizing list of deportment rules:

1. Don't fail to seat the prospect properly.
2. Don't point your finger or pencil at him.
3. Don't sit awkwardly on your chair.
4. Don't have a calendar on the walls. It may remind him of an appointment or a note falling due.
5. Don't put your feet on his chair.
6. Don't smoke.
7. Don't slap him on the knee or poke him with your finger.
8. Don't chew gum or tobacco.
9. Don't tell funny stories.[20]

At national conventions, after the fanfare of arrival, the honor guard herded salesmen to a lecture by Patterson, who ordered them to forswear cigars, coffee, and tea for the duration. "This is not a convention, it is a school,"[21] he admonished one session. And the banquet that followed was a far cry from the sodden debauch typically ascribed to businessmen turned loose at the annual corporate shindig. Patterson abominated meat and alcohol, so dinner was mashed vegetables and bottled water. Between gatherings, Patterson would descend on regional offices and test salesmen on their mastery of the *Primer*, staging a memorable tantrum if anybody violated one of the rules in the manual or strayed from the exact wording of the ordained sales pitch.

Watson, who imbibed Patterson's obsession with managing the human relations while working under him at NCR, applied it with a vengeance when, in 1914, he moved on to IBM, and helped turn it into a corporate giant without ever understanding—or evincing much interest in—computers. Watson rather built the modern IBM around a corporate culture, a set of officially promulgated "company beliefs," which, well into the Reagan era, remained at least the paper rationale for IBM's corporate existence. As IBM's 1984 employee manual, *About Your Company*, asserted: "when a company has established its credentials as a leader, challenges may confidently be taken as opportunities, and change as gain. But some things never change. The company's beliefs, the cornerstones of its success, are enduring." The most basic of these corporate dogmas, according to the manual, is "Respect for the Individual—Caring about the dignity and rights of every person in the organization."[22]

IBM admitted women to relative equality in the corporate hierarchy well ahead of the American business community at large, but put them—as it did all management trainees—through the company school near Binghamton, New York, where the training emphasized the same discombobulating mix of pride in one's status, humility before the company philosophy, and camaraderie among the members of the company team. The song written in 1930 by the pioneering women members of IBM's Customer Engineering Class #576 sounds all three notes:

> *We are lovable gals from IBM*
> *And Customer Engineers*
> *We're ladies enough, but know*
> *Our stuff, of that you have no fear.*
> *We take the place of fellows*
> *And grease up all the gears*

'Cause we're rootin' tootin'
High falutin' Customer Engineers[23]

The Patterson Paradox

Thus a basic contradiction entered business etiquette as an authoritarian management model began to yield to a more libertarian ethic in which workers were to be treated as apparent (if not always real) equals. The confusion—and the consequent uneasiness about proper workplace behavior—never evaporated, persisting in nearly every management fad of the last two decades. Alternately workers soar to the heights through frenzied programs of ego building, then as suddenly dive, becoming expendable serfs of workplace Darwinism. Such contradictions have become an inviting target for satire, most notably in Scott Adams's comic strip *Dilbert* and its best-selling book spinoffs, with their picture of workers first pummeled by the whims of autocratic bosses, then numbed by corporate visions of touchy-feely teamwork. Managers keep underlings in place by never allowing them to figure out just what their place is, empowering them one day, humiliating them the next, and humiliating them with empowerment programs the day after that. "The terms *team member* and *associate*," Dogbert advises in *Dogbert's Top Secret Management Handbook*, "should be used instead of the diminutive terms *pud* and *loser*, respectively. The new terms sacrifice nothing in accuracy."[24]

This isn't a new note. By the 1920s, business etiquette manuals had already become a distinct subgenre in manners literature, and from the outset they struggled with the implied contradiction between America's ideal of equality and the built-in inequities of the boss-worker relation. Class, the inherent insults of which mainstream etiquette experts often deplore, tends to emerge as a far more ambiguous issue among the business writers. Nella Henney, who wrote an early example in *The Book of Business Etiquette* (1922), began with a sketch of the stratified system Americans thought typical of the Old World.

> In other countries the manners have been the natural result of the national development. The strong who had risen to the top in the struggle formed themselves into a group. The weak who stayed at the bottom fell into another, and the bulk of the populace, which, then as now, fell into a third or was divided according to standards of its own. Custom solidified the groups into classes which became so strengthened by years of usage that even when formal distinctions were broken down the barriers were still too solid for a man who was born into a certain group to climb very easily into the one above him. Custom also dictated what was expected of the several classes. Each must be gracious to those below and deferential to those above.[25]

By the twentieth century, Henney asserted—just as AT&T's Walter Gifford was to assert a few years later—American business had replaced such invidious class distinctions with a sort of workplace republicanism. "When a man hires others to work *for* him," Henney wrote, "he invites discontent; when he hires them to work *with* him there may be dissatisfaction, but the chances of it are lessened. A business well knit together is like any other group, an army or a football team, bound into a unit to achieve a result."[26]

But elsewhere Henney betrays the same schizophrenia that beset John Patterson's NCR and afflicted AT&T's effort to bolster employee self-worth and foster an egalitarian team spirit on the factory floor. Bosses are rulers; workers, however deftly soothed, are inferiors. Bosses may behave considerately, but when they do, workers owe them deferential gratitude. Repeatedly Henney insists that a business depends on a dominant leader, whose strength lies in superiority, not inspired colleagueship. "The atmosphere of most business houses," she tells us, "is determined by the man at the top.

His character filters down through the ranks."[27] And what percolates up must be strictly controlled. "Each man is directly responsible to his immediate superior. He should never, unless the circumstances are unusual, go over his head and he should never do so without letting him know."[28]

This paradox has been a curiously tenacious one in modern manuals for business behavior. Yet rarely if ever do writers seem aware of it. In *Standard Business Etiquette* (1937), Justus George Frederick echoes Gifford and Henney:

> In older days business executives ruled by inspiring fear and by repressing the importance of the worker. Today functional organization has emerged, and business is an enterprise between people of equal dignity who learn the ways of equals working together. The old days when the boss considered himself far above the worker are very obsolete. But this *compels* education for equality and dignified functional place in organization.[29]

Nonetheless, a disguised authoritarianism lurks within such sentiments:

> The desk-thumping "Napoleon" type of business "boss" is "out" like the stern "heavy parent"—but of course so also is the clock-watching, chiseling, "soldiering" employee. The "must do" of older times is today replaced by "want to do." The employee is not "obeying"; he is "cooperating."[30]

An employee reading this might well wonder if the reality of authoritarianism has indeed changed, or merely its rhetoric. For the boss remains a controlling superior, imposing values and a code of behavior on workers. The novelty lies only in his newly acquired ability to interiorize commands in subordinates instead of barking orders aloud, mesmerizing the worker until she no longer knows where her own motivations leave off and management's begin. The lists of business etiquette rules that comprise the bulk of *Standard Business Etiquette* don't resolve the confusion. Liberating though it sounds when Frederick says that "any higher-up executive . . . is there merely to tally and give any assistance needed—he is almost unnecessary,"[31] *Standard Business Etiquette*'s workplace rules implicitly contradict this:

> Study carefully the disposition and temperament of the executive you serve because these are the main guides to the attitudes you must take.
>
> Study carefully also the habits and tastes of the executive you serve, in order to avoid clashing with them in any way.[32]

Indeed, the proper employee is independent only in having been brainwashed until he intuits orders and follows them as if they were instincts of his own. If this raises a worker's self-respect, it does so only by rendering him oblivious to the power controlling him. Which, surely, amounts to little more than slavery, perpetuated by mind control rather than law, whips, or chains.

Business Manners for the Nineties: Total Quality Personality Reengineering

Clothed in the quaint rhetoric of Depression-era business speak, the crude self-contradictoriness of Social Person management now seems both obvious and antiquated. The surprise, perhaps, is how robustly such strategies in fact survive, thinly disguised but essentially intact, behind contemporary American business fads like Total Quality Management (TQM) and Corporate Reengineering. Their apparent aims are radically different: management theory junkies who fled TQM when they read Michael Hammer and James Champy's tough-sounding business best-seller, *Reengineering the*

Corporation (1993), thought they were doing something revolutionary. But both approaches, carefully scrutinized, boil down to Social Person management; only the rhetorical clothing differs. In both systems the aim is to codify and control workplace behavior, regularizing relations among bosses, workers, and customers.

Ensconced though they often are in MBA programs, the real affinities of TQM and Corporate Reengineering lie with programs of behavior modification; their advice and their concerns overlap to an eerie degree with etiquette writing, and they share its conviction that there's a right and a wrong way to do things—yet without ever quite being able to articulate a set of clear ethical principles to guide that conviction. Total Quality Management, an amorphous system that is nonetheless given expositions of Proustian length by its proponents, is in essence an attempt to translate a perfectionist work ethic and a spirit of cohesive group cooperation (a blend Americans attribute to, and envy in, the Japanese) into an American business philosophy. To this mixture TQM advocates add a fat lexicon of management science jargon and a fatter yet armory of motivational rhetoric, often sports inspired, with which to bombard and acculturate workers. Employees, in one of TQM's favorite terms, must feel (and be) "empowered"—independent, self-starting, confident, and competent. Yet (equally important in TQM dogma) they must also form cooperative, spirited, mutually respectful teams. Finally, these fiercely independent, empowered, and ego-free team players must also yield to the charismatic aura of a high-voltage TQM executive—who bosses without bossing, leads fearlessly but remains everyone's friend, and tactfully lays down the law to anyone whose sense of empowerment prompts her to question the canons of proper TQM behavior.

Great business leaders, according to one TQM manual (Jack Hradesky's *Total Quality Management Handbook*), share five hallmark traits with names like Modeling the Way, Inspiring a Shared Vision, and Encouraging the Heart. Foggy these rubrics may be. Foggier yet are the directions Hradesky gives for fulfilling them. "Encouraging the Heart," for example, demands that (as brotherly colleague) the executive "make creative use of rewards," "be personally involved as a cheerleader," and "say 'thank you,'" but also that (as exacting boss) he "foster high expectations," "link performance with rewards," and "provide feedback about results." Modeling the Way, which on the face of it sounds more leaderly, does indeed demand that the manager firmly articulate "rules of the road" and "be expressive (even emotional) about . . . beliefs." But he is also called upon to "build commitment by offering choices."[33]

Reengineering, as outlined in Hammer and Champy's *Reengineering the Corporation*, is, in tone at least, leaner and tougher. "Reengineering," they explain, "seeks breakthroughs, not by enhancing existing processes, but by discarding them and replacing them with entirely new ones."[34] Still, while much of the book consists of case histories of two-fisted CEOs who jolted their companies into success by revolutionizing them, the executives themselves often report a motivational style remarkably like John Patterson's, alternating ego massage with displays of authority, and accompanying both with a steady barrage of snappy slogans and catchphrases.

Rhetorically, reengineering demonstrates a strong apparent preference for the warrior style. In *The Reengineering Revolution: A Handbook* (1995), Hammer and Steven A. Stanton warn explicitly about the dangers of too much politeness in business: "Another sign of weakness is slapping people's wrists instead of breaking their legs. Often, as a reengineered process is implemented, some key senior manager will perceive it as an intrusion on his domain. . . . If, instead of confronting this individual harshly, the executive leadership cozens [coddles?] him and gently urges him to reconsider his opposition, the game is lost."[35] In Hammer and Champy's original manifesto, *Reengineering the Corporation*, the CEO heroes whose case histories constitute much of the discussion at first seem a macho lot, like John E. Martin of Taco Bell, who rouses his comatose company with strokes of business-process genius like "K-Minus," a strategy that called (Martin explains) "for a kitchenless restaurant, evolved from our belief that we are a customer-driven, retail-service company, *not* a manufacturing company. We believe our restaurants should *retail* food, not *manufacture* it."[36] For any colleague skeptical about the wisdom of boldly visionary strategies like removing the kitchens from restaurants in order to improve customer service, Martin reserved a devastating response: "each time I would listen, smile, shake their hand, and thank them for being an important part of Taco Bell's successful *past*."[37]

Yet it would be much too simple to characterize reengineering as the final frontal attack on such civilities as the marketplace observes, with the CEO rampant as dominant beast in a corporate jungle. Hammer insists, for example, that reengineering is not downsizing. The point is to redesign the job, not humiliate or liquidate the worker, and both *The Reengineering Revolution* and *Reengineering the Corporation* are TQM-like in the stress they put on cooperation and group spirit. Reengineers are supposed to be leaders, but they are also supposed to excel in "the ability to work as part of a team, [and] the patience to listen to the needs, fears and concerns of everyone who will be affected by reengineering."[38] Such vacillation between the authoritarian and the humanitarian urges is endemic in popular business manuals, whatever their underlying management philosophy. "Top people *stand out*," announces Debra Benton of "Benton Management Resources" (headquartered in Fort Collins, Colorado). "But they also *fit in*."[39]

In mid-1997, there were 174 books currently in print on business manners. Many of these were practical guides to foreign (often Asian) business cultures, but the bulk of them deal with the abundance of false positions endemic in the American workplace. True-False quizzes abound, as if to imply that the conduct needed to win advancement is a question of scientific fact rather than instinct or guesswork. Pachter and Brody's *Complete Business Etiquette Handbook* (1995), for example, features an "Etiquette Awareness Quiz": a sample question asks how far apart two American businessmen should stand when talking to each other (the correct answer, they say—

without explaining why—is three feet).[40] In her 1991 book, *Professional Presence: The Total Program for Gaining That Extra Edge in Business by America's Top Corporate Image Consultant*, Susan Bixler ("president and founder of the largest corporate image consulting firm, The Professional Image, Inc."),[41] opens with a "PPQ" (for "Professional Presence Quotient") test, which runs the gamut from table manners at business meals to what kind of wool to look for in a business suit.[42] Yet the practical advice in the discussion that follows is familiar: the ambitious tyro must master the nuances of caste in a system where overt hallmarks of rank have been either blurred or obliterated:

> The head of the table is the "power perch." It is reserved for the most senior person present. The three other important positions are those to the right of the power perch, the seat to the left, and unless it is too far away, the seat opposite.
>
> If you are new to the organization and uncertain about your place at the table, hover around the coffee and doughnuts, examine the conference room's paintings, or admire the view.[43]

Business leadership depends on keeping employees socially inferior, maintaining hierarchical distinctions through a mixture of polite condescension and blunt rebuke. But it also depends on tact, with bosses taking pains to foster the emotional well-being of staff. The real difference between TQM and Corporate Reengineering lies only in which of these ill-matched duties receives the stronger emphasis, with TQM's partisans playing down the perquisites of leadership, reengineers trumpeting them. In a sign of just how overdetermined and socially confusing the situation is, *Dilbert* has been commandeered as a tool by the very forces it satirizes: Hammer and Stanton's *The Reengineering Revolution: A Handbook* features a number of *Dilbert* strips as comic relief. It should not surprise us, given this kind of atmosphere, that anxiety and ambiguity about proper business behavior have become institutionalized. Draconian dress codes that arbitrarily relax on Fridays (although only according to carefully calibrated guidelines); imperious CEOs who demand ducal compensation packages, along with employee obedience and homage to match, but who also pointedly christen themselves with hearty regular-guy nicknames—like General Electric's "Jack" Welch, or "Chainsaw Al" Dunlap, Sunbeam's erstwhile head (ignominiously lopped off in 1998).

Letitia Baldrige began her career in the State Department, and her *New Complete Guide to Executive Manners*, probably the most popular contemporary manual of business etiquette, emphasizes not just the inevitability but the desirability of rank and protocol: "Rank and deference sound un-American in a way, as though an artificial imposition of titles was more important than people's true value and worth, but that is not the case. Adhering to protocol, understanding and obeying its rules, brings order to the workplace and to society."[44] But when it comes to explaining what this means in practice, Baldrige waxes vague, as if reluctant to face the consequences of a serious return to rank. Mirroring proponents of an egalitarian workplace who nonetheless advise deference to a boss, Baldrige avoids a square confrontation with the issue. Instead of taking her example from the conference room or cubicle, where rank might sting, she ushers it onto neutral and painless territory: "stop to let a car from a side street . . . get in ahead of you. This is deference at its very best—kindness to a stranger in trouble."[45]

Business etiquette is civility with a bottom line, driven by the urge to achieve a hard-edged practical result: profit. It doesn't aim, at least not directly, for the deeper but more numinous benefits of civility in general. But in its contradictions, workplace civility dramatizes a conflict at the heart of contemporary manners, particularly acute in the United States, thanks to the dilemma posed by our traditional fondness for a culture of equality and our equally passionate pursuit of status. As a culture, we engage in a schizoid practice of which Walter Gifford, AT&T's president during the thirties, was a business pioneer—proclaiming the demise of the imperial executive, even as the anthropologists studying the Bank Wiring Room in his Cicero plant were discovering (and seeking, for the good of the company, to perpetuate) a rigid worker-boss hierarchy.

This merely reflects, with a clarity of outline not readily found elsewhere, a profound ambivalence about civility: a yearning for the predictability it brings, but a suspicion of the culture of privilege that supports it. Part of our history conditions us to demand a universal, classless, supposedly simple system of republican manners: which, could we only attain it, would be both beautifully and impartially simple, with everyone giving and claiming the same treatment. Yet in practice it has proved difficult if not impossible to devise a functional system of manners without reliance on the paraphernalia of rank. Despite the twentieth-century revolution in gender relations, customs that yield precedence to women remain common, though perhaps on the ebb. And would anyone want the elderly or the ill deprived of extra respect and consideration? Perhaps age and health are less powerful determinants of social status than birth or economic attainment, but in manners they do constitute a rank based on the Golden Rule if nothing else.

No: class of some kind is the very mold in which civility is cast. Yet with class distinctions dynamic and confusing if not in a state of actual decay, manners must inevitably become problematic and civility appear under threat. The struggle between autocracy and democracy underway in the American workplace merely mirrors, with an almost theatrical exaggeration, our general love-hate relationship with civility and etiquette.

chapter four

Bride, Groom, and Corpse:
Rituals and Rites of Passage

Weddings and funerals, the two great public rites left in the average American life, have been occurring at rough parity since the start of the twentieth century. In the 1990s, there have been about 2,800,000 marriages every year as against 2,100,000 deaths. And though it remains possible both to mate and expire without a ceremony marking the joyous or grim event, it is nonetheless rare. Mating and mortality seem not to have lost their impact as epochal life facts, and Americans, no matter how rootless, no matter how hell-bent otherwise on decivilizing and demythologizing life, still meet them with elaborate and expensive rituals. Jessica Mitford's razor-edged best-seller, *The American Way of Death* (1963; reissued posthumously in 1998), mounted a clarion and still-resonating attack on the excesses of the American funeral and the rapaciousness of undertakers. But thirty years later the industry, while changed in important respects, still flourishes. In 1994, it took in $8.5 billion, which resolves to an expenditure of just over $4,000 per corpse; in 1995, the national Funeral Directors' Association put the average cost of a funeral (exclusive of a grave site, burial vault, flowers, and obituaries) at $4,624, a 24 percent rise in the four years since 1991.[1] The wedding industry is far less formally organized, and reliable figures are thus harder to come by; plausible 1996 estimates of the average bill for an American wedding ranged from $6,000 to $16,000;[2] nationally we may spend as much as $32 billion on weddings every year.[3]

No other human activities, of course, are really comparable. And on no others do we spend so freely in pursuit of demanding rituals in which none of the participants or observers (save possibly the corpse) knows exactly how to behave. Mistakes are likely, public, memorable, and embarrassing (a whole genre of wedding books, like *Bride's Book of Wedding Disasters*, exploits this fact). Both permit, even require, behavior that in other contexts might seem rude. Crying is permitted, even expected, at both, a license granted at almost no other social rites. Both call for unfamiliar clothes, and breed multiple social situations in which almost nobody knows how to act at all, let alone impressively: even the professionals hired as facilitators sometimes seem at a loss, or come up with grotesquely tasteless advice. While one can, of course, marry at a county clerk's office or arrange to be sped, naked and on the cheap, from deathbed to crematorium, weddings and funerals stand out as a last bastion of stateliness in American life, marking transitions in which we make compensatory and sometimes bizarre obeisance to gods of formality elsewhere relegated to oblivion. Sixty-eight percent of Americans, for example, still opt for a formal, old-fashioned service and burial.[4]

Surely there is nothing absurd in the urge to counter the shock of such fundamentally wrenching experiences with ceremonies that reaffirm human dignity. Death is self-evidently pitiless. Marriage, while its roots are a matter of controversy among historical anthropologists, may well have originated in the forcible kidnapping of bride by groom—a harsh fact still obscurely commemorated in the honeymoon trip, and perhaps even echoed in the modern wedding's tendency to lavish attention on the bride, as if to compensate for an impending break with a comfortable past, a looming loss of power and independence. Some ethnic marriage customs allude openly to the atavistic barbarism of nuptials (Moroccan grooms, for example, ritually beat their brides with a dagger handle during the marriage rite).[5] It should not, therefore, surprise us that weddings and funerals are both prime concerns for etiquette authorities, and linchpins for sizable industries designed to guide paying customers through them. Everyone goes to weddings and funerals, yet almost no one does so often enough to be self-possessed at either, particularly in a multicultural nation where a gay marriage ceremony can differ as much from an Islamic wedding as an Irish wake does from a Jewish funeral, and where increasingly large percentages of the betrothed and the grieving or dying design—in whole or in part—their own rites.

Etiquette advisers have reacted to this growing anxiety and complexity with ever longer chapters and ever more detailed step-by-step advice—especially on nuptials. The 1995 *Amy Vanderbilt Complete Book of Etiquette* offers a massive 165-page wedding section, not untypical for post–World War II guides. Yet the most striking change from the etiquette manuals of the 1880s to those of the 1980s and '90s is a mushrooming preoccupation with buying, as the understandable anxiety caused by transitional rituals has shifted gradually away from how participants should act, battening instead on the apparently more congenial and preoccupying American question of what they need for the occasion and how to buy it. Civility— and not just at weddings and funerals—has increasingly become something sought and bought at retail rather than absorbed from the manners and mannerisms of a peer group. As a social force, class may be in turmoil; but marketers, profiting by the confusion, have transformed traditional emblems of status into selling tools, offering assurance as a commodity to be purchased rather than acquired by imitation.

Consumerism is, of course, ubiquitous, from car showrooms and home-decorating magazines to the cosmetics counters at department stores. But nuptial and funerary entrepreneurs have grown clever at hiding their kinship with the more flagrant forms of salesmanship, promoting themselves rather as advisers and counselors, raising anxieties about what's proper and then—for a stiff price— offering reassurance. Most brides (not, of course, all) resist buying a wedding dress at Sears, and Sam's Club doesn't—so far—sell caskets. Rites of passage seem to demand prodigalities of acquisition, but a specialized kind, appropriate to the gravity of the events being commemorated.

The Bride Wore Air

Weddings in general—nineteenth-century weddings in particular— evoke images of formality, grace, courtly elaboration. Yet the case was often far otherwise. Consider the following wedding notice, published in the Salem, Massachusetts, *Gazette* on April 21, 1818:

> At St. Johns, Mr. Samuel——to Mrs.——, widow. She was in a state of nudity while the ceremony was performed.[6]

As the notice went on to explain, this was a consequence not of bridal eagerness but rather the observance of an old custom: a widow married in clothes bought by her dead husband was thought to transfer responsibility for his outstanding debts to her new spouse. Marrying naked supposedly rid the bride of any liability she might be carrying unawares into the union. And while this is a curiosity, it is a significant one, dramatically illustrating one difference between weddings and virtually every other common ceremonial occasion of American life. Despite their complete respectability, marriage festivities are expected, in fact virtually required, to thread elements of rowdiness into the show of respectability. Garters are thrown, brides kissed by non-husbands, old shoes tied to limousines that speed through the streets, horns blaring. Such customs are vestiges of even franker ancient practices like the lewd all-night carousals that in Europe once obligatorily took place outside the bridal chamber door. Rude, surely, if considered in isolation; but in context what's expected, fit, and therefore polite. Perhaps the joyous optimism inherent in a new marriage is powerful enough to accommodate the expression of unruly instincts, the animal vitality pulsating underneath the veneer of civility. At the church door, controlled rudeness, even a certain ritualized violence, is an essential part of propriety.

Scholars disagree about the origins of human marriage. Edward Westermarck (1862–1939), the great Finnish anthropologist, argued in his classic *History of Human Marriage* that it arose from an innate human peacefulness, a hunger for safety and community. "I consider it probable," he wrote in 1922, "that it developed out of a primeval habit, . . . the habit for a man and woman (or several women) to live together to have sexual relations with one another, and to rear their offspring in common. . . . This habit was sanctioned by custom, and afterwards by law."[7] Other authorities have challenged this view, arguing that far from amounting to an expression of human solidarity, marriage essentially arose from organized rape, with a young man forcibly carrying off a woman, then reaching some kind of accommodation with her family and friends.

Customs, predictably, allow themselves to be read either way. In Wales, Scotland, and Ireland, as recently as the nineteenth century, a tradition survived according to which, on the day of the wedding, the groom descended upon his prospective father-in-law's house with a group of friends to claim the bride. The parents balked; a mock fight ensued; the father then galloped off with his daughter clinging to him, pursued by the groom. Finally the parent allowed himself to be overtaken, and the wedding ceremony duly followed. This might, of course, easily be taken as commemorating an ancient tradition of marriage by capture. Westermarck read it rather as a demonstration of the groom's bravery and the bride's parents' attachment to their daughter.[8] The meaning is impossible to resolve finally, boiling down to an inconclusive dialogue in nuptial rituals between the civilized and the violent, the refined and the rude, which in turn echoes a basic dilemma about the function of civility. Are civil customs the natural expression of an inborn human urge toward community and gentleness, or are they barriers thrown up against a natural drive toward conflict and violence?

Whether the ancient wedding celebrated the civilizing of a violent act or merely commemorated an amicable one, American marriage customs have, over the last hundred years, tended more and more to emphasize the genteel and repress the rowdy. As the nineteenth century gave way to the twentieth, this trend expressed itself in ever more determinedly opulent weddings, each demanding a maximum stretch of the budget to engirdle the biggest attainable inventory of made- or bought-to-order clothes, cakes, and memorabilia.

Many if not most of the widespread modern customs that now seem steeped in immemorial tradition were unusual, even unknown, until quite recently. In New England, at least, church weddings seem to have been exceptional in the earlier nineteenth century: typically a justice performed the ceremony for a token fee of one dollar, which he customarily returned as a gift to the bride.[9] The white wedding gown was an innovation that swept the English-speaking world only after Queen Victoria chose it over the traditional royal fur and brocade for her wedding in 1840 to Prince Albert. And it took longer still before white came to seem the only proper color for a wedding dress. Brides of the American mid-nineteenth century wore whatever appealed to them. And what appealed to them, by contrast with the modern fantasy gowns pictured in *Bride's* and *Modern Bride*, was often practical. Young women kept scrapbooks full of swatches of wedding dress fabric they'd traded with friends, and a typical Victorian example, kept in the 1840s and '50s by Laura Kendall Hoadley of South Woodstock, Vermont (and photographed in Linda Otto Lipsett's *To Love and to Cherish: Brides Remembered*), is an anthology of almost everything but white—

stripes, checks, plaids, and paisleys in shades of blue, pink, red, and black.[10]

The etiquette authorities of the nineteenth century—even though they most often aimed at relaying to their readership the practices of the urban social elite—tended to stress the wedding as a simple, practical, and dignified rite, veering into impropriety as soon as it became too obsessed with getting the details "right" or slathering on a too-thick layer of pageantry. The real danger to good breeding at a wedding lay, they seemed to think, in a vulgar overemphasis on pomp and display. In *Manners and Social Usages* (first published in 1884 and revised in 1905), Mary E. W. Sherwood devoted but 51 of her 468 pages to weddings, confining her attention to the social problems presented by the ceremony: how the party gets to the church, how to form the procession, where to stand, and what to do during the ceremony. She ignored entirely the mountain of announcements, showers, rehearsals, gowns, suits, and other appurtenances essential to the modern wedding. In fact, Sherwood disapproved even of receptions: "An attempt has been made in America to introduce the English fashion of a wedding breakfast. It is not as yet acclimated."[11] And she regarded wedding presents as optional. Received, they had to be acknowledged by a prompt thank-you note, but Sherwood disapproved violently of gift-giving flamboyance, and in fact seemed to look askance on the very idea of the custom:

> Wedding presents have now become almost absurdly gorgeous. The old fashion, which was started among the frugal Dutch, of giving the young couple their household gear and a sum of money with which to begin, has now degenerated into a very bold display of wealth and ostentatious generosity, so that friends of moderate means are afraid to send anything. . . . So far has this custom transcended good taste that now many persons of refined minds hesitate to show the presents.[12]

This note seems to sound repeatedly in accounts of weddings, from about the turn of the century through the 1920s. The all-out spendthrift wedding was plainly becoming a fact of life—*Godey's Ladies' Book*, for example, had begun featuring patterns for wedding gowns in the 1850s; Sherwood's disapproval, often echoed, suggests vulgar nuptial display was becoming commonplace. And in the early years of the twentieth century, even in a New York avid for fads and given to hyperbolic displays of wealth, the press often reserved its most enthusiastic wedding coverage for the ceremonies that affected a self-conscious simplicity, and dignified themselves by a respectful reaffirmation of ancestral links with the city's modest past.

There was, of course, a frank snob appeal here: the couples best positioned to invoke family history tended to be the scions of its oldest patrician clans. In 1905, for example, the Sunday, June 3, edition of the *Tribune* featured a wedding of which Mrs. Sherwood would surely have approved, between Helen White Stevens and Gilliat G. Schroeder at St. Mark's Church. The ceremony was brief and understated (the bride "in a frock of white radium and ecru lace, with which she wore a leghorn hat decorated with white plumes"), the reception that followed a low-key affair, only "for the relatives and intimate friends," at Delmonico's.

So much for the wedding notice; but despite its modesty, the *Tribune* considered the Stevens-Schroeder marriage remarkable, amplifying its coverage in a separate article on the society page. Lineage was its theme. Helen Stevens, the *Tribune* wrote,[13] was "a direct descendant of Peter Stuyvesant in the sixth generation and in the seventh generation from Governor Winthrop of Massachusetts." The white wedding gown, draped with antique lace belonging to the family, was her mother's, "of the old-fashioned Canton crêpe which was embroidered . . . in China. . . . The embroidery is not the kind seen on dresses today." But the centerpiece of Stevens's bridal costume, and the climax to which the *Tribune* story builds, was her fan.

Several months after the death of Mrs. White [the bride's grandmother], when her daughters ... were looking over some of her belongings, they came across a little box worn by age. Opening it, they found it to contain the fan which the bride carried. It was inscribed thus:

> This was the Wedding Fan of
> JUDITH WINTHROP
> Who Married
> BENJAMIN WINTHROP
> in 1785

What made this wedding noteworthy was its stark (though hardly impoverished) simplicity. Clothing and objects were plainly important, but only because they linked the couple to their ancestry, reaffirming the deep-lying network of social bonds antedating and extending beyond the marriage. It was the kind of eloquent merchandise that couldn't be bought at any price, impossible to find in the kind of splashy nouveau riche wedding Colonel Mann's *Town Topics* liked to describe with ironic fulsomeness.

When Emily Post published the first edition of *Etiquette* in 1922, she echoed Sherwood's hostility toward over-fancy weddings; her advice was brief and severely practical. Set the date, order invitations from the printer (Post gives no instructions about these except to specify they should be engraved), and assemble a guest list, a task which—in this first version, before the book became a massive bestseller and in subsequent editions grew to embrace the social needs of a burgeoning, socially ill-defined, and significantly downscale mid-America—was uncomplicated: "In cities where a Social Register or other Visiting Book is published, people of social prominence find it easiest to read it through, marking 'XX' in front of the names to be asked to the house, and another mark, such as a dash, in front of those to be asked to the church only."[14]

The assumption, then, is that a proper wedding is the privilege of a properly high-class couple. But high-class meant unpretentious and simple. In her one concession to the reader's probable desire for a description of an ideal wedding, Post cites as "perfect" the nuptials of a poor woman and a rich man, held at the bride's father's humble house, with a homemade wedding cake and a reception whose refreshments were sandwiches, bacon, eggs, and cookies. The music came from a Victrola.[15]

The Dawn of the Blockbuster Wedding

Yet even in 1922, the forces of social history had already undermined Post's plea (and Sherwood's demand) for simplicity. People, of course, have always lavished large amounts of money on extravagant weddings; but in the period from roughly 1880 to 1920, nuptial extravagance gradually shifted from being seen as an optional vulgarity of the rich to a proper exercise for everybody. Divorces, after all, had become public, expensive, and dramatic by the turn of the century, with the newspapers hounding participants and blazoning every detail of the more dramatic cases. If the explosive end of a marriage blazed before the public eye, why underplay the joyous beginning of one?

By the 1930s—and surely the deprivations of the Depression drove this urge—the American wedding had become the odd mixture of romantic fantasy and consumption unchained it largely remains today. Marcia Seligson, in her entertaining and still valuable survey of the wedding industry, *The Eternal Bliss Machine: America's Way of Wedding* (1973), sees this as the dominant theme of modern American nuptials, uniting all regions, classes, and ethnicities. "The American wedding," she writes, "is a ritual event of ferocious gluttonous consuming, a debauch of intensified buying, never again to be repeated in the life of an American couple."[16]

The phenomenon had become widely apparent by the twenties

and thirties. Women's magazines shifted up into wedding overdrive in February, March, and April, bursting with color photos and the lavender-pink writing that—with small refinements and variations— still characterizes wedding columns. Weddings, as the magazines presented them, were fairy-princess fantasies, dreamed up by the bride and actualized by her parents, whatever the cost. In its June 1935 issue, Edward Bok's *Ladies' Home Journal* featured another wedding at St. Mark's Church in Manhattan, and it was a far cry from the understated Stevens-Schroeder nuptials described a generation earlier in the *Tribune*. This time the bride, Nathalie Anderson, commissioned a color-coordinated extravaganza. The flowers alone demanded careful planning, a large investment, and occasioned a gush of copy:

> The bride's bouquet attendants showed the new tendency in wedding flowers—to have beautiful blossoms beautifully arranged without ribbon or other decoration and the exquisite lilies of the valley were actually nestling in a bed of malines, which helped each stem to stand out separately but effaced itself so that the bouquet appeared to be quite unstudied. . . .
>
> To keep the note of gay flower colorings against the deep stone, stained glass and wood of the church, the chancel was decorated with abutilon fern and smilax, and on the altar were masses of stock, repeating the lavender note of the maid of honor's dress and blending perfectly with her bouquet. . . . [17]

Condé Nast's *Bride's*, today billing itself as "the #1 Bridal Magazine" (with a 1996 circulation of 327,595),[18] first appeared in 1934 as a free handout in the northeastern states. Compared to the almanac-sized 580 pages in the June–July 1997 issue, the early numbers of *Bride's* averaged a mere 100 or so pages, but the content essentially resembled that of the magazine today: a relatively few service articles, whose subjects (usually including a section on wedding etiquette), naturally enough tend to reappear issue after issue, surrounded and dwarfed by a tidal wave of advertisements, inclusive but on the whole aimed at the higher end of the market. Stationers; department stores eager to supply dresses to the bride, gifts to her bridesmaids, and a bridal registry for the invitees; hotels and tourist boards selling honeymoons. But the theme, coursing through ad and feature article alike, is that a wedding is an extraordinary event, utterly beyond anything in the American bride's previous experience. No longer is the focus of anxiety on the social rituals associated with the rite itself or the mysteries of the marriage bed. Instead, the magazine stresses planning and purchasing a succession of goods-laden events, from the engagement to the climactic arrival at the couple's fully outfitted new home. The worst pitfalls threatening the bride aren't an inadvertent insult to a relative or guest, a misstep at the ceremony, or a failure of courtesy, but rather ignorance in the arcana of prenuptial shopping.

Throughout the 1930s, Chicago's department store Carson Pirie Scott advertised the free services of Miss Joan Adair, "The Bride's Secretary," whose prim countenance dominated its ads in *Bride's*. Customers gush with gratitude: "It's such a relief to find someone who will tell you what you really ought to wear. . . . The white fan made a lovely background for my flowers and everyone loved the bouquet."[19] By the 1940s, Miss Adair, still at it, had matured in the ads from "Bride's Secretary" to "Wedding Consultant," marking not only an advance in job status but perhaps a shift in perception, away from the social intricacies of matrimony and toward its business end, away from ritual and toward consumption. (World War II, with its burst of prosperity and unprecedented empowerment of women, no doubt supplied the momentum for this trend.) To romantic items like wedding dresses and dream Bermuda honeymoons, the ad pages had now added increasingly high-priced commodities like automobiles.[20]

In broader perspective the move toward etiquette as consumption emerges even more clearly. As edition followed new edition, the initially terse wedding section in Emily Post's *Etiquette* came reluctantly to terms with acquisitive exuberance, expanding its sections on clothing, food, presents, parties, stationery, personal and household trousseaux; by 1969, an 80-page wedding section had grown half again as long. And by 1997, the posthumous Emily Post trademark had exploded well beyond the pages of *Etiquette*, appearing on five separate book-length wedding guides (*Emily Post on Weddings, Emily Post on Second Weddings, Emily Post's Complete Book of Wedding Etiquette, Emily Post's Wedding Planner*, and *Emily Post's Complete Book of Wedding Etiquette Including Planner*), as well as two CD-ROM packages, *Emily Post's Electronic Wedding Planner and Etiquette Guide* and *Emily Post's Complete Guide to Weddings*. This, of course, represents only the Post division of the wedding etiquette industry; dozens of titles are available, and acquiring one or more guides and/ or planners has become the earliest harbinger of an avalanche of purchases.

A glance through the pages of any bridal magazine instantly reveals both the dimensions and the often tacky contents of the splurge; the gown alone is a study. First, one has to choose an overall style: Ball Gown, Mermaid, Sheath, Princess. Then, according to *Bridal Guide* magazine's *Ultimate Wedding Gown Guide*, there are twelve neckline styles (with names like Queen Anne, Illusion, Jewel, and Sweetheart), twelve acceptable sleeve designs, five possible waistlines, seven designs for the train, and ten head coverings to be topped by one of seven kinds of veils available in eight patterns of lace. In 1996, the *Wall Street Journal* estimated the average cost of an American wedding gown as $670;[21] in a 1997 photo spread in *Bride's*, prices for the dresses shown ranged from $296 to $7,000.[22] And the gown is only the beginning: the invitations, the ceremony and reception, the trawling for and hauling in of gifts, and the outfitting of a new home are all treated, with sometimes improbable extensiveness and authority, in every printed and software wedding guide.

It would, however, be precipitous to read this only as a triumph of gross acquisitiveness over sentiment. Etiquette guides to weddings and magazines like *Bride's* and *Modern Bride* dwell, surely enough, on things; yet consumption is motivated not by unmixed greed but rather the bride's palpable anxiety to buy wisely and *properly*. There is, in other words, a real if strangely directed ethical imperative driving marriage consumerism.

In its April–May 1995 issue, *Bride's* included a service feature on stationery (excerpted from the seventh edition of its *Bride's All New Book of Etiquette*). There are practical tips in the article: proofread carefully, order extra invitations to cover mistakes and forgotten invitees, allow up to two weeks if a calligrapher is hand-addressing the envelopes. But the real payload of the piece is to assuage the fear that this necessary purchase won't be handled appropriately. Like the ordering of a gown, wedding stationery has right and wrong uses that the bride is unlikely to have mastered. The line between acquisition and propriety is fine to the point of nonexistence. A prominent sidebar of Do's and Don'ts is heavy on points of the small morals: all invitations must be addressed by hand; abbreviations are forbidden; if a wife has a professional title, her name should occupy a separate line on the envelope, with the husband's title and name following.

Of course, a materialistic bride can make the purchase of a dress or invitations solely an excuse for a buying binge; but the literature of wedding etiquette suggests a subtler agenda, with public propriety now achieved by informed and tasteful buying rather than rites that imitate the customs of a social class with exalted status. Manufacturers offer wedding gowns in a huge range of styles and prices. Yet all the samples shown are studiously different from home and street wear. To buy them knowledgeably, the bride has to learn a new vocabulary of dress. However much they vary, all wedding gowns one way or another evoke formality, class, wealth, grace, tradition, and—perhaps as the summation of all these traits—a once-in-a-lifetime break with everyday style, an assertion of ceremony over routine. In this context, consumption is more than a Veblenesque display of superior wealth and status. Instead, it has become a medium for the expression of our desire for decency and order, our need to affirm a dimension of human worth beyond the amoral transactions of the marketplace.

Mary Roberts Rinehart (1876–1958), best known for her thrillers and mystery novels like *The Circular Staircase*, neatly caught this shift in a sentimental but shrewd 1935 *Ladies' Home Journal* story, "The Second Marriage," placed in the June issue to take advantage of the magazine's annual wedding drumroll. The heroine, Lilian, enamored but reluctant to give up her independence, embarks hesitantly on a union with Warren. Rinehart, with a firm grip on the susceptibilities of the mid-twentieth-century American reader, records the ambiguities of their relationship as a quiet duel of value-fraught possessions. On the honeymoon cruise, they occupy separate staterooms; Warren signals his forbearance from masculine brutality by appearing hesitantly at the connecting door every morning,[23] clean-shaven and decorous in dressing gown and slippers. But when they set up housekeeping afterward, trouble arrives. Will they sleep amidst Lilian's dainty taffeta hangings or in Warren's heavy wooden double bed, which clashes with the curtains and the rug? Warren's mahogany wins the first round, and the taffeta retreats to the attic. But the servants—who are Lilian's, female, and predate the marriage—sabotage the detente by refusing to put Lilian's gold and ivory toilet ensemble into this cave of woody masculinity. The climactic crisis comes when Warren buys a dog, which goads the servants into open rebellion. After a brief separation, loneliness convinces Lilian that male companionship is more important than satisfied servants or a feminine housescape. Warren returns.

"The Second Marriage" captures the role possessions have taken on in popular renderings of the mid- to late twentieth-century American wedding. Acquiring them is perhaps the central challenge of the extended ritual of getting married; oohing and aahing over them (as Rinehart clearly expected her readers to do) is an important part of that ritual, for participants and onlookers alike. Approve or disapprove of this phenomenon, it nevertheless forms a basis for a real social drama of give and take, supplying counters for a game by which the players ultimately decide which parts of their prenuptial lives they will keep, which will be sacrificed to the union, and which are negotiable. By 1935, the home-town social network that once would have monitored and might have dictated the couple's adjustment to each other was, if not completely gone, at least disrupted. Rinehart makes no mention at all of where or how Warren and Lilian live, who their friends and relations are. The only things left to sign them into some kind of mutual accord are the hints whispered by their furniture, silver, crockery, and dry goods. If these are tasteful and can be made to harmonize, the couple will settle their differences and end in happy companionability.

This is not quite acquisitiveness as an end in itself. The bridal buying binge generates a buzz, surely, but only as a means to an end, a way to smooth the potentially rough social and emotional transition from a single to a married state. Moreover, it bridges the shrinking but still significant power gap between the sexes. There are no groom's magazines. Wedding plans belong to the bride, who governs the epic splurge accompanying the marriage. From a feminist perspective, this is ambiguous. It could be seen as a delusive ploy, in which a spending spree blinds the bride to the inherent inferiority of her position and her impending loss of independence. It might, on the other hand, just as easily betoken a coming of age, an affirmation of her power in the relationship, and a symbolic righting of an otherwise endemic inequality between men and women.

For buying, in America especially, is a peerless leveler. Everyone, even the poor, can participate in it at some level. Ethnic, economic, and class affinities may have ceased to function as reliable guides to good ceremonial form, but consumerism has filled the gap left by crumbling barriers (and distinctive customs) of lineage, blood, and race, as these become increasingly confused and unreliable. Mass consumption doesn't always merit quite the scorn some cultural critics have heaped on it: it has helped to splice together a network of social manners even as the class system has become increasingly unstable, bewildering, and unreliable as an arbiter of manners. In weddings, commerce has helped to preserve some symbolic vestiges of an old-fashioned sense of propriety, dignity, and fitness on the solemn occasions of life.

The Final Binge: Death and the Tao of Shopping

As with weddings, so with funerals. Since at least 1963, when *The American Way of Death* became a best-seller, the American funeral has served as a ready-to-hand sign of our penchant for swamping the stark realities of life and mortality not with compensatory rituals but expensive, garish, and grating displays. Like weddings, funerals have been commercialized to the point where planning them has become a shopping trip, but an exponentially more surreal one: the casket display room at a funeral home is a full dimension of eeriness beyond the fitting room at a bridal salon.

Mitford offered a beguilingly simple explanation for the eccentricities of the American funeral: it was a scam, perpetrated on a grieving and gullible public by the funeral service industry. Mitford documented her case extensively and devastatingly, from embalming (a costly extra almost nowhere mandated by law and at best capable of preserving the corpse for a scant few weeks) to caskets with innerspring mattresses and appalling mortuary cosmetic jobs. Mitford, to her own delight, caused a national uproar, provoked a grassroots movement to regulate the funeral services industry more tightly, and ultimately helped bring about some significant reforms. Nowadays virtually all funeral homes at least supply customers with a disclosure form, making it more or less clear what they must pay for every proposed service and (in theory at least) giving them the chance to decline what they don't want and negotiate what they do.

Mitford's crusade didn't, however, significantly lessen the costliness or devulgarize the contents of American funerals. Nor did it loosen the grip of commercial funeral directing on American death.

In 1960 the industry, according to Mitford, took in $1.6 billion. By 1995, that had risen to $8.5 billion, a growth that outstrips the inflation of the 1970s and '80s (that $1.6 billion would amount to about $7.5 billion in 1995 dollars). Time and indignant satire haven't lessened the American public's willingness to buy what the funeral industry offers. We still invest in French Provincial caskets with posture-improving innerspring mattresses; embalming remains customary; funeral homes still offer (and often push) a wide array of ancillary services and goods: limousines, grief therapy for the survivors. Cooperative nonprofit memorial societies, recommended by Mitford as an alternative to the predations of greedy undertakers, have increased in number but have yet, in the United States at least, to threaten the dominance of the commercial funeral services industry. Cremation, in theory a simple and economical alternative to burial and the rigmarole that often attends it, is still relatively rare, though slowly increasing: nationally about 14 percent of the dead wound up as ash in 1985, 18 percent in 1992, and 21 percent by 1995.[24]

The inference is that on the whole, bereaved Americans really want a material display of some pretense, and get something beyond odd merchandise in return for spending heavily, even if they know the panoply is tasteless: the relationship between the customer and the funeral director is symbiotic. What are we getting out of $5,000 caskets, hostess gowns, and brunch coats for the corpse? Surely something akin to the reassurance conferred by a $16,000 wedding with a synthetically traditional gown and all the trappings: a bought version of the collective social and emotional rituals that once dominated rites of passage. In his classic study *Rites of Passage* (1909), the pioneering French ethnographer Arnold van Gennep (1873– 1957) drew a parallel between weddings and funerals. Both marked irrevocable shifts (from a single to a married state, and from life to death). According to van Gennep[25] and a successor, Victor Turner, both wedding and funeral customs tend to cluster far less around the states than on the disruptive transitions between them—in marriage the exciting and apprehensive time between the engagement and the exchange of vows (which is almost exclusively the concern of wedding etiquette, from Emily Post to *Bride's*), and the even more troubling period immediately after a death, when the deceased is so wrenchingly gone yet disturbingly present. From its earliest years as a self-designated profession, funeral directing's leaders insisted that the corpse be spoken of as if it was still alive, as if to prolong the transition and help the survivors adjust to the shock of the death. According to "Professor" W. F. Hohenschuh, whose "Quiz Class" columns enlivened the industry trade journal *Casket & Sunnyside* during the early years of the twentieth century, it was an unpardonable gaffe to call the corpse a corpse: "I make it a rule to receive the friends at the door, ask them if they wish to see Mr. Brown, supposing he is dead. I never ask them if they want to see the remains or the body. I always refer to them by name."[26]

Earlier, in the nineteenth century, Americans thought the corpse belonged at home; people strongly resisted any attempt to conduct funeral preparations and formalities anywhere else. Even when someone died at a hospital, the family would typically insist the body be brought home for a time before burial. Thus, whatever work the Victorian undertaker undertook was likely to be performed under the family's watchful eyes. This—as Mitford remarks—surely tended to hold costs down and minimize involved and grisly procedures like embalming or draconian (and often semisurgical) cosmetic makeovers. The family kept up an intimate contact with the deceased, and etiquette writers dwelt on how they should manage this stressful yet also therapeutic disruption in the customary conduct of the home. Mary Sherwood devoted a scant six pages to funerals,[27] five of which deal with the problems of mourning: how long it should be worn, how far it should restrict one's social activity. "Consideration of the dead body, so dear, yet so soon to leave us; so familiar, yet so far away," in Sherwood's words, is brief indeed, mentioning no role at all for the undertaker (her assumption seems to be that the body is properly an intimate family concern), and dwelling forcefully on the need for restraint. The proper coffin, for example, is

> simpler than formerly. . . . Made with care, it is plain on the outside—black cloth, with silver plate for the name, and silver handles, being in the most modern taste. There are but few of the "trappings of woe." At the funeral of General Grant [in 1885], twice a President, there was a gorgeous catafalque of purple velvet, but at the ordinary funeral there are none of these trappings. If our richest citizen were to die to-morrow, he would probably be buried plainly.

But starting in the 1870s and 1880s, undertakers began organizing. Their ambition, not unique at the time—doctors were in the process of doing exactly the same thing, though with far greater ultimate success—was to limit their numbers, raise their status, and hike their charges by claiming a hard-to-master professional expertise. In the 1890s and early 1900s, trade journals brimmed with high-minded rhetoric about the need to raise standards in (and control entry to) the trade. "The trend of the profession is onward and upward," *Casket & Sunnyside* editorialized in 1905. "The importance of fixing the terms upon which applicants may enter the profession can not be overstated."[28] Leaders agitated successfully for restrictive state licensing laws and the establishment of colleges of "mortuary science." Usually the rhetoric was impeccably high-minded, though occasionally a more naive and revealing note crept in, as when, in 1910, the British *Undertakers' Journal* confessed to "something very alluring in the prospect of rubbing shoulders on a basis of equality of status with doctors and parsons."[29]

In the United States, funeral directors staked their claim to professional status on a quasi-medical technique that (or so they persuaded the public) added dignity to the painful transition from life to death: embalming. It had become fairly common with the carnage of the Civil War, when embalmers gathered vulturelike around the battlefields in search of war dead whose corpses had to be shipped long distances home.[30] And, in a grisly echo of Queen Victoria's pioneering of the white wedding gown, it was Abraham Lincoln who helped make embalming a national fashion: his corpse underwent the process to preserve it on its thirteen-day-long rail journey from Washington to Springfield, Illinois. The pioneering issues of *Casket & Sunnyside* are loaded with ads for every appurtenance of the trade ("REAL HEARSE BARGAINS," blazoned a front-page announcement in the January 1905 issue), but competing embalming fluids dominated, often touted by testimonials from satisfied customers:

> I can find no fault with Ultimatum Embalming Fluid.
> —Saxton & Son, Cleveland, O.[31]

Embalming was the arcane process that—in the minds of funeral directors at least—necessitated moving funeral preparations and rites from the home to the mortuary. Once the rituals of death had been transplanted onto their own turf, they began devising and adding the array of pricey ceremonial addenda that gradually formed the standard of propriety for American funerals and that Jessica Mitford was far from first to decry.

In fact, as with weddings, so with funerals. In the first edition of *Etiquette*, just as she'd attacked kitsch-laden weddings, Emily Post laid into commercialized funeral directing as a crass operation. Her exasperation had the same root in each case. Material display had, she thought, supplanted a healthy preoccupation with fitting behavior at solemn and important rites. The "Best People," whatever their class, should resist the slide into materialism and commercial boosterism. Over the years, however, Post, her rivals, and her imitators—just as they'd done with weddings—began accommodating themselves to the inevitable. In the 1945 edition of *Etiquette*, Post was still offering counsel about how to manage and how behave at a home funeral. But she also included practical advice about how to negotiate with a funeral director, somewhat soft-pedaling (without retracting) her earlier conviction that much of the trade amounted to a predatory racket. "Because of the criticism of a certain not admirable type of funeral director in the earlier editions of this book," she wrote, "it must at once be said that this was not meant to apply to any of the directors of high reputation who are conscientiously considerate not only of the feelings of the family but also of their pocketbook."[32] Nonetheless, her overall tone is of reluctant accommodation to a powerful rather than admirable trend; her attitude heralded Mitford and the industry's other vocal critics. Explicit or veiled warnings—about controlling unnecessary costs, avoiding pretentious displays, and evading the clutches of an unscrupulous undertaker—are standard in most contemporary etiquette guides.

Yet historical and cultural anthropologists, reevaluating American funeral customs, have proved reluctant to view this as a simple morality tale of scavenging buzzard and brain-dead prey. Glennys Howarth, in a useful comparative study of American and British customs, *Last Rites: The Work of the Modern Funeral Director* (1996), emphasizes the mutually satisfactory nature of the relationship. Vulgar and insinuating or no, the local funeral director supplies visible tokens and packaged activities to contain grief and guilt toward the dead, easing mourners through the stressful time just after death when the deceased person isn't yet socially "gone."[33] Excessive expenditure is therapeutic; the survivors know, of course, that the corpse feels no gratitude for its plush mattress or the landscape painted inside the casket lid. But we need some way to articulate and validate our ambivalence, the illogical yet natural desire to think of the corpse as still connected to the world of living human needs and sensations, even as we acknowledge that the person has vanished from it.

In *Celebrations of Death: The Anthropology of Mortuary Ritual*, anthropologists Richard Huntington and Peter Metcalf argue in essence that the funeral's apparent vulgarity can, viewed dispassionately, amount to real if displaced delicacy. They point out that expensive and showy funerals aren't exclusive to modern America; elaborate and grotesque funerary customs are widespread, across cultures and throughout recoverable history. Several sociological surveys have been performed that suggest the bereaved derive real comfort from the funeral director; one study of Boston-area widows found they rated the undertaker as a more effective source of solace than either clergymen or doctors.[34] Huntington and Metcalf also remark shrewdly that funerals rarely if ever occasion truly uncontrolled spending. Even when the casket is swamped by floral tributes, custom regulates the display: no matter how much he may spend at the florist's, a casual friend does not, if he has a fit sense of the occasion, send an arrangement so extravagant it competes with the immediate family's. In fact, the range of what funeral directors offer and customers buy is far more limited than it would be if expenditure were the only object.

Funerals may be far costlier than strict need would dictate, but this seems to reflect the mutual consent of buyers and sellers, since innovations haven't caught on—as with Lafayette Gatling, the Chicago funeral director whose South Side funeral parlor pioneered drive-by body viewing;[35] a trend of following funerals with a lavish catered reception hasn't quite caught on (a dying Georgia man left $5,000 for a post-cremation bash served by black-tie waiters, but this struck the *Atlanta Constitution* as odd enough to warrant a 1995 feature article).[36]

Perhaps we should face the not necessarily damning fact that shopping, purchasing, and paying have become central and necessary underpinnings of American social comfort, inseparable from our visceral sense of what's right and fitting on momentous occasions. Pundits, even our own consciences, may tell us this is wrong, urging us back to a time when propriety meant following a time-honored religious practice or at least imitating the ways of the Best People. But the grip of religion has weakened and the Best People are increasingly hard to identify. Our sense of how we should live is, for better and worse, increasingly influenced by what we see for sale.

Wal-Mart Weddings, Home Depot Coffins?

All the same, Americans are far from easy in their acceptance of consumption as a medium for the propagation of civility. By the mid-1990s, the enclosed shopping mall, an innovation in the 1960s, was already becoming a slightly tatty and perhaps endangered artifact. A reaction had set in against its contrived illusions of affluence, safety, and village green amity. We've grown wiser, as evidenced by the publicity over Long Island's Green Acres Mall, which became a symbol of sorts for the decline of the shopping mecca—its name suggestive of rural calm, its actual location a swath of roughneck suburban blight (a widely publicized fatal stabbing happened in 1994 between the lingerie and bath departments of the mall's Victoria's Secret). Falling out of love with their malls, Americans have increasingly shifted their shopping to grim utilitarian boxes—category-killer book and home-goods giants, glaring fluorescent-lit discount warehouses, factory-outlet plazas whose very ubiquitousness has much diluted the cachet of the designer labels sold in them. Having once invested shopping with an aura of elegance and fantasy, we now seem perversely intent on pursuing it still more addictively while divesting it even of fake (let alone real) joy.

Might this happen with weddings and funerals? Some evidence suggests such a trend has already begun. Two chains of wedding superstores have recently appeared (David's Bridal, Inc., and We Do—The Wedding Store seem to be the biggest), occupying cavernous spaces of up to 26,000 square feet[37]—about half the size of a football field—and aiming to do for marriage what Home Depot did for hardware. A storefront funeral furnishings outlet—the Ghia Gallery—appeared in San Francisco in the late 1980s, offering off-the-shelf discount funeral goods: jewelry, caskets, urns (one in the shape of a liquor cabinet that played "How Dry I Am" when opened).[38] In 1994, Lloyd Mandel, a Chicago funeral director, opened a cut-rate showroom at a strip mall in Skokie, offering a guaranteed 25 percent in savings over the competition;[39] another company, New Hampshire–based Casket Royale, sells at a discount through its World Wide Web site (www.casketroyale.com). And in fact, the entire funeral services business, once exclusively the province of small local operators, has fallen increasingly under the domination of low-profile but aggressive conglomerates (the two largest of which, the Loewen Group and Service Corporation International, recently became embroiled in an acrimonious corporate slugfest).[40]

Even in the freighted world of mating and death, there is movement afoot to demythologize consumption, to wring the fantasy out of shopping, and to redefine it downward into a hard-eyed transaction, driven by a mutual and natural distrust between the buyer and the seller. Among the state-of-the-art nineties weddings featured in *Vows: Weddings of the Nineties from the New York Times* (1997), most seem determined to avoid the tacky excesses of the bride's-book fantasy:

> They cut out all but the essentials. There was no time for showers, cake tastings, bridesmaids' teas, cocktail parties or long deliberations over details. Margo chose her wedding dress in exactly an hour. "I had an appointment at eleven thirty at Vera Wang," she said. "Found the dress. Left at twelve-thirty."[41]

In 1996, one Glendale, Arizona, couple took this impulse to emblematic lengths (their wedding didn't make it into the *Times*, though it did merit a feature in *World Wastes*): their altar was a ribbon-bedecked garbage truck: "We'll be talking about this forever,"[42] the groom remarked.

And as the small, family-operated funeral parlor fades into history, replaced by the corporate death franchise, even undertakers sometimes seem seized by an odd ambivalence. As long ago as 1985, *Casket & Sunnyside* (its title now modernized and streamlined to *C&S*) featured a reminiscence by Thomas Finan, a St. Louis funeral director who joined the business in the 1930s. What, he seemed to be asking, hath Mammon wrought? "We give you a nice appearing body," he mused, "a nice memory picture to look at, perhaps after somebody's been in the hospital and not looked too good. We give you nice surroundings, an air conditioned building, you ride in a big car. It just seems to me that we want to deny death."[43]

It seems poignant and significant that even an advocate for the industry is dubious about the articles of its industrial faith. No sooner do we begin to come to terms with a manner of doing things than a trend sets in that begins to undermine it and redefine it.

The civility lesson taught by these eccentric excesses of the American wedding and funeral is twofold. First, civility is more adaptable and inventive than we give it credit for: it can take root even in the most unpromising soil. And second, as soon as we adjust ourselves to new manners, and begin to think them natural or even inevitable, they crumble in our grip, as if change and instability were part of their very existence, accelerating further in response to every attempt we make to immobilize them.

chapter five

Virtual Rudeness: Mass Media, Mass Communications, Mass Mannerlessness

Anyone persuaded that foaming rage is native to the human condition need look no further than the Internet. USENET—the huge public bulletin board open to anybody with access to a computer—may be the largest repository of obscenity and abuse the world has ever amassed. This unedited posting, culled from the "alt.flame.niggers" board in the summer of 1997, is by no means unusual, either in the moltenness of its rage or the stumbling incompetence of its English:

> I just had to wait over an hour to pay a traffic ticket. The line was at least 100 people long. Thanks to affirmative action, there were two fat nigger ladys working the counter. I know they got their job due to their color, because they sure as fuck didn't get their job based on qualification. The lazy cunts were as slow as death plus they were bitchy to the people in line. They would just shuck and jive back and forth totally ignoring the fact that there were people who REALLY work for a living,

waiting on them to do their job. It amazes me that no-one went bezerk and shot one of them . . . why are Niggers universally incompetant??? They really are a waste of Carbon.

A rebuke materialized almost instantly: "Look MAGGOT! You couldn't even qualify for the animal level of intelligent life." So too did a bellow of support:

You're are right on the fucking money! they never say thank you or nothing. their always mad about something.and they can't run the gas pumps at 7–11. i would never hire a black woman, their the worse. their brainless. i got this one black lady fired from the gas station. she was a rude bitch.[1]

The abuse in this particular thread broke after six postings, but there were plenty of other USENET controversies underway to affront the sensibilities. In August 1997, seventy-one bulletin boards bore the "alt.flame" heading. "Alt.flame.niggers" held about fourteen hundred messages; other groups bulged with as many as four thousand. "Alt.," in Internet terminology, designates a forum open to anyone, and generally not supervised by a moderator who excises obscene, racist, irrelevant, or libelous postings. "Alt." groups thus offer a window into the uncensored thoughts of USENET's 7 million subscribers worldwide.[2] As these not exceptionally rabid examples attest, the vista can be disturbing. Few people, no matter how consumed with inward resentment, would dare speak so unrestrainedly or woundingly in the living presence of strangers, but the personal computer seems to unleash the beast in those who have the urge to shatter social taboos but lack the courage or articulateness to do so viva voce.

Internet enthusiasts point to this simply as the unavoidable side effect of freedom. If hateful feelings and harebrained ideas make their way on-line, so too do original and valuable ideas that may find expression nowhere else. No needles' eyes restrict passage to an anointed few: the crackpot, Nobel laureate, buffoon, and sage compete for attention as equals. But not everyone finds this exhilarating: in its scant two decades of existence, computer-mediated communication has generated more than its share of debates between the conflicting claims of unconfined free speech and censorship. In 1997, the Supreme Court struck down a law regulating the Internet for obscenity, thus reassuring First Amendment purists willing to tolerate the inevitable quotient of rudeness untrammeled free speech entails. But cyberspace has also run amok with license on occasion, pushing tolerance to its limits, from Matt Drudge to a troubling recent incident in Canada, in which graphic testimony from a sex murder case, closed to daily press reporting by the judge in an attempt to ensure fairness, found its way onto the Internet. And the ease with which adults can gain access to such material has raised acute concerns about children. Any six-year-old with basic computer (and rudimentary reading) skills can, left to herself, surf instantly onto shoals of junk, obscenity, or hatred, and become a defenseless target for exploitation, whether sexual or merely commercial.

How Real Is Virtual Viciousness?

On-line invective is shameless because its perpetrators feel shielded from consequences. Chat-room natterers and bulletin board ranters are not immediate human presences, but packets of digitized data zooming across a network of machines and cables. This affords a minimum of safety: no one, after all, can be physically assaulted in cyberspace, which is space only in a metaphorical sense. But a few hours welded to the monitor and tapping at a keyboard can deceive. One can—although at present the systems for doing so are often primitive and always balky—listen to someone's voice, converse aloud, view a still or moving picture. In a device now common on the World Wide Web, a Colorado Springs software company's web site trains a camera on Pike's Peak,[3] feeding a new image to the site every minute, so the browser can "go," in a virtual sense, and see what's "there." A tyro exploration of the World Wide Web can exhilarate in its illusion of world travel: clicking on a link to Paris's municipal web site (www.paris-france.org) seems to accomplish a speed-of-light journey across the Atlantic, without even incurring the small cost of an international toll call.

Yet, of course, the journey is imaginary and the traveler planted at home before a PC screen; the images scrolling past may come not direct from France but through an intermediate storage point in Ohio. A site purporting to originate in the Rockies may be a fraud perpetrated from someone's Newark basement. "Virtual" has become popularly interchangeable with "computerized"; more tendentiously yet, it has become synonymous for many people with "real." Yet its exact meaning is far more provocative: "in essence or effect," according to the Oxford English Dictionary, "*although not formally or actually; admitting of being called by the name so far as the effect or result is concerned*" (emphasis added).[4] In a strict sense, then, *all* convincing images and representations are virtual. Computer simulations are linked by the principle of virtuality to movie and television images, indeed to all made-up but persuasive imitations of reality, from Balzac novels to Disney World thrill rides.

Loosely, colloquially, we use "virtually" to mean "really." To most people, "virtual reality" is reality, save only for the accident of its having been filtered through an electronic medium. Yet in the dictionary sense, "virtually" means "*not* really." In cyberspace, this paradox takes on serious—and not very widely understood—moral implications. The virtual person whose words, voice, or image come through a PC can affect the viewer much as a real person would. Yet in truth he's an electromagnetic phantasm; there is no sure way to ascertain that he has presented himself accurately. In a custom borrowed from the Citizens' Band craze of the 1970s, denizens of cyberspace often communicate using invented handles: real or false names, numbers, sometimes an eerie nickname (one contributor to

USENET's rec.games.board forum signs him- or herself "Pallida Mors"). On an adult chat channel, Twelve Inches in Toledo, who claims to be twenty-eight, may be seventy-five. Foxy Chick, the supposed topless waitress, could be a thirteen-year-old with a prosecutor father who materializes over her shoulder just as she is arranging an assignation. Nor can one be sure a virtual correspondent is even human: an increasingly large volume of electronic mail originates not from people but "bots"—robot programs that collect e-mail addresses and distribute automatic messages with contents ranging from mere junk to obscenities and threats.

In this carnival mixture of fantasy and reality, ids easily gain the upper hand over superegos. One speaks through a machine from the apparent safety of home to interlocutors virtually real but in practice as imaginary as aliens in a Nintendo game. The insult, let fly, seems virtual in the sense of "real" when one dwells on the satisfaction of venting anger, virtual in the sense of "not actual" when it comes to reaping consequences. But the hurt suffered by the person it lands on can be painfully real, and the anger thus aroused uncontainable. Hence, often, the origins of a flame war, and the not unreasonable concern about the deleterious effect computer communication can have on manners.

Worry dates back to the earliest years of the Internet. Norman Shapiro and Robert Anderson explored it in a 1985 Rand Corporation study, *Toward an Ethics and Etiquette for Electronic Mail*,[5] and it has persisted ever since as a nettlesome issue. No matter how arcane, technical, or exclusive the posting site, etiquette sooner or later becomes a topic of discussion and debate. Like every book of its genre, *The Internet for Dummies: Quick Reference* (1996) features a "Chatting Etiquette" section, which captures the ambiguity of virtual interaction. "The first rule of chatting," it says, "is that a real person with real feelings is at the other end of the computer chat connection. Hurting him or her is not okay."[6] Yet the second rule urges caution, "because you really have no idea who that other person is."[7] In real space the five senses, intuition, and experience supplement the exchange of language, and collaborate to warn us when the interpersonal temperature rises into a danger zone. On-line, one's interlocutor can all too easily figure either as an approving alter ego who duplicates one's thoughts exactly, a barbarian who deserves verbal massacre, or a substanceless phantom without vulnerability or a taste for vengeance.

Cyberspace multiplies the freedom—and the risk—of a costume party, where disguise liberates, encouraging people to act on impulses they'd normally suppress,[8] in a release of anarchic energy that can, despite the risks, be socially useful. Carnival license boasts a venerable history in Western culture—in the crude horseplay traditionally allowed at weddings, the feasts of misrule traditional at the winter solstice, or the Fat Tuesday celebrations that preceded the penitent self-deprivations of Lent. The modern American Halloween and New Orleans Mardi Gras are pale relics of the unzipped festivals countenanced by our European forebears (before the French Revolution, even under the generally authoritarian eye of the ancien régime, carnival revelers were permitted to dress up a piglet as Louis XVI and a goat as Marie Antoinette, then parade them, bleating and squealing, through the streets).[9]

But the traditional carnival is a limited indulgence, brought to a timely end before it leads to chaos. At the traditional French Mardi Gras, an effigy of the *Bonhomme de Carnaval* who presided over the festive misrule was, when the celebration ended, tried, hanged, and finally drowned,[10] marking a decisive return to the status quo. But the Internet is worldwide (though some governments, like Singapore, restrict access to it, and in the Third World it remains a luxury for the few). It runs all year, twenty-four hours a day; no ceremony ever returns it to the subjection of a monarch. And few if any of its louts, often pseudonymous, with e-mail addresses that can be difficult or impossible to trace, ever pay for their offenses against order.

A now classic account of a painful Internet manners fracas first appeared in John Seabrook's 1994 *New Yorker* article "My First Flame," which later furnished the narrative centerpiece of a book,

Deeper: My Two-Year Odyssey in Cyberspace (1997). Seabrook had
found to his own surprise that even as a computer novice he was
easily able to start, then continue at improbable length, a cordial e-
mail colloquy with Microsoft's William Gates (this was in the days
when Gates still figured in public opinion as the genial prophet of
a coming cyber-Nirvana rather than a robber baron). Their
exchange seemed at first to confirm the Internet's promise as a
status-blind forum where the obscure and great could confer on an
equal basis. Seabrook's article describing the experience provoked
the flame—from a technology writer who thought Seabrook had
not acknowledged him sufficiently. "Crave this, asshole," was the
greeting. The message itself began with "listen, you toadying dipshit
scumbag . . ."[11]

Anyone used to the peculiarly conventionalized pileups of obscenity de rigueur in on-line flaming will instantly recognize this as
nothing unusual for the genre. But Seabrook records vividly the
misery that washed over him when, unsuspecting, he retrieved it
from his mail file.

> The same intimacy that inspired people to speak their hearts
> also inspired them to say things that would be literally un-
> speakable in any other medium. Words that could not be spo-
> ken to my face (I would have walked away, or yelled back, or
> charged) or on the telephone (I would have hung up) could
> be typed and sent through the computer, and since the tech-
> nology had made this form of human expression possible, peo-
> ple were naturally going to take advantage of it.[12]

Printing the screed out seemed to cool it a little: paper somehow
neutralized the venom.

But not for nothing is the home computer called "personal." It
responds instantly to commands, or perversely refuses them by
crashing or freezing, an accident that usually feels as if it were an
intentional tantrum. PCs ask questions and demand confirmation

when issued an order. ("Are you sure you want to permanently remove these items?") Television can't compete as a simulated companion; rarely if ever does it force a viewer to interact with it. The car is the only other machine so twined into our personal lives and emotions. Even so, it can neither talk back as a PC appears to nor bring the virtual presence of strangers, friendly and hostile, into one's home. A couple of years ago, as a CompuServe subscriber, I began getting unsolicited junk e-mail, mostly touting lunatic investment schemes. On CompuServe's advice, I replied to these with a curt "DELETE," shorthand for a request to be removed from the sender's list. Then one of the mailers, a malicious genius, hit upon the inspiration of compiling an e-mail address list of everyone who'd replied with a negative, whether matter-of-fact or irked, and sending everyone on that list a copy of every negative and/or obscene e-mail received. Within days, my e-mail in-tray was a maelstrom of outraged protests from complete strangers, originally directed no doubt at the anonymous cyberpredator, but all addressed to me. At a loss to figure out what was going on, I replied to each missive expressing my bewilderment and dismay; the recipients would then answer, compounding the confusion.

Absurd in retrospect, it was harrowing at the time, and the only solution was to quit CompuServe and take refuge with a low-profile Internet provider, whose small subscriber base seemed less attractive to scam artists and sociopaths.

If the PC's immediacy sharpens the pain of an insult, its unquestioning obedience to the operator and its potentially global reach seem correspondingly to exaggerate the insulter's adrenaline rush. Anyone with Internet access can issue orders or demands for information to the world's nerve and power centers—the Treasury Department, the Pentagon, the Centers for Disease Control, the FBI, the CIA. And the ensuing exchange of information may commandeer, if only for a few milliseconds, dozens of intermediary computers at sites anywhere in the world: the Internet's signature technology breaks a message up into packets, each of which may travel a different route. The feeling of power this confers is an illusion, but a potent one, and a quick survey of the sorts of on-line nicknames users choose for themselves confirms it: Dick Dastardly, The Prince of Lies, Overlord Big Daddy Zeus.[13] Many of these names seem meant as jokes, though the intention is often unclear, since the bearers are inarticulate and confused. But Internet culture, whether its participants are waxing literal minded or ironic, seems to encourage vaunting grandiosity.

If movement destabilizes manners, computer-mediated communication often seems to destroy them, thanks to its instant continent-leaping mobility and the promiscuous linking of anyone with anybody. Strangers lurch into each other's homes, unchaperoned by the vigilance of a fixed, permanent community. Anyone can cobble a persona together out of reality and fantasy mixed. Class barriers cease to exist, except insofar as the truly disenfranchised can't afford computers at all and one's command of written language—sometimes—divulges telltale evidence of wealth, education, or status. Punishments, in the rare instances where they happen at all, are as virtual as the offenses: at worst, banishment by one's Internet provider. Culprits suffer real pangs for misbehavior only when they commit real crimes or torts on-line, and even then only if the courts can track them down.

Civilization and Carole Lombard: The Moral Dilemma of the Virtual

Yet—uniquely able though it seems to deliver us into terminal barbarism, and despite the hype attending it—nothing in the Internet's morally unstable world is fundamentally new except for the speed, ease, and cheapness with which it transports a class of commodities humans both revere and revile: images. At least since Plato, artificial representations of reality have been alternately praised as vital to human enlightenment and cursed as seductions to vice. Images entertain, of course, and they help us to shape and interpret the world. But they can also decoy, mislead, and corrupt.

Iconophiles think of image making as a powerful human faculty, forging attractive examples of virtue and warning pictures of vice. For iconophobes, images are, simply, perverting lies. Over the course of history the controversy has waxed and waned, recurring in dozens of forms, from the early Christian Church to Shakespeare's theater, from the Breen office (Hollywood's organ of self-censorship, established in the 1930s) to America Online. To Reformation-era Catholics, devotional statuary and stained glass fostered piety; to purist Protestants, they were idols, coarse productions of human vanity that interfered with prayer and contemplation. To contemporary feminist opponents of pornography like Andrea Dworkin and Catharine MacKinnon, images of abusive sexuality whet male lust and encourage real-life imitations. To its equally impassioned defenders, smut is at worst harmless fantasy, and perhaps a safety valve, a source of therapeutic release for dangerous appetites. A debate has alternately simmered and raged over movies since the 1920s, television since the 1950s. Cultural critics like Susan Sontag (in *Against Interpretation, On Photography*, and *Illness as Metaphor*) have argued that representations are inherently dangerous because they substitute imaginative invention for reality, both cheapening it and staining it with the image maker's prejudices.

The dilemma of the image carries important implications for civility. Images, unless regulated by law or social pressure, can figure forth anything, moral, immoral, pleasant, or repellent. Yet assuming that images do indeed influence us, it is harder to imagine them eroding bedrock moral principles than matters of relatively indifferent custom, like manners. A snuff movie that glamorized murder, even if it eluded the censors, would hardly lead most viewers to find torture and killing acceptable. But what of a film that makes *manners* look ridiculous? The strictures of etiquette lack the moral clout wielded by ancient and near-universal commandments. Customs are often arbitrary, bordering on the comic even before artful satire points up their absurdity. Mightn't manners, shaky in their grip to start with, prove far more vulnerable to manipulation than morals?

This is not a theoretical question. Screwball comedy, coming into its heyday in the 1930s, seemed refreshingly new to audiences and generated some of the enduring classics of film, like *Bringing Up Baby*, *The Philadelphia Story*, and *My Man Godfrey*. All of these are comedies of manners. And in all of them traditional social customs fall under comic attack. As its title suggests, Ben Hecht's coruscating screenplay for *Nothing Sacred* (directed in 1937 by William Wellman) attacks every shibboleth imaginable, from small-town values to the sanctimonies of the press to medical ethics, and it endured a brush with the Breen censorship office before being approved for release.[14] Its most memorable scenes depend upon the screen chemistry between the stars, Fredric March and Carole Lombard. Their romance is a characteristically screwball reversal of traditional boy-girl courtship roles. March plays a cynical newspaper reporter who, desperate to save his job, concocts a publicity stunt, a whirlwind Manhattan glamour tour for Lombard—supposedly a poor dying radium worker from Vermont, actually a normal, healthy American opportunist, providentially misdiagnosed by her drunken doctor.

The plot culminates in a hotel-room fistfight, March knocking Lombard senseless with a right hook to the chin. The scene entertains precisely because it so blithely savages traditional gender chivalry. Yet it also reflects a distinctly revisionist twentieth-century version of the romantic. Flouting the traditional civilities of courtship makes Lombard and March sophisticated, classy, and sexy: *Nothing Sacred* exaggerated to comic effect—or did it actually contribute to bringing about?—a shift in male-female manners that was already well underway by the 1930s (though gloves-off sparring as a courtship ritual dates back at least as far as Shakespeare's *Taming of the Shrew*).

In real life, a drunken boxing match hardly seems the medium by which two thoroughly attractive people might seal their lifelong passion. But in an image world, confined only by the inventiveness of the creators and the tolerance of the viewers, the heretofore shocking can be made to seem natural, refined, and right; formalities, once useful or even obligatory, can quake and topple in a moment, without stress or apparent effort. As played by Lombard, Hazel Flagg, the humble Vermont factory drudge, breezes effortlessly into a svelte late thirties New York, and adapts without missing a beat to nightclubs and luxe hotels; she easily tames a retinue of ruling-class metropolitan males. The heady insult is a staple of screwball romance, with variations in *It Happened One Night*, *The Lady Eve*, *Ball of Fire*, *His Girl Friday*, and many others. Wisecracking anti-chivalry has been a cliché of sophisticated romance ever since.

Concern that engaging images may distort, confuse, and destabilize real-life values is not wholly misplaced. *Nothing Sacred* reinvents violence as sophisticated romance; with no apparent effort it reinvents class too, embodying its hayseed heroine in perhaps the suavest actress of her era, Carole Lombard. The alchemy works effortlessly on film, and the identity between Lombard and her character is as seamless in appearance as it is improbable in fact. But a guardian of manners might well be alarmed: mightn't the power of Lombard's beauty and sophistication to transfigure Hazel Flagg's cynicism and boorishness become a deceptive lure to the audience, encouraging a multitude of loutish real-world Hazel Flaggs to believe themselves Carole Lombards, and vent their boorishness with a clear conscience? Such representations, seen and perhaps imitated by millions, are potentially an academy of bad manners, legitimizing ill conduct by linking it (arbitrarily and perniciously) with glamour, beauty, money, and sophistication.

Virtual rudeness on a computer differs from the gilded loutishness of a screwball comedy not in kind but rather in degree. Only a select few have ever worked in film, a gated industry, granting entry to only the privileged among creators, who are usually highly attuned to their social responsibilities even if resistant to outright control by censors. But there are millions of potential image makers lurking anonymously in cyberspace. As John Seabrook and legions beside him have discovered to their chagrin, on-line anything and anybody go. The PC monitor is a potent mischief maker because it thrusts deeper than film (or television, or any other virtual medium) into one's personal territory.

Measuring Mayhem: Adventures with the Electrical Pneumocardiograph

The fear that cyberspace is unprecedented, in both its novelty and its danger, is unfounded: the virtual has always inspired worry about its effects on public and private behavior. Carolyn Marvin, a communications theorist, documents this point forcefully in her book *When Old Technologies Were New: Thinking About Electric Communication in the Late Nineteenth Century* (1987). American Victorians, she demonstrates, were as nonplussed by the telegraph and telephone as the twentieth century has successively claimed to be by film, television, and now the personal computer. Our forebears too saw seductive new inventions as presenting dangerous challenges to civility, and for reasons not dissimilar. The United States had three thousand installed telephones in 1876; the number had multiplied to nearly a million and a half by 1900,[15] and the rapid growth occasioned a minor crisis of social adjustment. A whole strain of early jokes about the telephone, Marvin reports, involved the confusion it caused between real and virtual presence: many early phone stories involved a bumpkin who nods silently in reply to a caller's increasingly agitated "Are you there?"[16]

Guardians of morals worried seriously about the effect an uncontrollable explosion of hard-to-monitor and possibly deceptive communication might have on family relations. "The doors may be barred and a rejected suitor kept out," the magazine *Telephony* observed in 1905, "but how is the telephone to be guarded?"[17] Stories abounded in the press of elopements planned, even crimes committed, by telegram and telephone. Parents stood warned. "The serenading troubadour can now thrum his throbbing guitar before the transmitter undisturbed by apprehensions of shot guns and bull dogs. . . . The new means of communication has its disadvantages, and must be used with caution."[18] Even as they embraced it, Americans seem, Marvin argues, to have felt a real ambivalence about the changes instant electric communication had wrought in the human landscape. To the pessimistic, it portended anarchy, ease in deception, an irreversible erosion of traditional values, a new highway by which the corrupt could gain access to the impressionable minds of the innocent. Even the standard "Hello" with which we now unthinkingly answer a phone call was a defense against a hidden danger inherent in the technology. It's safer—as Emily Post explained[19] in the earlier editions of *Etiquette*—than answering with "This is Mary Smith," which exposes you to a stranger about whose intentions you may know nothing.

Acceptance of the telephone did not erase this fear of the virtual, which resurfaced with the advent of every new technology for bringing people, ideas, and images together. Was it really unreasonable to fear that rude speech and/or images, instantly disseminated to the masses, might destabilize and corrupt real-life behavior? Scientists, hard and social, have been trying for decades to detect such a power in virtual representations, thus far without conclusive results. Perhaps the pioneer effort commenced in the 1920s and 1930s, in the wake of rising alarm about the burgeoning commercial film industry and its possible effects on the public. Beginning in 1928, the Payne Foundation funded a series of university studies of the effects of movies on the behavior of audiences. Some of the key experiments were published in 1933, and though the results were at best ambiguous, they ultimately contributed to the establishment in 1934 of an industry-supported office charged with enforcing the motion picture production code.

One of the studies, *The Emotional Responses of Children to the Mo-*

tion Picture Situation, by Wendell Dysinger and Christian Ruckmick (University of Iowa psychologists), involved hooking children up to an "electrical pneumo-cardiograph" (a cuff that measured pulse and respiration rate), and a "Wechsler psychogalvanograph,"[20] which gauged emotional responses through changes in electrical resistance on the skin. The sensor was a box with two salt-water wells into which the subject dunked his or her index and third fingers. With the investigators perched behind them in the theater, the children watched movies: *Hop To It Bell Hop*, *Charlie Chan's Chance*, and *The Feast of Ishtar*. The last, a bodice-ripper with a Bible story fig leaf, particularly interested the researchers, since it exposed the subjects to scenes like the following:

> The picture opens with a view of the feet of the dancing priestess, Tisha, followed by a full-length view. . . . After the dance she lies on a divan. . . . and her maids fan her. . . .
>
> (Jether, a country youth of wealth, is introduced. He enters the palace with awe and is admitted through luxurious curtains to the presence of Tisha. He approaches bashfully as Tisha responds boldly.) He slowly comes nearer to her. She reaches out with her foot, touching him on the hand. . . . He takes her extended hand and walks nearer to her, sitting beside her. A servant peers through the curtains. She guides his lips to hers . . . and then turns her scantily clad back. After hesitation he kisses her back and she reclines in his arms . . . where he kisses her lips. . . . Another scene shows her displaying her wiles as she reclines on the idol, Ishtar.[21]

Infant pulses thumped; breathing thickened; Jether and Tisha treated the Wechsler psychogalvanograph to a strenuous workout. Dysinger and Ruckmick thought this proved that film images of behavior could affect impressionable observers, even if they couldn't quite demonstrate that, having reacted perceptibly to licentious scenes, the children would imitate them in real life.

In a companion study, *Motion Pictures and Standards of Morality* (1933), Charles Peters, a professor of education at Penn State, polled focus groups of adults to determine what sorts of film scenes fell in with community standards of propriety, and which violated them. He devised a numerical rating system: zero indicated a scene neutral to average social mores; a positive number denoted social approval of graduating intensity; negative numbers meant disapproval.

One of these scales measured reactions[22] to the "AGGRESSIVE-NESS OF A GIRL IN LOVE-MAKING." Where "A GIRL LETS HER ROOMMATE, AN INTIMATE FRIEND, ARRANGE A DATE FOR HER, FOR A DANCE," evaluators approved, assigning a value of +.34. A girl who "JOKINGLY INVITES A MAN TO CALL UPON HER AT HER HOME" still rated marginal acceptance (+.03), but if the "jokingly" drops out and "GIRL INVITES MAN TO COME TO HER HOME," she elicited a censorious −.12. The most negative response (−1.63) attended the following:

RELATIVE NUDENESS, HINTS IN CONVERSATION, ETC., AC-COMPANIED BY CERTAIN GESTURES, SUGGESTS NO GREAT RELUCTANCE TO BE APPROACHED WITH SEX ADVANCES.[23]

Peters believed his system measured scientifically what Americans thought either acceptable or improper in make-believe renderings of social behavior. But the logical gaps and unacknowledged assumptions of both his and the Dysinger-Ruckmick experiments, obvious at this remove, afford useful cautions about the difficulty of connecting virtual representations with real human behavior. Dysinger and Ruckmick did, I suppose, identify the kinds of movie scenes that stimulated children physically, Peters the sort that moved adults to express disapproval. But neither study reveals a thing about whether Tisha, Jether, the Relatively Nude Lady, and their ilk contribute to a decline in social decorum or morals. Such questions, perennially debated, seem stubbornly impervious to resolution by science, and more recent methods, though increasingly sophisticated, have found the possible link between the virtual and the real just as elusive.

Contemporary expert opinion, beset by public worries about rampant violence and sex on television, has tended to side with the iconophobia implicit in the Payne Foundation's Depression-era studies. A 1993 report by the American Psychological Association (APA), for example, asserted that "there is absolutely no doubt that higher levels of viewing violence on television are correlated with increased acceptance of aggressive attitudes and increased aggressive behavior."[24] The TV-era lab methodologies are indeed clever, the experiments more carefully and ingeniously constructed than was once the case. And yet, despite the APA's confident pronouncement, the results are in practice no less ambiguous if one examines them closely.

A classic 1963 study by the University of Wisconsin's Leonard Berkowitz and Edna Rawlings,[25] often cited as establishing a link between violence viewed and violence acted out, illustrates. In an effort to test the iconophilic proposition that seeing violent images might actually purge and thereby dissipate aggressiveness in a viewer, Berkowitz and Rawlings brought groups of undergraduate volunteers together to watch a violent film clip—a prizefight scene from *Champion*—and then measured their reactions. The ingenious twist in their design was that before the movie, the volunteers were given a brief talk and then a test by a supposed graduate assistant who was actually following a script. To some groups, he behaved courteously; others he calculatedly insulted (by telling them that midwestern college students were known to be less intelligent than their eastern counterparts). Following this setup, designed either to anger the group or leave it in a neutral emotional state, the experimenter entered, and just before the screening, threw another whammy, prefacing the film with a talk that—depending on the group—either presented the violence to follow as justified by the victim's earlier misbehavior in the film, or not justified.

In evaluating the questionnaires they had collected at various points during the experiment, Berkowitz and Rawlings concluded that the students who were first riled by the behavior of the phony test administrator, and who were then shown a representation of violence that they'd been primed to think of as justified, became less inhibited in acknowledging and accepting their hostile feelings. The study, so carefully contrived, apparently convinced many of its readers of a real-life link between violent images and heightened aggressiveness in a viewer. But the Berkowitz-Rawlings experiment touched only on the *feelings* subjects reported as a result of their experiences, and concluded nothing firm about how they might subsequently be expected to behave. And their method, however sophisticated, left in complete mystery what actually goes on in the biochemistry of the brain when an image is processed there and translated (if indeed it is translated) into an emotion and a consequent action. The neurosciences have made great strides in the twentieth century, but they have yet to establish a persuasive model for the physiology of the image.

Moreover, for all the studies purporting to show that images influence behavior directly, others point strikingly in the opposite direction. One example: in a 1986 demographic analysis,[26] Steven F. Messner of the State University of New York at Albany showed that population groups that watched disproportionately large amounts of television violence in fact exhibited disproportionately *low* rates of violent crime. Our current cultural milieu, conservative and apprehensive, certainly favors the belief that images are dangerous. But the truth of such beliefs has by no means been established.

All of which does not mean that worry is wholly misplaced, particularly as it pertains to cyberspace, a new and volatile medium. Film and television, however dangerous they may be, are at least stamped indelibly as conduits of fictional entertainment: at some level audiences know that what they view shouldn't be mistaken for reality. Cyberspace is more insidious. Entertainment and merchandising may increasingly dominate the Internet, but it began as a research tool, a medium for the dissemination of knowledge and fact. The World Wide Web, for all its current advertising clutter, was conceived by its inventors as a scientific forum for the transmission of diagrams and technical illustrations too expensive to print in journals. The people one encounters in chat forums usually seem to be (and in most cases probably are) who they purport to be. The danger, then, is that this aura of science, objectivity, and fact may attach itself (and lend credibility and respectability) to the false and damaging. Pornography is one thing in a trash-littered downtown combat zone, where the ambiance is frightening to the innocent and clearly off limits to anyone who cares to seem decent. It is wholly another on the Macintosh in a nine-year-old's bedroom, where odious material passes unbranded by the warnings of an adult or the self-evident tawdriness of its surroundings.

A search for "American Nazi Party" on a World Wide Web browser elicits hundreds of hits, some frankly fictional, but most claiming to be factual. The first I unearthed was an adulatory biography of the party's founder, George Lincoln Rockwell, presenting itself as authoritative, with nothing on the screen to distinguish it from the soberest assessment by a published and university-anointed scholar. In the real world, the author of this page would probably be denied the seal of social approval implied by an academic appointment. If allowed to speak in a reputable forum, he would do so surrounded by an array of signs that, fairly or not, cautioned the audience that to the establishment, his ideas were cracked and dangerous. On-line, however, the fanatic's web page can in theory look as good as UCLA's, and anyone, knowledgeable or ignorant, can peruse it. A casual browse can, with little effort, hunt up recipes for nerve gas and instructions—not all of them tongue-in-cheek—for making an atomic bomb. The moral and intellectual gatekeepers—libraries, schools and colleges, reputable publishers—patrol no frontiers on the Internet.

Automatic Emily: The Self-Regulation of Manners in Cyberspace

No wonder the more nervous guardians of order would like to find enough hard evidence to shut the whole thing down. At its worst the Internet seems to portend a final anarchy, in which the rudest, meanest, and lewdest seize initiative from the most refined—virtual mob rule, ominous not just for manners but civilization. And yet, perceptions aside, apocalypse does not really seem imminent. As an experiment in freedom, the Internet, despite outbursts of naked hostility and a culture of distaste for restrictive codes, has nonetheless spontaneously generated a powerful system of restraints, by which civility ultimately reasserts itself, pushing wayward manners up toward a level everybody can live with. If cyberspace is the ultimate experiment in the power of the virtual image, experience thus far suggests that disturbing images cannot, all by themselves, push significant numbers of people into misbehavior. Some mysterious but merciful herd instinct for peace prevents it.

Whatever shock he felt and the sender may have intended, John Seabrook's flame illustrates one of this system's key features. The classic flame's piled-up obscenities—"asshole," "toadying dipshit scumbag," "remove your head from your rectum," "ass-licking"[27]— are established rituals of Internet flaming, formulaic fraternity-style abuse where the first excremental epithet quickly launches a rodomontade. The e-mail flame is at once taboo in every formulation of on-line etiquette, and a venerated, near-universal institution. The cyberlout's self-administering comeuppance is that the more numerous and indiscriminate his obscenities are, the more they seem a rote exercise, without real animus behind it.

This doesn't, of course, neutralize the on-line insult, but does tame it; Internet scatology is like grand opera violence—so stylized that it reads as more silly than shocking. Attacks on one's parentage, the staple of insult for most of modern Western history, are unusual in flaming. Rather, on-line invective endlessly recycles body parts, excretory products, and knee-jerk repulsives (like maggots). But with only a finite number of organs and secretions to invoke, the rude terms repeat themselves until they lose their force—like "fuck," which unrestrained repetition has turned into a staple movie expletive on the verge of becoming acceptable in everyday conversation. "RTFM" ("Read the Fucking Manual," a brush-off for a dumb question) has become standard and perfectly acceptable usage, found just before the section on e-mail etiquette in *The Internet for Dummies: Quick Reference Guide.*[28]

Also paradoxically reassuring is the passion even the rudest contributors evince for civility. The flamer's most cherished role is, ironically enough, as a self-appointed scourge of rudeness and ignorance: the race-baiting diatribes I quoted at the beginning of this chapter are both protests against perceived rudeness, and sincere, if twisted. Few flames hurl abuse for the frank pleasure of it; most claim to be reacting to an offense against manners. And while resorting to rudeness in the defense of good form is morally problematic, it attests to the abiding power of civility as an ideal. Common though flames are, they are nonetheless rarer than painstaking attempts at politeness. Chat rooms, e-mail, and bulletin boards brim with anxiety about how easily an innocent remark can provoke misunderstanding and retaliation. Postings often begin with painfully constructed propitiatory prefaces and stumble into stylistic abomination in the effort to pre-placate. Boilerplate acronyms like IMHO (for "in my humble opinion") and emoticons like :-), the sideways-read smiley face, are common insurance devices, meant to disarm hair-trigger tempers from taking umbrage at a joke.

Finally, the potent myth of Internet democracy hides a contradictory reality: the enduring power of class. Hierarchy constantly reasserts itself on-line in the status gap between novices and seasoned users. Apologies from those who don't know the ropes and sneers from those who do (or who claim to) are common. No matter how egalitarian, informal, or even disreputable the venue, natural leaders almost always emerge, either by self-appointment or common consent. In the deluge of on-line gossip surrounding the Bill Clinton–Monica Lewinsky story, Matt Drudge rocketed overnight from pariah to pundit status because his crudely designed web site broke the scandal. USENET sites often divide into subgroups, identical save that one acquires a moderator who prunes out patently crazy or offensive postings and eliminates commercial clutter, while the other remains uncontrolled. These moderated groups quickly attract more and better informed participants, while unsupervised sites fill with verbose ads and lunatic maunderings, languish, and eventually go inert.

The Internet began in the late 1960s as ARPANET, an elite project sponsored by the Defense Department's Advanced Research Projects Agency. The first experimental trials of the system in 1969 linked computers at UCLA and the Stanford Research Institute in Palo Alto. The net soon spanned the continent, but (except for early nodes at the University of Utah and the University of California at Santa Barbara) in its early years it remained the near-exclusive preserve of science aristocrats at top-tier endowed research universities and think tanks—Harvard, MIT, the Rand Corporation, Carnegie Mellon, and Case Western Reserve.[29] The system's technological vocabulary was status laden from the start: the conventions by which machines communicate with each other became (and remain) "protocols." Computers themselves, depending on their role in a network, have rank: they're either in a "peer-to-peer" or "master-slave" relationship.

This once exclusive system ultimately fell into the clutch of the masses (plausible guesses about how many people currently use the Internet range between 25 and 50 million).[30] Yet apparent democratization has led to a recrudescence of authority and central control—as evidenced, strangely enough, by the very advance that turned the Internet into a mass-market phenomenon: the advent in 1992 of the World Wide Web. Devised at CERN, the European nuclear research center, the web was meant initially to serve up technical diagrams, illustrations, and quick one-click cross-references to related research. But its ability to mount full-color high-resolution images, sound, and video—along with the appearance of easy-to-use web-browsing software like Mosaic, Netscape, and Microsoft's Internet Explorer—quickly turned it into a mobbed marketplace. The science is still there, but now jostled by kitsch, crass commercialism, lunatic ravings, and slick corporate promotions.

The ascendancy of the web has opened the Internet to a huge new population of consumers. But at the same time it has worked to limit the number of providers, by the simple device of swamping the unschooled rather than eliminating them. It takes no skill at all to post a rant on USENET. But it requires a modicum of expertise, considerable time, a certain amount of sustained attention and maintenance, and usually an outlay of money to run a web site. An attractive one demands both taste and intelligence. The web is thus inherently prone to colonization by the possessors of money and talent. Sites with arresting, professionally designed graphics or video and sound clips pull in a disproportionate number of browsers; marginal mom-and-pop sites often vanish after a few months. So the web has already begun to imitate the distinction long established in other media between a small elite of anointed creators and a subservient public of passive, disempowered consumers. One can—for free—read substantial portions of *The New York Times* and the *Washington Post* on their web pages; record labels offer sound clips from their latest releases; games are available at the Disney web site. Of course there are plenty of cracked, crude, and obscene pages; but the difference between a corporate site and an amateur's vanity production is usually obvious, unlike postings on USENET, where, apart from its intrinsic merit, eloquence commands no visible advantage over rambling lunacy.

Despite the web's vastness, category-killer sites have drawn a disproportionate amount of attention, like dominant brands that crowd competing products off the shelf in supermarkets. And the very vastness of the web contributes, paradoxically, to the centralizing of control over it. The range of choices is so huge that it quickly created a demand for on-line search engines—web sites that allow viewers to generate lists of pages on topics of interest. The most popular—Yahoo, Alta Vista, HotBot, Infoseek, Lycos, and Excite—have quickly become powerful web institutions. And while they don't exercise censorship, they do serve as gatekeepers. I looked up "sex" on Lycos while writing this, and found 166,945 references: a catch too plenteous for use. So, to stay competitive, the search engines all offer short lists of preselected or recommended sites on popular subjects and selective guides to new sites. This makes sense out of the chaos; but guidance exacts its price in a loss of anarchic freedom. Newspapers have introduced World Wide Web review columns, singling out sites for praise and criticisms. And the newest search engine charges web sites a listing fee.

None of these developments enforces good behavior. But they all represent a vanguard of standardization and create a system of manners. Canons of good and bad taste are emerging. It doesn't necessarily require laws, police, or vigilantes to create civility. The impulse, if cyberspace is any guide, forms itself naturally, even where the climate appears initially hostile. This suggests a hypothesis comforting to anyone worried about manners: A law of the conservation of civility, holding that any new social space—even one conceived in complete freedom and potential anarchy—sooner or later, thanks to a stubborn human urge, generates leaders, laws, and civilizing conventions. This is no less true where, as in literature, film, TV, and the Internet (the most extreme case thus far), imaginative invention can run riot, untrammeled in its power to imagine no-holds-barred beastliness. Even in the virtual world of the image, where freedom is a shibboleth and the consequences of miscreancy aren't instantly calamitous, the civil reasserts itself. Rudeness tends to rein itself in by becoming conventionalized.

Etiquette is a far less fragile construct than pessimists are inclined to think. If, thus far in its short history, cyberspace is any guide, censors should relax and creative nihilists have reason to worry. Images are simply not a lever capable by itself of prying our social world off its axis.

PART TWO

Private Life

chapter six

Mr. Bok and Martha: The Triumph of Lifestyle

In a 1995 commencement speech at Boston University, John Silber bewailed the collapse of modern American manners. Civility, he argued, lay under assault; "mindless and indiscriminate violence," "unbridled hedonism," "filthy language," and gratuitously nasty-minded films (like Quentin Tarantino's *Pulp Fiction*)[1] were among the worst offenders. Such evils, he said, aren't grave enough to warrant legal prohibition or even outright moral condemnation. But neither are they harmless habits, rightly left to individual taste and passed over without judgment, since they do serious damage to social comity. Rather, they fall into a no-man's-land that divides obligatory public duty from the proper freedom of private life—where, good, graceful, or loathsome, our behavior is determined by free personal choice. Manners ought to be observed, yet can't be made compulsory, and so belong in a unique category Silber defines as a "domain of obedience to the unenforceable."[2]

Silber credited both this striking phrase and the idea behind it to John Fletcher Moulton (1844–1921), a British jurist and mathematician who coined it in a 1912 address to the Authors' Club in London. Silber, a stalwart cultural conservative, understands Moulton to be affirming the importance of obedience to such unenforceable laws. Yet in reality Moulton's talk staked out a more nuanced, ambiguous, even libertarian position. He voiced far less concern over mounting public unruliness than a growing— and to him pernicious—trend toward ever more intrusive laws, trampling ever more heavily upon private liberties. "The tendency of Modern Legislation," as he put it, "is to expand the area ruled by Positive Law."[3] Silber, predictably, condemned the rebellious American propensity to flout any stricture that wasn't narrowly enforced. But Moulton celebrated manners precisely because he thought human beings were naturally willing to observe them *without* being compelled to. As an illustration he cited the *Titanic* (which had sunk on April 14, 1912, a scant seven months before his talk). Moulton took the "ladies first behavior on the *Titanic* as evidence that Obedience to the Unenforceable was alive and well," and remarked that despite the absence of any enforcing authority, "the men were gentlemen to the edge of death."[4] (He seems not to have known that J. Bruce Ismay, the director of *Titanic*'s parent firm, had—along with a number of other gentlemen on the cruise—elbowed his way into a lifeboat past women and children, leaving them to their fate.)

However deluded Moulton's faith in human nature, he was surely prescient to pick *Titanic*'s sinking as a touchstone. For the ship united dramatic opposites in the understanding of civility. On the one hand, however abysmally some men failed to rise to the occasion, it did indeed furnish a stark and harrowing illustration of the need for moral imperatives that can't be legislated or enforced, like succoring the weak in a disaster. But another and very different sort of manners floated on (and sank with) *Titanic*. It bulged to the gunwales with the vainglorious but delightful appurtenances of the Good Life: bone china, silverware, crystal carafes, engraved menu cards announcing seven-course meals, gold-plated chandeliers, hand-carved oak paneling, allegorical clocks, mirrors, wines, jewels, gowns.⁵

The glamour of life on the *Titanic* fascinates modern Americans as much as its human tragedy (and both garnered rapt attention in the hugely successful James Cameron movie starring Kate Winslet and Leonardo DiCaprio). Insofar as manners involve morality, a case can be made for demanding obedience to them, voluntarily or otherwise. But what of the important (in fact to many observers dominant) aesthetic branch of manners—that devoted to the sometimes expensive cultivation of elegance, polish, and sophisticated display? "We are justified in enforcing good morals, for they belong to all mankind," G. K. Chesterton remarked in 1908. But, he added, "we are not justified in enforcing good manners, for good manners always mean our own manners."⁶ His point becomes instantly compelling if one turns from the violent movies and rap lyrics that (perhaps rightly) concern social critics like Silber to the proprieties of the middle-class American home as laid down by *House & Garden*, Martha Stewart, or their many twentieth-century forebears in that peculiar and undeservedly neglected division of manners, the art of gracious living. Their advice is clear, and their rules are meant to make life more civilized. But such domestic manners carry no ethical weight whatever; they are simply what some people find tasteful, gracious, pleasing, or conducive to social ease and pleasure.

Many such customs are strange indeed: unenforceable because obligatory obedience would be absurd. What we do in the privacy of the home, among family or such outsiders as we invite, is surely a matter of personal preference, the one corner of life where freedom ought to reign secure. The choice between paper and linen napkins, dressing formally or otherwise for dinner, issuing invitations by telephone or mail—these are central to manners but laughable as moral issues. At most, following such customs signifies complaisance, the willingness to conform to the usage current in a given group. Fish knives, for example: they intimidate the novice at formal dinners, and it's illuminating to know that in truth intimidation is their only apparent function. Nothing about their design suits them particularly to the eating of fish; they became standard in formal place settings only after the nineteenth-century silver-smiths who invented them inveigled the affluent and fashionable into buying them.[7]

A strong American impulse to fetishize this morally indifferent branch of manners was well in evidence before the current century, with many Victorian etiquette experts already straying into proto-consumerism and away from the purely moral emphasis they usually claimed as their lodestar. Though most renowned for her stiff-necked and sensible *Manners and Social Usages*, Mary Sherwood was also an unrepentant gourmande, and author of *The Art of Entertaining* (1893), in which her raptures over bonbons approach the por-nographic.

> I received once from Montpellier a box holding six pounds of these marvellous sweets which were arranged in layers. Begin-ning with chocolates in every form, they passed upward by strata until they reached the candied fruit which was to be eaten at once. I think there were fifty-five varieties of delicious sweets in that box. Such lovely colours, such ineffable flavors, such beauties as they were! The only remarkable part of the anecdote is that I survived to tell it.[8]

The twentieth century, despite nagging and sometimes sharply ex-pressed laments at the crassness brought on by affluence, has only sharpened this obsession with the art of living beautifully (as op-posed to merely living decorously). Magazines may—as many do—publish an etiquette column. But these are usually overshadowed by a profusion of articles about home decoration, personal self-presentation, or the wowing of guests with inventively prepared and beautifully served food.

This phenomenon is far too pervasive to trace to a single source, but one benchmark, a salient example if not the origin of the trend, was *Art in Everyday Life*, a book first published in 1925 by two less well known contemporaries of Emily Post: Harriet and Vetta Goldstein. It went through many editions, the latest in 1954, remained in print through the sixties, found wide use in high schools and colleges, and argued with conviction that manners are at least as much a matter of domestic good taste as duties of kindness or tact. For the Goldsteins, clothing, interior decoration, setting the table tastefully, and serving food attractively, far from being merely optional attainments, constituted an important aspect of morality. "It has been said," they wrote approvingly, "that good taste is doing unconsciously the right thing, at the right time, in the right way."[9] Searching for an apposite quote, they struck upon *Joseph Vance* (1906), a successful popular novel by the British potter-turned-novelist William De Morgan (1839–1917). De Morgan had first become famous for his exquisite blue and green lusters, and brought to fiction the same devotion to taste he had earlier applied to crockery making. The Goldsteins approved, citing a passage where Vance's mentor says, "I keep on hoping for the development, in Joey, of the faculty of Good Taste. . . . It's a quality of the inner soul."[10]

The classic etiquette expert prescribes which side of the plate the forks should go on, in what order, and what way of eating soup conforms to polite usage. But for the Goldsteins, the plates and spoons themselves were touchstones of good form. In one illustration of three floral-design dinner plates, they dismiss a splashy, realistic, and detailed painting of a bouquet because it is "in no way connected, either in placing or treatment, with the plate which it is meant to adorn." This violates a principle: "harmony of ideas."[11] Two competing plates pass muster because their flowers are small, stylized, and tastefully centered.

Even food was supposed to embody good design: "Any food which gives the impression of having been overtrimmed is distasteful to most people, and so even for the most festive occasions the hostess will be wise if she avoids overemphasizing decoration. . . .

Chopped pimentos in cheese, or the green of a lettuce leaf with white cheese would make a pleasant color pattern for a sandwich and would be enjoyed by the most fastidious person."[12]

Except perhaps in the air of authority conferred by its textbook format, *Art in Everyday Life* was far from unique in aestheticizing manners. It was rather a quasi-academic statement of a long-gestating idea that by the 1920s had emerged full-blown and become the basis for the humming commercial growth engine we now call— in an annoying but useful locution—the lifestyle industry. In the decades before commercial broadcasting became a dominant economic force, the pioneer boosters of lifestyle most readily found voice in mass-market magazines aimed at women but ambitious to influence everybody. Manners, in this new consumerist dispensation, remained the property of an elite, but a limitlessly expandable one based on good taste rather than wealth, irreproachable morals, or social prominence. Moreover, this antielitist vision of good taste pitched by the magazines could, with ingenuity and determination, be achieved by anyone of normal sensibilities and average means.

Edward Bok and the *Ladies' Home Journal*

Nineteenth-century books on the management of home life offered plenty of help with table etiquette and home entertaining, but the most influential and perduring of these had ranked gentility far below religion in the hierarchy of domestic concerns. Such, certainly, was true of the American home's predominant authority, Catharine Beecher (1800–1878). Her influential *Treatise on Domestic Economy* passed through sixteen editions between its publication in 1841 and 1856; in 1869, collaborating with her younger and more famous sister Harriet Beecher Stowe (1811–1896), she revised and expanded it as *The American Woman's Home*.[13]

The Beechers dispensed advice on setting the table, entertaining, designing an efficient home ventilation system, and personal hygiene ("After bathing, the body should be rubbed with a brush or coarse towel, to remove the light scales of scarf-skin, which adhere to it, and also to promote a healthful excitement").[14] They even supplied plans for a house that could function as a combined dwelling, school, and church (the chimney doubled as a steeple). But in both the *Treatise* and the larger *American Woman's Home*, these domestic arts served a higher goal. Religion, ethics, and social responsibility—not taste—defined their most important precepts. To the Beechers, the home anchored the entire American system. Commanding it, the housewife was thus not a charwoman, cook, or charm instructor, but a moral educator, and as such the very pivot of the democratic system. Entertaining and table manners, Catharine Beecher thought, were best seen as natural outgrowths of sound moral principle rather than exercises in aesthetic display justifiable on their own terms: "Good-manners are the expressions of benevolence in personal intercourse, by which we endeavor to promote the comfort and enjoyment of others, and to precept which requires us to do to others as we would that they should do to us. It is saying, by our deportment, to all around, that we consider their feelings, tastes, and convenience, as equal in value to our own."[15] All Beecher's strictures on behavior at the table proscribe behavior that treads on the sensitivities of others. "Politeness," she says, "requires us to welcome visitors with cordiality; to address conversation to them; and to express, by tone and manner, kindness and respect."[16] What's beseeming and beautiful is, simply, what's good.

This earnest approach sorts naturally enough with passionately reformist moral crusaders like the Beechers; but it surfaced also in seemingly frivolous organs like Louis Godey's *Lady's Book*, the pioneering American women's magazine, which by the onset of the Civil War had drawn an unprecedented 150,000 subscribers. Under the editorship of Sarah Josepha Hale (1788–1879), *Godey's* offered practical housekeeping tips and model architectural drawings for houses as well as its trademark hand-colored fashion illustrations— proto-pinups that made *Godey's* popular among Civil War soldiers on the battlefield. But Hale starched the fluff with strong infusions of moral seriousness, crusading forcefully for women's education, female independence, and a succession of charities (such as a fund for the widows of sailors lost at sea).[17] Lifestyle, insofar as the term denotes the blend of materialistic fantasy, manners, and shopping tips that dominates contemporary magazines from *Martha Stewart Living* to *Elle Decor*, was a budding preoccupation in *Godey's* but not a defining one: it yielded precedence to the proper moral conduct of life. And that balance was also a common note among World War I–era etiquette writers. In *Etiquette: Good Manners for All People, Especially for Those Within the Broad Zone of the Average* (1911), Agnes H. Morton, typically, insisted that the true glory of home lay in sound values, not ostentation: "Hospitality shares what it has. It does not attempt to *give* what it *has not*. The finest hospitality is that which welcomes you to the fireside and permits you to look upon the picture of a home life so little disturbed by your coming that you are at once made to feel yourself a part of the little symphony. . . . When people assume to entertain socially they should not give a false showing of themselves or of their means."[18]

But new currents had begun flowing, and no entrepreneur navigated them with more skill or enthusiasm than Edward William Bok (1863–1930). In 1889, as an obscure but self-assured twenty-six-year-old Dutch immigrant, he assumed the editorship of the *Ladies' Home Journal*—a magazine founded in Philadelphia by Cyrus H. K. Curtis in 1883 as a supplement to a newspaper, *The Tribune and Farmer*.[19] Together, Bok and Curtis concocted an innovative marketing plan aimed at lifting the *Journal's* class profile by soliciting carriage-trade ads, surrounding them with sophisticated and status-conscious copy, and thereby drawing a core of privileged and affluent readers. Ultimately, they hoped, the cachet these subscribers brought would—along with modest subscription prices—attract a mass audience of average but aspiring women. In 1890, the *Journal* stopped accepting patent medicine solicitations, which were a profitable mainstay of periodical advertising, but also a source of vulgar clutter. The *Journal* replaced the ratty, jumbled appearance then characteristic of American newspapers and magazines with a new svelte look imparted by ample white space and cleanly designed, understated advertisements.

Still more astutely, Bok transformed the magazine into a friend, adviser, counselor, and improver of its upward-aspiring new readers. This was his real passion as an editor. The *Journal*'s monthly advice features—with titles like "Mrs. Sangster's Heart to Heart Talks"[20] and "Side Talks with Girls," by Ruth Ashmore[21]—built loyalty by exhorting readers to write personally to the columnists; the *Journal* guaranteed a fast reply and unlimited follow-up correspondence. By World War I, thirty-five staff editors were fielding nearly a million such appeals every year.[22] Bok oversaw the effort, sending fake letters from phony addresses, and coming down sharply on replies he thought tardy or slovenly ("Your letters to me have shown rather careless typewriting and two of them have gone unsigned," he wrote to editor Emma Hooper in 1901. "These are points which I do not like").[23]

Alluring ads, the patina of sophistication, and the show of personalized concern for the well-being of readers conspired to give the *Ladies' Home Journal* an unprecedented authority with its audience. By 1903, already the nation's biggest-selling magazine, it passed the million mark in subscribers. Bok exploited this unprecedented success in the service of some quite bold civic crusades. The *Journal* pioneered the frank discussion of venereal disease and editorialized in favor of sex education (though until 1910, when it finally yielded to the momentum of public opinion, it fought vehemently against woman suffrage).

But Bok's longest-sustained campaign aimed at improving not the health or morals of American women but their taste. His passion was to beautify their homes, improve their gardens, civilize their tables. Bok was, in his way, as earnest a moralist as Catharine Beecher, but his ethical sense took an aesthetic rather than an evangelical turn. Under his leadership, the *Journal*'s sense of social responsibility found its fullest expression in a sustained and many-faceted campaign in favor of the Good Life, indoors and out. Writing of himself in the third person in his best-selling, Pulitzer Prize–winning (and monumentally self-congratulatory) autobiography, *The Americanization of Edward Bok* (1920), he put it thus: "Bok had begun with the exterior of the small American house and made an impression upon it; he had brought the love of flowers into the hearts of thousands of small householders who had never thought they could have an artistic garden within a small area; he had changed the lines of furniture, and had put better art on the walls of these homes. He had conceived a full-rounded scheme, and he had carried it out."[24]

The *Journal* was quick to adopt new four-color press technologies, which gave it the ability to illustrate its advice vividly. Bok inaugurated a popular series of architect-designed house plans, striking interior decoration schemes, colorful serving ideas for food, and even a subscription series of old masters' prints. "Before he was through," Bok wrote of himself, "he had presented to American homes throughout the breadth of the country over seventy-million reproductions of forty separate masterpieces of art."[25] In 1904, J. Horace McFarland inaugurated a monthly "Beautiful America" feature, attacking various urban eyesores and organizing a campaign against billboards, already an annoying roadside nuisance. There were interior decoration features like Edith W. Fisher's "How I Made My Home Pretty."[26] There was a regular department called "The Court of Last Resort," not a forum of advice for the desperate or a human relations column, but a lyceum of good taste, which answered questions ranging from "Why are there so few blue flowers?" to "What are the functions of a man who conducts grand opera?" and "I do not understand Raphael's 'Transfiguration.' Can you help me with a brief history and explanation?"[27]

The *Journal*'s food columns were particularly noteworthy for emphasizing presentation over preparation. Recipes tended to yield precedence to serving suggestions; a meal was often as much a work of domestic art and an excuse for display as it was an occasion for cooking and eating good food. In 1905, Hester Price contributed a photo display on "Festive Tables for January," and her accompanying instructions demonstrate that strenuous elegance in dining and entertaining aren't an obsession new to the 1980s and 90s:

> This chafing-dish feast is planned for the mystic hour when the old year merges with the new. The color scheme is yellow. The yellow candles are capped with orange-colored tulle shades, decorated with small oranges. A small pine tree, trimmed with imitation oranges, is in the center of the table. These "oranges" are made of cotton and orange-colored crêpe paper. Within each is a scroll of heavy paper decorated with a gilded wishbone. Some beautiful wish for the New Year should be written upon each scroll. At each cover is a small triangular cake. At twelve o'clock each person should blow out his candle while making a wish.[28]

Three quarters of a century before Martha Stewart, Price anticipated all her trademark themes—the recherché concept, the exquisitely pointless touches like gold paint on a wishbone and cotton-wool oranges, the air of long-standing tradition fadged together ad hoc but designed to seem venerable, dignified, and nostalgic, the skillful evocation of entertaining as the center of a warm and sophisticated circle of family and friends.

Even during the Depression, the *Journal*'s food editor, Ann Batchelder (who continued in the job until her death in 1955),[29] specialized in recipes that kept up appearances, no matter how cheap the ingredients became in deference to the times. Bargain prices, she said, need not imply lack of elegance. In the September 1935 issue, she presented a cheese ring—plainly a budget recipe, since all it contained was grated American cheese and gelatin. Plebeian it might be, but patrician it was supposed to look: colorfully served, with a green salad filling and surrounded by a wreath of halved tomatoes. Batchelder was frank about her priorities: the dish, she said, had "somewhat of appetite appeal and more than a little good looks." The secret of severing its ties with cafeteria food and making it into the centerpiece of sophisticated celebration was to create a mise-en-scène: prepare it in the morning and eat it at leisure on the porch, watching the evening stars as they rise. "It will be Venus the queen of Heaven, for a little time in September, and after a while Mercury, the fleet, will shine over the horizon for your enchanted eyes."[30]

Bok's *Ladies' Home Journal* wasn't alone in turning practical homemaking into a putative art by investing it with fantasy, nor was it unique in its determination to ballast such arguably trivial themes with serious social commentary. *The Delineator*, one of the *Journal*'s chief rivals among the women's magazines, began in 1872 as a catalogue of sewing patterns designed by Ebenezer Butterick, but in time yielded to the demand for at least some serious cultural content. Theodore Dreiser became its editor in 1907, and introduced among his writers such weighty names as Rudyard Kipling, Arthur Conan Doyle, even Woodrow Wilson.[31] Mixing quotidian concerns with the graver questions of the day lent the magazines credibility, the relatively serious writing lending credence to adjacent visions of graceful and pleasurable living. The blend now seems less peculiar than it really is because it has become so entrenched in the American cultural scene. For better and worse, we owe its invention to Edward Bok.

The Assault on Martha Stewart: Gracious Living in the Nineties

Martha Stewart began her ascent to fame as a Connecticut caterer. But by 1990 she had become an institution, both a national symbol of the epidemic American infatuation with gracious living and the scapegoat of a nascent backlash. Miss Manners, at present probably our most influential etiquette authority, has a widely syndicated newspaper column and a number of books in general circulation. But Martha Stewart represents an altogether different order of fame, with dozens of titles in print, her own monthly magazine, *Martha Stewart Living*, a daily syndicated half-hour TV program, an interactive World Wide Web site, a mail-order shopping service, an eponymous home products department in Kmart stores, even an umbrella corporation with a suitable business-octopus name: Martha Stewart Living Omnimedia, Inc.

Stewart is only the most visible figure in a thriving lifestyle industry that churns out books, magazines, and exemplars of every other medium from television to CD-ROMs. It has mirrored the growth of retail chains like Crate and Barrel, Pottery Barn, The Gap, and Williams-Sonoma, which sell the trappings of designer-anointed home life in mall outlets and mail-order catalogues. Stewart stands out because of her relentless drive; also because her audience is so large and devoted. She has even achieved the dubious apotheosis of academic attention (a cultural studies anthology is in the works, to be titled *The Martha Stewart Collection*).[32] And, in the culminating proof of her ascent to institutional status, she recently provoked a best-selling unauthorized biography, Jerry Oppenheimer's *Martha Stewart—Just Desserts*. Both her popularity and the negative reaction it has inspired warrant a closer look.

Oppenheimer dwells relentlessly on what he sees as Stewart's pathological ambition and cutthroat business competitiveness, but—hostile though his portrait is—he never questions the sincerity of her dedication to raising the aesthetic tone of American domestic life. Stewart has a reputation for fussy and expensive elegance, but her interests span cooking, gardening, decorating, entertaining, even family relations and finance. And her dominant theme is not costly luxury, but rather studious care—taking pains to make one's daily life pleasant, artful, dignified. The acutest pleasure, in Stewart's world, lies not in buying elegance (though she offers multiple shopping opportunities), but in achieving it through skill and thoughtfulness. In early 1997, she and Kmart inaugurated a new "Everyday" collection, cornerstone of a design-it-yourself department for the budget-minded devotee of good taste. There are no carriage-trade pretensions in these store displays, no attempts to ape the moneyed ambiance of expensive retail stores like Bergdorf Goodman or ABC Carpet and Home.

At Kmart, a near-life-sized cardboard Martha stands at the main entrance, directing customers to the home furnishings department. At the Astor Square branch in Manhattan (a recent immigrant from the suburbs), in the fall of 1997, Martha Stewart Everyday abutted a pre-Halloween display of plastic pumpkins, Reese's Peanut Butter cups, vinyl trash cans, and zebra-striped polyester rugs. Stewart's wares were well made, subdued in color, simply designed, and unpretentious: a line of trademarked paints, some terrycloth bathrobes (modeled by Stewart with a matching towel wrapped around her head), table linens, bedsheets. Amidst it all stood a TV monitor reeling out a promotional video loop in which Stewart, smiling and husky voiced, touted her merchandise: not, however, with a hard sell, but a characteristic emphasis on technique. "Our fitted sheets," Stewart purred, "have extra-deep pockets. . . . Do you know the secret of folding a fitted sheet? I learned this from my mom. . . ."[33]

Martha Stewart Living, her monthly magazine, conjures a colorful yet gauzy panorama of amiable, sun-dappled home life, a blend of casual, sentimental, and elegant. Longer established home life magazines like *Architectural Digest* or *House Beautiful* tend to embody their visions of the lush life in detailed spreads of aggressively "done" rooms and distinctive, almost always expensive houses, more or less exhaustively documented in photographs, often accompanied by floor plans and replete with tips about where to buy the furniture and accessories pictured. Artful touches, often contributed by a stylist, suggest human occupancy—a just-this-side-of-slovenly heap of books and magazines on the night stand, or a dining-room table with candles ablaze and one chair casually pulled aside, as if drawing the reader to fantasize himself into the scene. With Stewart, it's usually not the design concept that draws the reader or viewer in, but rather Stewart's presence, sometimes in a photo but always hovering in the text and offering hints about how to create an atmosphere of elegance. Her advice is on the whole heavier on labor than expense: instructions for how to make miniature hamburgers for parties, or for donning dust mask and rubber gloves to color linen napkins with natural dyes like fustic and madder root (two projects included in the September 1997 issue of *Martha Stewart Living*). Her message is that beyond a merely passable way of doing things glimmers a classy and distinguished way, discoverable if one pursues it with the dedicated perfectionism of the artist.

Stationery, for example. The undiscriminating may buy it off the drug or convenience store shelf; the more ambitious may splurge on the expensive formal letter papers ready boxed at a stationery store; the still more *raffiné* can have them printed or engraved. But all these upward increments in taste leave one short of the Stewart standard.

Martha Stewart looked for years for just the right emblem for her stationery. Last year, she found an image she liked: a cornucopia engraved onto the frontispiece of a rare seventeenth-century book called *Worlidge's Husbandry*. She brought it to Joy Lewis, who recognized the drawing as a banknote-style engraving. Lewis hired a retired employee of the bureau that engraves United States banknotes to recreate the design. Martha's monogram was blind-embossed, or impressed onto the paper without color, in classic Roman type. The cornucopia was engraved and inked in "van Dyck Brown," the color black fades to after a hundred years.[34]

Snobbery and materialism? That has certainly become a major theme in the attack on Martha Stewart that began in the early 1990s. Oppenheimer's *Just Desserts*, for example, juxtaposes Stewart's unremarkable Polish-American childhood in Nutley, New Jersey, against her supposed pretensions, implying that the determination with which she climbed out of it and her obsession with style constitute an attempt to hide sordid beginnings, break out of the humble sphere she belongs in by right, and elbow her way in among the wealthy elite.

But this exaggerates Stewart's snobbery and ignores her attentiveness to the hard work behind good taste. The distinguishing characteristic of her stationery, after all, lies not in its cost but rather in the ingenuity and painstaking research that went into its design, as well as in its rejection of the mass-produced. And nowhere does Stewart try to conceal either her lower-middle-class origins, or painful events in her adult life, like her 1990 divorce.[35] Indeed, she writes quite candidly about them in the "Letter from Martha" that opens, and the "Remembering" column that closes, every issue of *Martha Stewart Living*. In one such column, she recalls a childhood memory of her family poring longingly through Sears and Montgomery Ward catalogues,[36] which at the time seemed the utmost reach of upward-aspiring fantasy. Oppenheimer, with an air of having discovered a closely guarded secret, reveals that Stewart's parents shopped at Two Guys from Harrison, a now defunct and decidedly low-rent New Jersey discount outlet; but Stewart herself has reminisced almost nostalgically about Two Guys in "Remembering."[37] Stewart's agenda seems not to imitate upper-class manners, but rather to *separate* the art of civilized living from class; to relocate it—in the tradition of Edward Bok and the Goldsteins—from a sense of belonging to a particular status group to a schooling in good taste that anybody might acquire with thought and careful study.

Stewart's stationery is described—and readers seem to take it—not as a possession to drool jealously over but rather as an illustration of the forethought, care, and discrimination everyday life deserves. When Stewart photographs a house, she usually emphasizes not the likely-to-be-intimidating whole, but rather a nook, a corner in the garden, a space small and intimate enough for anyone to imitate no matter how unprepossessing the property or how unexceptional one's means. Her locations exude a leisure and luxury that encourage imitation, and don't remove the reader to an envying distance. Like Emily Post before her, Stewart tries to universalize rather than restrict the accomplishments of class. Post's difficulty lay in never being quite able to explain or decide who the "Best People" were, even though she believed in their existence. Stewart, however, represents a contemporary effort to solve this difficulty. Her criterion for admission among the Best People is a readily learnable ability to appreciate and create what she likes to call "Good Things," an approach more apt to break down social barriers than fortify them. One recent feature in *Martha Stewart Living* covered an impeccable soul-food luncheon served in a Harlem apartment.[38] Good taste and an appreciation for "Good Things" are, as Stewart presents them, meant to cross cultural, ethnic, and class lines, becoming accessible to everybody everywhere.

The democratizing of good taste has been decried: Pottery Barn, for example, has been taxed by critics for offering mass-produced good design at bargain prices to mail-order customers in the hinterlands as well as to well-heeled urbanites. The implication—rather unflattering to design considered as a serious pursuit—is that a beautiful object loses its aesthetic value as soon as it gains wide appreciation. Beauty, in other words, is a quality conferred by an elite rather than created by an artist, and the patina vanishes as soon as the masses admire it. Stewart, I suspect, would disagree. Do her critics mistrust her because she encourages snobbery or because she undercuts it?

Twilight of the Goods: The Decline of Etiquette as Conspicuous Consumption

Lifestyle in the Stewart mold differs markedly from the consumerism so garishly on view in contemporary American weddings and funerals. The undertaker and the wedding consultant offer a simple bargain: put money down—usually quite a lot of it—and the expert will free you of anxiety by guaranteeing a respectable display. The customer participates by choosing from a menu of caskets and cakes, burial robes and bridal gowns. But the choice, though wide, is limited, winnowed down by the expert to a manageable list of acceptable selections. Stewart's aim—and this is a refinement that gives her a spin wholly different from that of other lifestyle gurus—is to educate her reader or viewer into expertise on her version of good taste, but through attractive example rather than the stern professionalism affected by the Goldsteins. Self-consciously upmarket organs like *Architectural Digest* sneer by omission at anything not owned by a demimogul or designed by a celebrity of the vanguard. Downmarket venues content themselves with easily followed and mostly rudimentary how-to tips, like a remodeling feature in the *Ladies' Home Journal* (nowadays considerably more coach-class in feel than it was in Bok's time), where homeowners win prizes for supposedly ingenious remodeling strategies such as knocking down a wall to make the kitchen bigger, or finishing an attic for an extra bedroom.[39]

Of course, Stewart is hardly above commerce. Her Martha By Mail subsidiary sells a $58 "Metal Projects Kit," a $99 bag of garden tools, and an assortment of $22.50 cookie cutters.[40] But in her virtual Elysium, shopping has shrunk from a central cultural activity into a subsidiary one. Indeed, Stewart's grip on her audience may lie in her having intuited, at exactly the most opportune historical moment, the onset of a goods hangover. Americans gave way to buying frenzies in the 1950s and 1960s, survived the mini-dearth of the seventies, then indulged themselves in another binge in the mid-eighties, before the recession of the early nineties. But the heretofore pure mindlessness of consumer orgies may be evolving; perhaps the buying public has gradually acquired a brain, even a memory; and consumerism, if we have yet to break a settled addiction to it, is beginning to haunt us with nasty morning-after headaches. Not that consumer spending has lessened: total retail sales in the United States rose from $957 billion in 1980 to $2.5 trillion in 1996.[41] But among those who consider themselves evolved and sophisticated, the mere act of spending no longer confers ipso facto a feeling of classiness.

Emily Post's etiquette debut in 1922 seemed auspicious for the appreciation of civility as a matter of moral sensitivity and the considerate behavior that should follow from it. But even as her book climbed to best-seller status, the American sense of good manners was moving from a preoccupation with the ceremonies of interpersonal behavior into a persuasion that one demonstrated sophistication and polish by buying either classy merchandise or a cut-price imitation thereof. In later editions Post tried to accommodate this trend by offering some advice about how, for example, to tell the difference between good and inferior silver.[42] Yet she never really seems to have approved, and she may have been prescient, because retail, in a still nascent development, now seems to be losing some of its once potent magic. This is heartening insofar as it suggests that ideas of civility, ever more firmly glued to money over most of this century, may finally be coming unstuck from it. The mid- to late 1990s have seen a sustained boom, but in this one the appearance of sophistication and the air of belonging to an elite seem to demand that no matter how caught up in it, one keep an ironic distance from consumerism. This, surely, had something to do with Calvin Klein's decision in the nineties to feature anorexic, grubby, and drugged-looking models in his ads; it was a subtle way of trashing money and desire (even while grabbing the former and peddling the latter).

The recent history of Condé Nast's *House & Garden* documents this shift. Founded in 1901 as a middle-of-the-market contender in the lifestyle field, it targeted a more affluent readership in the status-crazed Reaganite 1980s, renaming itself *HG*. Buffeted by a generally rough market for home-decorating magazines in the recession of the early nineties, *HG* folded in 1993. But the genre had bounced back energetically by 1995,[43] with titles like *Architectural Digest* and *House Beautiful* reporting strong revenues and a rejuvenated demand for advertising space. Condé Nast recruited a new editor—Dominique Browning from *Mirabella*—and spent $40 million on a relaunch of *House & Garden*, which made its debut with the September 1996 issue.

Browning's new *House & Garden* exudes affluence, with advertisers like Steuben Glass, Portico, Gucci Home, George Smith furniture, Baccarat. The featured houses and gardens—unlike Martha Stewart's understated locations—tempt the reader to melt with greedy envy. "My husband and I," Judith Krantz writes in one issue, "have wrapped a beach house around a dance floor."[44] Another article showcases an 18,000-square-foot Charles Gwathmey erection in Pacific Palisades ("the library shelves display the owners' collection of first editions. . . . The hall leading to the bathroom has a sensuous double curve. . . . The island in the kitchen is made of European unsteamed beech. . . . The husband's bathroom has a Jacuzzi tub, while the wife's is equipped with a steam shower").[45]

But alongside the expensive consumables, there lurks—of all things—what might be called an Irony Department: "Past Perfect," written by Véronique Vienne. Each month it revisits an old issue of *House & Garden* and proceeds, sometimes with rather self-conscious pomo mockery, to deconstruct the vision of luxury there offered. One such column highlighted a 1958 "living garage," in which a family demonstrated pride in its new Edsel by setting up a dining area and lounge beside it. Another spread, from 1942, showed a World War II–vintage photo of a mildly indisposed housewife, stretched out on a divan and coddling herself on a sick day:

> At the mere suggestion of a head cold, the well-prepared woman will pull from her closets an arsenal of trays, a moiré bedrest, a taffeta-covered hot-water bottle, a fleecy Wellington blanket, and a cashmere throw—monogrammed, of course—and deploy them like so much ammunition.[46]

Vienne seems here to have gone rather over the edge in her

determination to read wartime semiotics into this picture: the model and her collection of comforts are essentially indistinguishable from anything in the 1997 magazine, save that the photo is black and white and her hair marcelled rather than moussed. But however belabored, the point of "Past Perfect" is that, without our conscious consent, possessions can trap us unawares into expressing the corny or even invidious cultural meanings they carry. The resuscitated *House & Garden* seems to want to wink at its readers, as if to intimate that today's true sophisticates keep a due perspective on their possessions. Self-awareness, *House & Garden* implies, inoculates against the tacky misstep that—unless it looks intended—brands the perpetrator as a witless slave of trends.

The current of most twentieth-century American taste has run strongly in favor of material display, with refined consumerism competing against and sometimes overshadowing interpersonal relations as the touchstone of domestic good manners. Yet in the 1990s one can detect the possibility of an incipient reaction, not in the form of a return to the moralism many would prefer, but in a kind of consumer stoicism, a nibbling awareness that conspicuous consumption can make one ridiculous as well as enviable. The fashionableness of retro styles like Art Deco or 1950s moderne is double-edged—a conjunct of mockery and sentimental nostalgia. We long for the unself-conscious and untroubled affluence of these styles, yet also find ourselves amused by their excess and the fantasies they seem to reflect. Do avid watchers of *Leave It to Beaver* and *Ozzie and Harriet* reruns long for a bygone era of financial ease and domestic quiet, or are they sneering at the naïveté with which such shows link affluence, innocence, and civility?

Martha Stewart treads with quite sensitive ambiguity over the tempting and disquieting connection between money and civility. Her solution—sublimating crass acquisitiveness into an obsession with personal craftsmanship—may not be for the ages. But it shows an astute awareness that materialism, which often goads manners toward the coarse and vulgar, may not be a totally irreversible force.

chapter seven

The Lady in the Boutique and the Man in the G-String: Etiquette, Race, and Gender

Rudeness, usually a minor annoyance, can trigger a wounding explosion when it blunders onto a cultural minefield. Class, ethnic rivalries (perhaps not so flammable now as earlier in the century, but still prone to flare), the miscues that so easily divide old and young, gay and straight—all can generate rancor. But perhaps the deepest and stubbornest wounds to civility are those inflicted using race and gender as weapons. Any group, even a casually bonded one, cultivates distinctive habits, which can provoke incomprehension or hostility among those whose customs and identifying traits differ. Sailors cringe when a landsman calls a ship a boat; Asians dislike the Western habit of maintaining frequent eye contact in casual encounters. But women and men, blacks and whites, are riven by far more powerful and dangerous misunderstandings. Immemorially different, fated to interdependence yet mutually suspicious, their differences in behavior are underlined somatically: their bodies bear indelible testimonies to difference. And their relations have been poisoned by the massed forces of an abusive political, social, and economic history, whose shadows never seem to dissipate even where the worst oppressions have abated or even evaporated.

In 1996, Karen Grigsby Bates and Karen Elyse Hudson published *Basic Black: Home Training for Modern Times*, an etiquette manual aimed at the emerging black American middle class. Taken by itself, that constituted good news. There is such a class, and demographers agree that it has been growing in size and economic power; its self-confidence appears to be growing apace (though there is less unanimity on this point). In their much-discussed *America in Black and White: One Nation Indivisible* (1997), Abigail and Stephan Thernstrom noted that since 1940, the percentage of black families living in poverty had declined from 87 to 26 percent.[1] But there has been sharp dispute about whether or not such statistical advances have eased interracial tensions or soothed the divisive memories left by the American racial past. Bates and Hudson appear ambiguous. Much of *Basic Black* is a guide to the arcana of bourgeois entitlements, as if in acknowledgment that a growing number of affluent blacks want to live at ease with the social amplitude their new status entitles them to. Bates and Hudson explain how to book passage on a cruise ship; how, once aboard, to deal with a captain and crew; how much to tip the masseuse at a resort hotel.[2] Yet they also concede that painful throwback situations may still arise where racism survives, either in full-blown or vestigial form—and offer advice about what to do, for instance, if someone tells racist jokes, suggests a colleague would never have been hired but for affirmative action, or behaves in any other way that suggests a continuing belief in some false or hurtful stereotype. The tenor of Bates and Hudson's advice is generally that such incidents, while disturbing when they happen, have faded in frequency and so should not normally be made an issue of. They don't recommend overlooking racial slights, but do warn against overreaction, advocating a pointed but cool and civil response.

Yet, as is often true in matters of manners, a sensible general rule laid down a priori seems problematic as applied to real life. In a

Washington Post article written shortly after the publication of *Basic Black*, Bates chronicled some actual instances of racial insult that seemed to those on the receiving end all the more grating for being unintended. A deliberate put-down, after all, implies that one counts for something. But a slur emerging unconsciously from reflex prejudice about a group suggests the offender is incapable of recognizing the victim as an individual. As an example, Bates cites "a former first lady's press secretary who, when browsing posh boutiques, is routinely asked 'does this come in size 8?' by other shoppers who carelessly presuppose that since she is black, she must, ergo, be there to serve."[3]

Incidents like this bear closer examination. While minor—they involve no anger, no deliberate insult—they are nonetheless not trivial in quite the same way that using an oyster fork to eat shrimp might be. Race is not lifestyle; any conflict arising from it raises troubling moral questions, and strikes a raw nerve in human relations. If we take account only of the press secretary's feelings, she certainly suffered an insult. She might, of course, resolve to ignore it on the ground that it was thoughtless. But in one sense that worsens it: only a deeply ingrained, widely shared, and institutionalized stereotype can be applied without forethought. To pass over an unconscious snub of this sort means caving in to an entrenched prejudice, and—in this case—acceding as a matter of course to the unpremeditated assumption that anyone who happens to be black must be at least a social inferior and probably a servant.

Even thus far the dilemma is hard to resolve; but our difficulties are only beginning. Who, after all, really authored this affront—the insulter or the insulted? The press secretary assumed that other customers addressed her as a saleslady because she was black. But could she really be certain it was her race that elicited this response? Anyone staring idly into space in a store, anyone not intently picking over the merchandise, is liable to be taken for a salesperson. An impatient and self-absorbed customer might hail anyone in sight, oblivious to race or apparent class status. In an expensive store, the entitled and therefore typically inconsiderate clientele may well presume anyone they see—black, white, male, or female—is there to serve, and then ignore the feelings of anyone addressed mistakenly: boorishness, surely, but a race-blind version. Nor is it impossible that such an incident might stem from simple stupidity: an incapacity to arrive at *any* judgment about a person's status from his or her appearance, and a blissful heedlessness that anyone might care.

In *A Country of Strangers: Blacks and Whites in America* (1997), David Shipler recounts a like incident[4] in which a black friend (a professor at George Mason University) met Senator John Danforth, who instantly addressed him by his first name. The friend, offended, read this as a casual, perhaps unthinking slur. Shipler (who is white) experimented by introducing himself to Danforth, who promptly called him "David," leading Shipler to conclude that Danforth's overfamiliarity was color-blind, an American politician's rote backslapping rather than casual racism. In the end Shipler saw the import of this incident as lying in his friend's touchiness: it was, he thought, an illustration of the nation's abiding racial tension and misunderstanding. No matter how honorable our intentions, he argues, we Americans have failed to haul ourselves out of the pit of mutual suspicion dug for us by slavery and its aftermath.

If everyone could be brought to agree not only that our past history bears a burden of racial injustice, but that we inherit that burden in a pervasive syndrome of instinctive prejudices that govern our present-day behavior, we could posit some simple rules for interracial etiquette. We could agree, for instance, that black people have reason *by definition* to bristle at any remark that appears to presume them socially inferior. Refrain, then, from making such remarks. Ask the woman at Bergdorf's whether or not she's *seen* a sales clerk; call no adult black person by a first name unless explicitly invited to. And if you find it irksome to reserve this courtesy only for blacks, avoid first-naming anyone above the age of twelve.

No calculus, of course, can determine whether—over the course of written history and before—worse pain has been inflicted in the name of race or gender. But whatever their relative importance as occasions of oppression, gender is clearly different from race in one respect: it presents a more universal manners problem. There are, after all, many places on earth where different races are not in daily contact, but none where males and females don't mix intimately, and surely none where the mixture is trouble-free. Anthropologists disagree about whether or not the widespread and ancient hierarchical dominance of men over women is absolutely universal, whether this was a creation of society or a consequence of biology, and how far other hominids share it. But, universal or not, as the anthropologist Barbara Diane Miller has written, "human gender hierarchies are one of the most persistent, pervasive, and pernicious forms of inequality in the world."[5] In contemporary American manners, they vie with race hierarchies as the greatest (or at least the most common) cause of misunderstanding.

Nor does everyone agree that race and gender oppression still infiltrate and thereby define our every unconscious utterance and gesture. A groundswell of reaction has risen against the very idea; it has become a contemporary cliché to resent the once oppressed as the new oppressors, ever-whining demanders of special consideration, always espying imaginary depths of prejudice behind every chance gesture and empty remark. Who, demands the anti-P.C. backlash, gave women, blacks, or gays unlimited license to detect and rebuke an intentional slur behind any gesture or utterance that irritates or displeases them? Moreover, isn't it rude all by itself even to claim such exaggerated consideration, to deem oneself entitled to set up absolute imperatives and taboos, dictating aggressively what others may or may not say?

This note of exasperation first sounded, predictably, on the right. But by the early nineties it had spread well beyond cultural conservatives. In *Culture of Complaint: A Passionate Look into the Ailing Heart of America* (1994), Robert Hughes—shrewd, humane, a figure not readily associated with the forces of reaction—insists on his sympathy with women, African Americans, homosexuals, the disabled.

But he also decries the monsters of jargon and contorted utterance that, he thinks, sensitivity to their sensitivity has foisted on public discourse. "Racist," "sexist," and "homophobe," he notes, have become the neutron bombs of insult, instantly lethal and unanswerable. Conversely, when striving to be polite and steering apprehensively among the hair-trigger sensibilities of the once insulted, we torture our language into the kind of absurd finicality that gives etiquette a bad name:

> Just as language grotesquely inflates in attack, so it timidly shrinks in approbation, seeking words that cannot possibly give any offence, however notional. We do not fail, we underachieve. We are not junkies, but substance abusers; not handicapped, but differently abled. And we are mealymouthed unto death: a corpse, the *New England Journal of Medicine* urged in 1988, should be referred to as a "nonliving person." By extension, a fat corpse is a differently sized nonliving person.[6]

Hughes denounces as vacuous sanctimony the American twentieth century's queasy cycling of socially acceptable synonyms for "Negro."

> If these affected contortions actually made people treat one another with more civility and understanding, there might be an argument for them. But they do no such thing. Seventy years ago, in polite white usage, blacks were called "colored people." Then they became "negroes." Then, "blacks." Now, "African-Americans" or "persons of color" again. But for millions of white Americans, from the time of George Wallace to that of David Duke, they stayed niggers, and the shift of names has not altered the facts of racism.[7]

Complaints like this have resonated widely. Even the politically correct now show due embarrassment at the smarmy euphemisms of political correctness. And insofar as plain English and a healthy loathing for jargon destroy cant and hypocrisy, they buttress real (as opposed to merely formulaic) civility. If words drift free of realities, whatever aura of politeness they generate is doomed to be specious, empty, in the end irrelevant. Yet plain English, as Colonel Mann illustrated, is also the natural medium for insult, and to soften it doesn't always corrupt it into euphemism. The widespread exasperation so eloquently voiced in *Culture of Complaint* is understandable as an outburst of irritation with the demands of whining victimhood. But in extremer forms it can become a reprehensible impatience with the restraints of good manners, a selfish unwillingness to spend time and effort accommodating the feelings of others, and a willful blindness to anything in their experience that might warrant the effort.

Manners are, after all, never obligatory in the same way that obedience to a traffic light is obligatory. Their meaningfulness derives in part from our perception that they have been observed voluntarily. Etiquette is thus always supererogatory, a taking of more than necessary pains in order to create an atmosphere of consideration and respect. Mastering the use of a fork takes an investment of patience, time, and skill; bare hands would, though less polite, be more natural, more efficient, and probably no less sanitary. The real mystery, and the moral issue before us, is how we decide when such extra efforts are warranted, which human situations deserve the extra care and forethought required for politeness.

The Ladies' Night Strippers: The Secret Symbolism of Public Display

Critics of political correctness are not always hostile to the idea that the accumulated insults of our race and gender history justify a compensatorily heightened sensitivity. Rather, their quarrel seems to lie with both the extent and the content of the gestures prescribed as appropriate courtesies. How much consideration is enough; when does extra effort become overkill; where does the obligation to make amends for our forebears' cruelty impose an unfair burden on us? And then, what do the contorted expressions and baroque obeisances demanded by political correctness really mean? Are they truly courteous, or do they mask unconscious or covert condescension? Or do erstwhile victims exact them as a form of revenge ex post facto, with the once-insulted claiming a right to force the innocent heirs of dead oppressors through humiliating rituals of penance for crimes they didn't commit?

The tergiversations of smoking etiquette in the 1980s and 1990s illustrate how easily matters of etiquette can become playing pieces in a slippery game of one-upsmanship. At first, increasingly restrictive social rules about where it was permissible to smoke seemed to rise from genuine concern for the health and comfort of nonsmokers. But as public sentiments grew ever more hostile, smokers were successively banished (first by convention and finally by law) from schools, offices, cabs, restaurants, hotel rooms, rental cars, and in California briefly even from bars. What commenced as consideration for nonsmokers increasingly began to look like the gratuitous persecution of smokers. The atmosphere became so intolerant that a few acts of almost Soviet-style historical revisionism occurred. The town of Hyde Park, New York—Franklin D. Roosevelt's birthplace—actively considered painting out the jaunty cigarette holder from the FDR silhouettes that mark the town limits (so far the cigarette has stayed in place).

Customs are laden with symbolic meaning, and symbolic meaning is mutable, prone to change radically with the times: banishing cigars from the office may have begun as an expression of the stogie-chomping boss's noblesse oblige, but it seems to have turned into the administrative assistant's revenge. And time is not the only solvent of meaning: much depends as well on the personal eccentricities of whoever gets to define it. What one person intends as a light pleasantry may be someone else's idea of a stinging insult, and a gesture of apparent deference can easily mask a concealed slight. Erving Goffman (1922–1988), the great sociologist and analyst of social self-presentation, observed this mordantly in his book *Relations in Public* (1971), noting for example that "in the early days of drop hanging, the victim apparently was allowed to govern the moment of his own demise by being put in charge of the signal (a handkerchief) for the drop. . . . Today, apparently, persons being gassed are allowed to signal for the pellet and are encouraged to breathe deeply on their own. . . . Routinely in American practice, the police *ask* the subject to empty purse and pockets instead of doing this themselves."[8]

Goffman thought such grating courtesies served both as tacit apology for an intrusion against the self and a way to ease the victim into cooperation. But they could also amount to calculated insult: the master, by requesting what he can plainly command, underscores and rubs in the extent of his power. And in controversial or sensitive realms like gender and race relations, where people jockey anxiously to preserve their own dignity while according at least a show of deference to others, the indeterminacy inherent in the symbolism of manners can make them seem not just problematic but confounding. Two anthropologists, Maxine L. Margolis and Marigene Arnold, supply an intriguing case history of this in their 1993 study of a cultural novelty of the 1970s, a once-a-week male strip show, in this instance put on at Ginnie's, a small-town American disco. If female strippers represented the subjection of women to male desire, Margolis and Arnold asked, might this apparently novel transformation of men into commercial sex toys for women amount to a therapeutic settling of old scores, and a symbolic righting of an ancient imbalance in gender power?

The shows made some efforts to convey exactly that message. "Ladies, this is *your* night," was the announcer's repeated tag line as the performers, the "Feelgood Dancers," shed their Charlie

Chaplin suits, Conan the Barbarian fur pelts, and Kung Fu leather gear.[9] But careful observation, according to Margolis and Arnold, revealed a subtle countertheme contradicting the carefully built up illusion that on Ladies' Night at Ginnie's, women were the dominant sexual consumers and men the passive providers. In the traditional strip joint, where men look on as women perform, the strippers are the supplicants, cajoling drinks from the men. Customers are expected to be unruly and a certain amount of aggression toward the women is tolerated. But at Ginnie's the staff were the aggressors, ordering the women to line up docilely outside before being admitted. A disc jockey (male) ran the performance, barking orders to the audience ("they won't take it off if you don't scream").[10] The dancers dressed not as wheedling boy toys but as sexual predators—ex-cons, lion tamers, sailors just off the ship. And the performance culminated with the disc jockey demanding that the women "dive-bomb": that is, kneel before a dancer and stuff money into his G-string with their mouths. "This action," as Margolis and Arnold perhaps unnecessarily remark, "is symbolic not only of women's subservience, but of their sexual availability and vulnerability."[11]

But how, finally, are we to decide whether dive-bombing was a minor triumph of feminism or a sneaky end run around it by men? The apparent compliment, as William d'Alton Mann knew, can in fact be a snub, and a seeming put-down can in fact betoken smittenness (a fact without which screwball comedy would scarcely exist). The meaning of a social gesture depends on who interprets it, who decides its moral significance. Disagreements about the meaning of behavior create no profound ethical problem where long-continued injustices have not abraded social nerves. But race and gender are highly sensitive, morally fraught, and cannot be ignored or finessed, except by boors. Our communal life is irreversibly saturated with awareness of them.

In a recent book, *Passing By: Gender and Public Harassment* (1995), Carol Brooks Gardner, an ethnographer at the University of Indi-

ana, interviewed more than five-hundred people in downtown Indianapolis between 1988 and 1993, in search of underlying patterns
in public rudeness toward women. Gardner dealt with a wide range
of obnoxious behavior—"pinching, slapping, hitting, shouted remarks, vulgarity, insults, sly innuendo, ogling, and stalking"[12]—but
underneath it all she discerned a persistent atavistic belief, symbolically expressed in a variety of aggressive gambits, that a woman
ought not to be a public creature, and any female who ventures
outside the shelter of home unaccompanied by a defending male is
asking for trouble. This was so common an idea in the nineteenth
century as not to be worthy of note. What is remarkable, Gardner
points out, is how obstinately it has held on. Sylvia Plath complained
about it eloquently in her journal in the 1950s: "I am a girl, a female
always in danger of assault and battery. My consuming interest in
men and their lives is often misconstrued as a desire to seduce them
or as an invitation to intimacy."[13] And even consciously feminist
contemporary etiquette manuals like Mary Mitchell's *Complete Idiot's
Guide to Etiquette* inherit it. Mitchell, advising the woman who travels alone, varies between postmodern boldness (encouraging, for
example, conversation with strangers) and slightly anachronistic-
sounding caution (noting that to some men, a woman who accepts
a dinner invitation is implicitly assenting to postprandial sex).[14]

In one revealing incident recounted in Gardner's study, "Sally,"
a college student, reported being approached by a young African-
American man on a summer day while sitting over her newspaper
on Monument Circle in downtown Indianapolis. The man, who had
been riding a bicycle around the circle, dismounted, perched nearby,
laughed to himself, mumbled about what a nice day it was, and
seemed to be eyeing her covertly. Increasingly anxious, she shunned
eye contact and pretended to read, until finally—with a muttered
comment that might have been either "Haughty" or "Hoity-
toity"—he remounted his bike and rode off. Sally reported herself
upset not only by the presumptuousness of the unsolicited flirtation
but also by its disquieting and embarrassing racial undertones. She

was worried that, as she put it, he might think she'd kept silence because "he was Black instead of because I was afraid"[15]—a reading that would, of course, instantly reverse the poles of offense, with Sally now the transgressor and the man on the bicycle transformed from harasser to victim.

In the end, Sally decided against this reading of the incident: her boyfriend, as it happened, was black, and this (she seemed to feel) absolved her both of real racism and of any obligation to avoid the appearance of it in casual encounters. Gardner seems to agree with Sally in viewing this encounter purely as an instance of gender harassment, albeit one complicated by cultural complexities that rather blur its outlines. But the reality seems considerably more doubtful to me. The black cyclist's side of the story remains untold: he might well disclaim any intent to flirt, and plausibly interpret Sally's grim attention to her newspaper as a symptom of the panic whites often indulge in the presence of a strange young black man (several of Gardner's black male interviewees reported crossing the street when they saw whites approaching, so as to avoid provoking such humiliating displays of fright).

What makes such incidents so hard to parse is the contemporary flux in the values by which—if they only kept stable—we might hope to judge. If the young man had been white, he would certainly have figured as the sole offender, and the incident as an example of bad gender manners. But if Sally had been a white male and the cyclist a black female, for most observers the possible dimension of gender harassment would instantly vanish because women, in conventional belief, cannot possibly be harassers; the episode would then appear simply and unambiguously racist.

Sensitivity: Anodyne or Irritant?

Few would deny, I think, that we owe an extra debt of consideration to groups traditionally oppressed, or that we raise the standard of contemporary civility by paying special deference to those denied it in the past. The challenge is to decide which of these all too familiar histories was the worst, and whose claim should therefore take precedence in the knotty cases where they come into collision. But approaching manners in such a way forces us to whittle a many-branched and ambiguous reality down to a rigid and reductive formula, upon which we have to agree as deciding absolutely the right and wrong of any given situation. By such logic, anyone who addresses a black woman in a store as if she were a sales clerk is *by definition* voicing a prejudice that all blacks are menial. Any man who tries to strike up a conversation with an unaccompanied woman is—QED—a harasser. No other reading of either incident is then admissible. In the cases where racism and sexism both come into play, we must set priorities: if racism is deemed the deeper and therefore determining American historical injury, then Sally failed in politeness; if sexism, then the culprit was the man on the bike. There are very potent attractions in this way of thinking. It simplifies some otherwise confusing and emotion-laden situations. And to make a habit of purging even the appearance of condescension from everyday behavior arguably stiffens one's resistance to injustice in great ones.

In *The Etiquette of Race Relations in the South: A Study in Social Control* (1937), Bertram W. Doyle showed vividly how manners can function as a disguised instrument of intimidation, exploring black-white interchanges from the antebellum period through Reconstruction and into the earlier twentieth century. In the era of slavery Doyle found patterns, often local rather than regionwide, of apparently amicable interaction between white masters and black slaves. Addressing their owners, slaves would soften "Master" into "Massa" or "Mars" and "Mistress" into "Mistis" or "Miss."[16] In the intimate relationships that often developed, particularly between house slaves and the whites they served, the slave might follow such a title with the white's Christian name. The owner might then respond by calling a male "Uncle" or a woman "Auntie."[17] To some degree, such caressing terms might indeed appear to mitigate the inequities of the relationship, but of course they also rubbed it in: "etiquette," as Doyle put it, "is the very essence of caste, since the prestige of a superior always involves the respect of an inferior."[18] Defenders of slavery could—and of course did—cite such courtesies as evidence that it was in fact a benevolent institution based on a familial bond between a conscientious master and affectionate dependent. Thomas Jefferson was perhaps the most illustrious practitioner of such expedient hypocrisy: opposed in principle to slavery, he nonetheless sustained his notably ill-run Monticello plantation with the labor of over a hundred slaves, but compensated by attempting to treat them humanely (he evinced reluctance, for example, to order them beaten for infractions, and attempted to keep families together).[19]

During Reconstruction, interracial manners lost even the appearance of harmony and became openly tense. Emancipated blacks began to resist white expectations of deference; former slaveowners, newly disempowered, found common cause with poor whites eager to claim a respectable status they had never before enjoyed. With the social landscape in earthquake, the fragile antebellum fiction of civility between the races cracked and shattered, provoking incidents like one Doyle records from 1866, on the Mississippi near Vicksburg, when a freedman attempted to board a steamer. "God damn your soul!" was the captain's response; the passengers chimed in variously with "Kick the nigger," "He ought to have his neck broke," and "he ought to be hung."[20]

With the end of Reconstruction, interracial manners ebbed into a more superficially equable but inwardly hostile pattern, in which prewar codes of master-slave manners, no longer supported by institutionalized slavery, survived in segregation laws that marked whites (whether aristocrats or rabble) as a superior caste and blacks as an underclass. Behaviors not regulated by statute tended to follow those that were: thus it became a social impossibility to address a term of respect like "Mrs." to a black woman. Doyle provides a wrenching example from the Scottsboro case, in a 1932 *Nashville Banner* item on Ada Wright—mother of two of the boys accused of rape though almost certainly innocent. Wright had embarked on a lecture tour in an attempt to arouse concern for their predicament, and in announcing this, the *Banner* put itself into contortions to avoid according her any title of respect:

> Europeans will hear of the highly publicized Scottsboro case through the lectures of Ada Wright, mother of two Negro defendants in the case. . . . The Alabama Negro sailed Wednesday. . . . One of Ada's sons is under death sentence.[21]

Reverberations of the past continue to echo present-day exchanges between blacks and whites. David Shipler's examination of race in America, *A Country of Strangers*, cites a well-intentioned white college administrator who complimented a black colleague by comparing her to a sapphire; the colleague instantly took offense, detecting (she believed) a disparaging allusion to Sapphire, Kingfish's nagging wife in *Amos 'n' Andy*, an almost proverbially grating example of racial stereotypes.[22] In truth the white woman had only the dimmest memory of the series, and none whatever of Sapphire, but the damage had been done. The black woman, acutely sensitized to slurs, simply disbelieved anybody who claimed not to remember. And forgetting, even if one conceded the possibility of it, was all by itself a sign of insensitivity.

Do this and like incidents demonstrate the need for the twisted-like-a-pipe-cleaner caution that characterizes political correctness, or do they rather point up its dangers? Millions of whites guffawed thoughtlessly at Sapphire in the fifties; millions today would be mortified if caught watching (let alone enjoying) her. And the change in attitudes surely represents an advance in civility. Doesn't it then follow that "sapphire," with or without its capital letter, should be—by definition—radioactive in interracial contexts? It would certainly be clarifying to govern the casual use of words by ironclad rules of good form, branding certain terms or expressions as off-limits, no matter what the intention of the person uttering them. But there is no small admixture of tyranny in such benevolence by ukase. People instinctively resent having their right to decide what they mean trumped by the judgment of self-appointed manners police. If conscience pronounces you innocent of racism or sexism, who has the standing to judge your behavior otherwise?

Accepting the premise that certain social situations require an extra effort of tact entails the danger of a paradoxical result: heightened sensitivity may add to the very discomfort it hopes to assuage. Much contemporary literary and cultural criticism is animated by the idea that the act of failing to confront something paradoxically marks it for attention; omission makes the thing not mentioned loom all the more pregnantly just beyond the borders of the spoken and admitted. By this logic, the stressful walking on eggshells so common in contemporary interracial and intergender interchanges may only perpetuate suspicion and hostility. Manners work best when not laden with moral significance. Related to and supportive of ethics they surely are, but they are useful just to the extent that they attenuate morals into casual habits, customs we can observe with the kind of half attention the distractions of daily life require.

Etiquette, speeding us expeditiously through the chances of routine, could never achieve that aim if every brush with a stranger became a moral watershed. Erving Goffman thought that although manners began as religious rituals of obeisance to sacred objects, they usefully decayed over time into perfunctory vestiges, their totemic origins having all but disappeared from consciousness. Once portentous, Goffman believed, such customs had dwindled into small courtesies, "attesting to civility and good will on the performer's part and to the recipient's possession of a small patrimony of sacredness."[23] Shrunken from their ancient grandeur, perhaps, but highly useful in making a connection ("Hello!") or remediating an encroachment ("Excuse me!"). Manners release us from the need to cogitate over every casual phrase we utter, smoothing social encounters by rote, useful and effective precisely to the extent that they avoid conscientious agonies.

This is a nuance, but a vital one, and the more thoughtful etiquette writers seem to appreciate it. Bates and Hudson's *Basic Black* neither ignores nor plays up the possibility of racist subtexts behind certain kinds of gaucheries, but suggests that people exposed to them will find it more functionally satisfactory to presume they betray ignorance rather than malice. "Our preference," they remark, "is to do the culturally uninitiated a favor by straightening them out—gently—and relieving them of their stereotypical baggage at the same time."[24] Their assumption, repeatedly echoed in the treatment of male-female manners commonest in twentieth-century American etiquette guides, is that if one doesn't make a monomania of it, civility can be worked to the equal advantage of both parties in a charged relationship, and need not endlessly stumble over the memory of past wrongs.

Even early twentieth-century books on gender etiquette evince some ability to treat the remaining echoes of past discrimination as an opportunity for diplomatic reform rather than an occasion for outcry; docilely sexist on the surface, in practice they treat customs implying the inferiority of women as vestiges. Having lost their real power, such customs can be tolerated, and even cleverly used as stratagems to advance the cause of equality. Margery Wilson's 1935 charm manual, *The Woman You Want to Be*, for example, repeatedly argues that by taking male behavior as it comes, and not bridling even when it seems deliberately offensive, a woman can work a prejudicial situation to her advantage. Interestingly, Wilson cites examples from the history of race as instructive for gender relations—recalling, for example, Roland Hayes (1887–1977), the great black American tenor, who faced down a hostile crowd and fended off a riot when he sang in Nazi Berlin. Hayes had his accompanist play Schubert until the murmurs and catcalls subsided, whereupon he quietly resumed the program. "As the last note of the last number died away, the audience realized how both he and they had been unselfed, and in their wild demonstration of approval he was carried on their shoulders around the Beethoven Hall twice before their fervor was spent. They had met on the common ground of music."[25]

The principle, Wilson argues, translates easily to less obviously supercharged contexts, like male-female conversation. *"You must participate in a conversation in order to influence it,"* she insists, and asserts that this can be achieved without venturing from the turf conventionally assigned to females: the emotions. If the conversation turns to music, a woman may know nothing about the technicalities of the subject, but may nonetheless contribute a remark "if it applies to the *emotional effect* of the type of music being discussed."[26] What if a klatch of engineers turns to diesel engines? "You may know nothing of the details and yet be perfectly sensible in remarking how one might feel when riding in the new contraption. You can say, 'What a thrill to shoot through space like that.' " Or, if the males happen to be doctors discussing new drugs, "be quite in the talk by commenting on the probable *emotional reactions* of mothers."[27]

I can already hear howls of outrage at this advice, and if Wilson's hypothetical engineers and doctors had been engaged in serious discussions of medicine or diesels, the eye-batting bimbo's comments she prescribes would be both insulting and silly. But her presumption is that in many such conversations, nothing serious is at issue; she is implicitly questioning the politicized mentality that reads the whole history of oppression into every unconscious slighting remark. Her stance does not dismiss the moral lessons of history simply because it views them as impediments in casual contexts. Put beneath a moral microscope, Wilson's counsel is hopelessly sexist. But manners are not the arena best suited to battling out momentous questions of right and wrong; their power, rather, is to maneuver delicately and hesitantly in the right direction, without provoking controversy—it being prudent to postpone the sermon until the prospective convert has been lured into the chapel.

Etiquette writers, while they don't always articulate this point, often seem to have assumed it. Doubleday's 1922 series of *Redbook* advertisements for Lillian Eichler's *Book of Etiquette* had represented Violet Creighton, Ted's doormat wife, as pathetically eager to prostrate herself before the snotty Brandons and the tin idol of her husband's career ambitions. But these ads were deceptive. In the book itself, Eichler proved—far more than her rival Emily Post—a firm advocate of gender equality. "Years of blind adherence to false tradition have robbed woman of her proper development along business lines," she wrote. "It may take many years of slow development before woman is considered man's absolute equal—in business as in politics. . . . It behooves every woman who is interested in the progress of womanhood, to do her little share in hastening that glorious time of complete equality."[28]

According to Eichler, falling in with old-fashioned expectations of female propriety, though it may occasionally appear to perpetuate the old order, in fact hastens the dawn of the new. Thus there is nothing retrograde about taking pains to avoid unladylike lapses, like allowing oneself to become a "slattern." "By a slattern we mean a woman who shows lack of care and thought in clothing. The girl whose blouse sags is a slattern. The woman whose dress hangs loosely and does not fit well is a slattern."[29] "Jean Rich" (a pseudonym for Frances Thompson), also a partisan of equality, nonetheless echoed Eichler's tone in her *Do's and Don'ts for Business Women* (1927). But her terms were even more traditionalist: "Don't try to acquire a mannish stride. It is most ungainly, ungraceful, and unattractive, and invariably will lower you in the estimation of your employer. Watch all your mannerisms and keep them free from mannishness. Never let your business life rob you of the niceties of life which belong distinctly to your sex."[30]

But the niceties of life are no easy study. No tact is too exquisite to conceal condescension; no insult too crude to rise from unacknowledged affection. The natural polyvalence of manners accords them an important but uneasy place in human affairs. Deftly used, they can ameliorate the pain left over from real wrongs; with thoughtlessness or ill will, they can worsen it. What civility simply cannot do—apparently ever—is to arbitrate fateful issues of right and wrong. Manners can help to soothe the hurt left by long-institutionalized injustices, but they can't single-handedly enact human equity or achieve the complete reparation demanded by the ethicist. They must instead be allowed to work in their own incremental, improvisational, indirect, opportunistic, and less than simon-pure way.

If borne down on too hard, they fail to work at all.

chapter eight

From Jean-Jacques to Dr. Spock: Parents, Children, and Discipline

In the 1960s and 1970s, cultural historians began floating a perverse and quintessentially postmodern idea, pleasing to theorists but baffling to the average parent: that the child doesn't really exist. Surveying his field in 1979 for *American Psychologist*, Yale's William Kessen wryly confronted the possibility that childhood, into whose mental and emotional secrets psychologists had been assiduously prying for well over a century, was nothing more than an artificial construct, "essentially and eternally a cultural invention."[1]

Of course no one denies the presence among us of human beings younger and smaller than adults and wired differently from them in intellect and emotion. But the underlying nature of these differences has become a matter of controversy: ideas are wont to diverge radically, depending on the time, place, and idiosyncrasies of the observer. A child's capabilities, vulnerabilities, the extent and limits of her moral sense, may seem self-evident to a father or mother scrutinizing her with the intimacy that carries unshakable conviction. But experts, ranging in approach from philosophical abstraction to laboratory science, have undermined such experiential confidence, devising irreconcilable theories about childhood, from Locke and Rousseau in the seventeenth and eighteenth centuries to Piaget and Erikson in the twentieth.

Their assessments are often counterintuitive. Historians, like the late Philippe Ariès (1914–1984), whose study *Centuries of Childhood* (1960) raised a landmark for postmodern skepticism, have been combing history, and emerging with evidence that the lives of medieval and early modern children and adolescents were startlingly different from the modern norm. In Ariès's view, childhood acquired its deceptively eternal-appearing current shape only in the 1700s. In earlier centuries, children had been treated more or less as miniature adults. A belief in their innate weakness first began to arise, Ariès thought, in the 1400s, and this led over time to a conviction—new in Western history—that their frailty demanded discipline. Later, as they came more and more to be perceived as inferior in ability and status, their parents began increasingly to expose them to regimens of physical correction, which had traditionally been meted out only to weak, dependent, and socially inferior adults.[2] Ariès has not gone unchallenged,[3] but his work illustrates the degree to which, over the last three centuries, ideas about children have caromed between dramatic opposites.

Perhaps the most basic of these perennial oppositions touches on manners: are children reprobate savages or naturally civil innocents? To adherents of the first belief, an adult's duty is to purge the child's inborn rudeness. For partisans of the second, the learning vector reverses: children should be observed and even imitated, not harshly corrected. Pessimism dominated much of the early modern era, particularly in Christian child-rearing advice: the doctrine of original sin implied a child naturally inclined toward mischief from birth and thus requiring a strong hand.

> *Speak roughly to your little boy,*
> *And beat him when he sneezes,*[4]

advised the Duchess in Lewis Carroll's *Alice's Adventures in Wonderland* (1865), and while doting Victorian parents might have laughed at her absurdity, nineteenth-century British culture, on the whole, saw eye to eye with her. Beatings were not merely routine but incessant, even—indeed, especially—in the British Empire's elitest public schools, where caning was a routine educational device.

Softer attitudes, however, had already begun to appear in the eighteenth century. One could regard the child as a blank slate, to be inscribed with any desired trait, whether humanity and tact or aggression and surliness. And the Enlightenment fostered a tendency to romanticize and idealize both infancy and childhood. William Wordsworth (1770–1850), perhaps the defining English Romantic poet, gave optimism a still-resonant expression in his "Ode: Intimations of Immortality," completed in 1804:

> *Our birth is but a sleep and a forgetting:*
> *The Soul that rises with us, our life's Star*
> *Hath had elsewhere its setting,*
> *And cometh from afar:*
> *Not in entire forgetfulness,*
> *And not in utter nakedness*
> *But trailing clouds of glory do we come*
> *From God, who is our home:*
> *Heaven lies about us in our infancy!*[5]

And apart from the alternatives offered by censoriousness and idealism, a parent could take the more urbane but possibly cynical position that manners had no moral function at all. Rather, they were a self-serving accomplishment to be studied and mastered, like riding horseback or playing the lute, as a way of impressing people and getting on in the world. This, in essence, was the stance taken by the Earl of Chesterfield (1694–1773) in his letters to his son.

However trifling a genteel manner may sound, it is of very great consequence towards pleasing in private life, especially the women; which, one time or other, you will think worth pleasing; and I have known many a man, from his awkwardness, give people such a dislike of him at first, that all his merit could not get the better of it afterwards. . . . Attention is absolutely necessary for this, as indeed it is for everything else; and a man without attention is not fit to live in the world.[6]

No matter what one's opinion about the child's inborn tendencies or the purpose of training in manners, most parents surely want to see their offspring civilized. But the fractured heritage of Western ideas about child rearing leaves us stumped about whether the educator's task is to nurture tender shoots or rip out noxious weeds by main force.

From Sesame Street to the Big House: The World of the Nineties Child

In the years after World War II, the titillating image of the innately evil hell-child reappeared incessantly: *Rosemary's Baby; Lord of the Flies*; the soulless automata of *Village of the Damned*; Rhoda Penmark, the pigtailed murderess of William March's 1954 novel *The Bad Seed* (later a successful play and an even more popular movie). Yet most postwar child-rearing literature, whether popular or academic, seems saturated with the belief that children are well-meaning if not angelic, and likely to act on their born good nature if only treated with tact, forbearance, and gentleness. Well over two hundred years have passed since Jean-Jacques Rousseau (1712–1778) set the standard for rosy views of childhood in his didactic novel *Émile* (1762); but his quivering sentiments match the content if not the vocabulary of much contemporary convention:

Nurture childhood; encourage its play, its pleasures, its instinctive kindness. Which of us doesn't sometimes long to go back to that time of life when laughter is always on the lips, and the soul ever at peace? Why ever should one want to take away from these little innocents the sweet enjoyment of a time that so soon escapes them?[7]

Rousseau's florid effusion, rendered in the flat accents of American pragmatism, is essentially the stance of the late Benjamin Spock (1903–1998), the patriarch of contemporary American child care. His attitude toward corporal punishment illustrates the similarity. Uneasy about spanking even in 1945, when *The Common Sense Book of Baby and Child Care* first appeared,[8] he had evolved into unambiguous opposition by the 1992 edition, observing that other cultures raise children successfully without resort to force, and linking a too-ready appeal to the rod with the generally high incidence of violence in American life.[9]

Another contemporary figure of commanding authority, Robert Coles, is similarly a believer in the moral dignity of childhood; he emerged from extensive interviews with children convinced that a normal upbringing fosters a powerful impulse in them toward well-doing. In his much-read *The Moral Life of Children* (1986), Coles argued that children are characteristically obsessive about conscience and cases of right and wrong. "In elementary school," he wrote, "maybe as never before or afterward, given favorable family and neighborhood circumstances, the child becomes an intensely moral creature, quite interested in figuring out the reasons of this world: how and why things work, but also how and why he or she should behave in various situations."[10] Coles concedes that the dark lessons of adult combativeness, envy, and suspicion can and do erode a child's born altruism; but the norm is a Wordsworthian beneficence, emanating first from a memory of maternal love in infancy and ultimately from a collective memory of prelapsarian happiness: "It is our nature,

St. John of the Cross knew . . . to hope against hope, and in doing so to be reminded of the first such episode—those strongly felt days, weeks, months when hope seemed (in retrospect) so simple, so forthcoming, so free of impediments, obstacles, impasses, commands, threats, criticism, not to mention self-criticism."[11]

Measured by such idealized models, violence by adults against children, even in the name of discipline, becomes not only inadvisable but reprehensible, and stirs outrage. Sappy Mister Rogers is an idealized and widely shared modern American image of how one ought to treat children; the mainstream media have erected a near taboo against calls for physical punishment, and seem ill-disposed even toward harshly expressed disapproval. Adults who transgress can become scapegoats in self-righteous mass witch-hunts. Consider, for example, the hysterical eruption of public hatred against Susan Smith, convicted in 1995 of strapping her two toddler sons into her car, rolling it into a lake, and drowning them. The apparent madness of the act and the desperation of Smith's life before it aroused little sympathy. Sixty-three percent of the respondents in a *Newsweek* poll thought she deserved the death penalty, not much less than the four fifths who wanted execution for Timothy McVeigh, the Oklahoma City bomber.[12]

Still more suggestive perhaps was the case of the Arizona couple arrested and tried in 1997 for attempting to discipline the two rampaging four-year-old girls they had adopted in Russia and were bringing home on a transatlantic flight. During their trial, the parents denied any wrongdoing; witnesses conceded[13] that the children were frantic and uncontrollable; and they suffered no physical injury from the episode. Yet there was little if any public sympathy for the accused adults. A Queens, New York, Family Court found them guilty of scolding and slapping the children, who then spent months bouncing from foster home to foster home before finally returning—conditionally—to their adoptive parents in early 1998.[14] The child, public reaction to such incidents seems to be saying, is sacrosanct. Physical punishment, no matter how mild, is both counterproductive and morally indefensible.

No sooner does one wave of righteous outrage dissipate than another rolls in. The year 1997's biggest such sensation was Louise Woodward, the Massachusetts *au pair* employed by two ophthalmologists and charged with the murder of the infant under her supervision, a case that plainly evoked the gnawing fear and guilt working parents feel at daily abandoning their children to the care of strangers. But are such public frenzies really what they seem to be, an affirmation of the importance of cherishing and nurturing children? Or are they attempts at denial, a collective sublimation of the disturbing truth that young children—shameless, boundless in egotism, irresponsible, amoral—can easily goad even a patient and loving adult into rage? An infant shrieking an octave and several decibels above the threshold of pain, a toddler in mid-tantrum in a supermarket parking lot, the overactive five-year-old who turns every day into an ordeal—every adult has been around one or two, and lives uncomfortably with the knowledge of how nearly overpowering the urge can be to retaliate. Thus we turn with implacable vengeance on those who seem to have yielded to provocation, like the New York physician who in 1997 stood trial for shaking his baby to death. He insisted the act was an attempt to get rid of an obstruction in her breathing. Prosecutors, unmoved, attributed the death to anger and charged him with murder.[15]

Not all the modern experts, of course, hold with Rousseau's Panglossian view of childhood. Orthodox religious and social conservatives are always on the qui vive for signs of inborn taint in the young and ready to purge evil, by force if necessary, seeing children as less than pure founts of sweetness and light. Exemplary manners can conceal lurking evil, as with *The Bad Seed*'s Rhoda Penmark ("she was," as a puzzled teacher remarks of her in the novel, "the only child in the history of the school who'd made a hundred in deportment, each month, in the classrooms, and a hundred in self-reliance and conservation, each month, on the playgrounds, for a full school year").[16] Sometimes, of course, infant Bacchism wears no mask at all. I can recall a memorable Christmas tree–decorating party: just as the guests crowned the tree with a tinfoil star, the hosts' five-year-old daughter appeared at the top of the stairs, gazed down at the sight in wonderment, and sighed, "Can we pray to it?" Her parents, appalled, immediately abandoned the party and hauled out her Sunday School workbook for a remedial session.

In fact, a long tradition acknowledges the child's disruptive energy. In their now classic 1959 study *The Lore and Language of School Children*, Iona and Peter Opie offered a bracingly unsentimental view in surveying the irreverent lore children invent and then share under the gaze of unsuspecting adults. Manners are prime targets:

> *Ladies and gentlemen*
> *Take my advice*
> *Pull down your pants*
> *And slide on the ice.*[17]

Children, the Opies said, are "the greatest of savage tribes and the only one which shows no signs of dying out";[18] and few adults, however strong their powers of denial, lack for corroborating evidence. The 1960s, predictably, affirmed this tendency not just to recognize the eruptive, Dionysian side of childhood, but also to celebrate it for its freedom from cant and hypocrisy. In a delightfully waspish 1963 *Commentary* article, " 'Good Bunnies Always Obey': Books for American Children," Jason Epstein chided the officious adults who controlled mid-twentieth-century children's books for lacing them with moral sugar and surreptitious lessons in conformity. Epstein thought this noxious school-of-education mentality annoyingly common in books awarded Caldecott and Newbery medals, the Oscars of the genre, citing as an example Mary Stolz's *Belling the Tiger*, which claimed a Newbery in 1961. In the story, some young mice, setting out to bell the cat, trap a tiger instead, but prudently decide not to tell their elders about the adventure.

Epstein saw the smug ending as propaganda against imagination and originality. Aesthetically stronger and in the long run healthier, he argued, were strong-minded if shameless classics, like Lewis Carroll's hallucinatory fantasies, Swift's misanthropic *Gulliver's Travels*, and even—in the not-to-be-despised domain of pulp—the lurid see-things of horror comics and the kiddie noir of Nancy Drew, Tom Swift, and the Hardy Boys. In their different ways all face dark terrors and accommodate rebellious urges. All acknowledge the child's real experience rather than a squeamish adult's prim prejudices, and all reaffirm literature's role as a goad to the imagination and the intellect rather than a means of mind control.

Indeed, the real-life behavior of children rarely conforms to the expectations, as evidenced by the juvenile section of the crime blotter, where children figure not as victims but perpetrators, sometimes outdoing adult competitors. The parents of the 1950s may have accepted Spock's easygoing ways as appropriate for their own off-spring, but newspapers and magazines panicked them with ever-worsening news about juvenile crime. This was not, apparently, hype: delinquency does seem to have mounted after World War II, rising especially sharply in the mid-fifties. Police arrested 37,259 children under eighteen in 1951; the number had more than doubled, to 86,128, by 1952, and nearly doubled again by 1953, to 149,806 (in those same three years the population of ten- to seventeen-year-olds rose only about 7 percent).[19] Then came rock music, smoldering with the sullen yokeldom of the redneck South, full of primitive lyrics, pounding rhythms, sex, and easy to imagine as a prelude to social chaos. How, parents might well wonder, could Spockean avuncularity tame and civilize a rising generation drawn toward such barbarism? The improbably decent and winsome TV world of the Cleavers, the Nelsons, and the Andersons may have been partly a self-celebratory portrait of postwar American family life, but it was also, surely, a wishful reaction against a threatening reality.

By the eighties and nineties, angst about juvenile crime had ebbed (though organized gang violence continued to be a worry). But suspicion and hostility persist, rarely acknowledged in the open, yet recurring again and again in symbolic form. Despite the sanctimoniousness of public outrage over adult cruelty to children, we seem increasingly willing to tolerate (indeed, to encourage) institutional mean-spiritedness toward them, as long as someone puts forth a moral pretext for it. Consider Newt Gingrich's call for a return to the era of the orphanage,[20] or the nasty recent fashion of criminalizing ever younger children who get themselves into trouble. Colorado pioneered the humane treatment of juvenile offenders as early as 1903—when, under the prodding of Benjamin Barr Lindsey, a Denver judge, it enacted the nation's first juvenile court law. But we seem to have been voluntarily regressing to an earlier and harsher era, thinking more like the Georgia court that in the 1890s sentenced a thirteen-year-old to twelve months of hard labor on a chain gang.[21]

Perhaps the most unsettling instance of this new urge to put the warden in charge of the nursery was the Oakland six-year-old who generated national publicity when, after dumping a newborn out of its bassinet and trying to beat it to death,[22] he was charged with attempted murder in early 1996. He was arrested, and the fact publicly revealed, as if he were a fully responsible adult: no anomaly in an atmosphere of impassioned demands for laws that allow juvenile offenders to be tried and punished as adults, and a resurgence of youth curfew ordinances (despite lingering doubts that curfews really curtail rowdiness).

Whatever the long-term historical trend, a queasy ambivalence runs beneath it, wavering between worship and suspicion. Widespread public concern about the mistreatment of children makes an appealing show of humanity, but some key statistics suggest an undeclared guerrilla war, with adults as the aggressors and children as victims. In a recent Heritage Foundation report, *The Child Abuse Crisis: The Disintegration of Marriage, Family, and the American Community* (1997), Patrick Fagan and William Fitzgerald argue that the

1980s and 1990s have witnessed an epidemic of assault on the physical and mental well-being of children, citing (for example) U.S. Health and Human Services Department studies that reported a 149 percent increase in incidents of abuse and neglect between 1980 and 1993.[23] As their title implies and the Heritage Foundation's conservative agenda would hint, Fagan and Fitzgerald blame this steep rise on the decline of the stable nuclear family, though they themselves admit that in the United States at least the best research evidence links child abuse most clearly to poverty.[24]

Yet—without minimizing the tragic dimensions of mistreatment of the young as a reality—at least as interesting culturally is the strangely inverse relation between our histrionically compassionate public attitudes and the way we seem to treat children in private (with ever more neglect and brutality, often disguising the latter as discipline). In retrospect, the mid-eighties panic over missing children seems clearly to have been a symptom of bad collective conscience rather than a measured response to real crimes. The disappearance in 1984 of Kevin Collins, a San Francisco ten-year-old, sparked it; his face was the first of thousands to blazon milk cartons, igniting a panic that masses of American children were vanishing into the clutches of lurking predators. At length it turned out that many if not most of these "missing" children had been abducted by a parent embroiled in a custody dispute with his or her spouse. Were we disburdening ourselves of guilt in a public auto-da-fé, a spectacle that diverted attention from less sensational but more disturbing Reagan-era realities: spreading poverty among children, distracted workaholic parents, ramshackle schools, underpaid and semiliterate teachers? Likely so, since over the next few years the milk carton craze faded. The Kevin Collins Foundation, formed to publicize the supposed kidnapping epidemic, ceased operations in 1996[25]—though the fact that the number of genuine disappearances had been exaggerated never circulated quite as widely as the rumors of vanishing kids.

Contemporary attitudes toward children are an anxious and unsettled mix, part nostalgia for the sentimentalized childhoods and peaceable families of the 1950s sitcom, part a lust for melodrama (supposedly secret yet shrilly publicized and crammed with tales of hatred, violence, and sexual exploitation). Such adult dithering isn't wholly neurotic, since real-life children partake of both worlds. Some are embarked on careers that will end in sainthood; others are already demonic and likely to grow more so. Most, like most adults, are a mixture, intriguing in its complexity but bewildering to anyone bent on devising all-purpose rules for moral and social betterment.

Slovenly Peter, Rainbow Brite, and the Bart Simpson Perplex

Ambiguousness about children may be a natural reaction to the realities of child behavior. But it also reflects a lurking ambivalence about civility. A child's momentary reversion to perceived savagery is a reminder, half-tempting and half-repellent, of the universal urge—repressed in adulthood but abidingly powerful—to let rip with our most antisocial instincts. Visions of childhood innocence, on the other hand, call up gentler, more tactful, more altruistic feelings, and remind us why we yearn for the civil state, desiring a safer and pleasanter life for ourselves and those we care about. The literature, television programs, even the toys we invent for children, are small allegories of these uncertain attitudes, showing us, like barometers, the state of the atmosphere at any given historical moment.

The contemporary American note is gingerly caution, an anxious eagerness to touch all possible bases. *Sesame Street* (which premiered in 1969) is a realm of cuddly Muppets and sugary communality, but, steeped in a recognizably gritty urban environment, it at least acknowledges the multiethnic and multiracial American reality, and admits measured doses of irreverent wit. Dinosaurs, a perennial source of fascination to children, of course evoke anarchy, though popular treatments show a strong (if not universal) tendency to tame them. In the 1950s, these monsters rampaged with crude force through movie fantasies like *Godzilla, King of the Monsters* (1956). But soon, without losing quite all their scariness, they fell victim to domestication. Maurice Sendak's hugely popular *Where the Wild Things Are*, first published in 1963, struck a particularly shrewd balance, its monsters at once sharp toothed and cuddly. Even Barney, the signature preschool craze of the 1980s, isn't wholly saccharine, since as a dinosaur he invokes the violence, danger, and unruliness children find both frightening and irresistibly attractive. But his creators have gone far beyond Sendak, upholstering over almost every trace of his ancestral Mesozoic ferocity. His teeth look like dentures or a row of Chiclets, his hide is plush purple and green, his form doughily Rubenesque rather than muscular, his voice goofy, and his affect slurpy. Whatever he shares by way of threat or lawlessness with his saurian cousins in *Jurassic Park* he has successfully sublimated. Many parents, creatures of the rebellious sixties and seventies, are openly revolted by Barney (Dave's Anti-Barney World Wide Web page—one of several—features an animated Barney repeatedly blasted to bits in a gush of blood). But children love him: for them he seems just the right mixture of slightly naughty spontaneity and reassuring safety.

Yet children's entertainment was not always so studiously inoffensive. Victorian creations for children were often far less well groomed than their twentieth-century created-by-committee descendants. *Struwwelpeter* (1847), the immortal, hair-raising, yet enduringly popular children's book by a German physician, Heinrich Hoffmann, with its bloodthirsty instructional verses and macabre drawings, appeals both to the adult disciplinarian and the child's embarrassing but well-documented love of gore. (Hoffmann and his book have even been immortalized in a Frankfurt museum.) A boy sucks his thumb; a man appears with a pair of scissors and shears it off. Little Harriet insists on playing with matches and incinerates herself, surviving only as a mound of ashes mourned by cats. Augustus, refusing to eat his soup, wastes away and perishes of starvation within a week. Compared to Barney and other innocuous latter-day children's idols like Strawberry Shortcake (the miniature doll whose designers intended her to exude "security and affection"),[26] or the Cabbage Patch Kids, *Struwwelpeter* (Englished as *Slovenly Peter* and still in print)[27] looks sadistic and cynical. Children, of course, love it, just as they loved the Garbage Pail Kids trading cards, marketed in the wake of the Cabbage Patch fad and featuring graphically vile characters like Valerie Vomit, Virus Iris, and Russ Pus.

In his intriguing scholarly history of American toys, *Kids' Stuff* (1997), Gary Cross remarks that some classic playthings, like the Jack-in-the-Box, seem perversely aimed at scaring children, as if in fulfillment of latent adult sadism.[28] Others are just business: Louis Marx, the legendary early twentieth-century toy manufacturer, bought up scrap metal on the cheap during the Depression, and cared little if children knew it. "It was a common (and perplexing) childhood experience," the toy historian Richard O'Brien has written, "to peer inside a Marx product and find evidence of its prior incarnation as a soup can."[29] The 1960s and 1970s saw a short-lived fad of tenebrous and lurid toys, in the spirit of Jason Epstein's complaint against the blandness of fifties children's literature: in 1969, Aurora Plastics introduced a working model guillotine, complete with beheadable plastic victims.[30] Nor have grotesque and violent products disappeared from the market in our own hypervigilant era, though they are usually not quite so explicitly morbid as the Aurora guillotine, and they tend to display an atavistic sexism, with the nightmarish worlds-in-conflict offerings like Mighty Morphin Power Rangers aimed at boys and the maudlin ones, like My Little Pony and Rainbow Brite, appealing to girls.

In the story of toys lurks a buried theme: an uneasy wavering between wary sentiment and guilt-ridden cynicism, a note of queasy irresolution, an indecision about whether to deny or celebrate the savage in children. This mirrors, of course, an equally troublesome ambivalence about manners, which is reflected with uncanny sensitivity in perhaps the definitive childhood hero of the 1990s: Matt Groening's Bart Simpson. He is not a wholly novel creation, echoing as he does a long line of popular caricature brats. The earliest of these was probably Richard Felton Outcault's wisecracking Mickey Dugan, the "Yellow Kid," who first appeared in the *New York World* in 1896, clad in a yellow, handprint-smudged nightshirt ("You ain't so warm," the Kid announced to the Sphinx on a visit to Egypt in an 1897 panel).[31] The tradition continued with the Our Gang series; the glowering and hard-bitten grade-schoolers immortalized in W. C. Fields movies; Rudolph Dirks's "Katzenjammer Kids" (Hans und Fritz, who debuted in 1897 and continued to inflict themselves on der Captain, der Inspector, and Momma for generations); Hank Ketcham's "Dennis the Menace."

More often hapless or hyperkinetic than truly malevolent (the Katzenjammers and the Fields children were refreshing exceptions), all these hellions, whatever the state of their morals, nevertheless cut up within strict and surprisingly stable limits, never venturing beyond what a conventional adult would judge as conceivable in childish misbehavior. Bart Simpson, however, broke new ground, claiming a whole new world of once exclusively adult vulgarity for childhood use. Bart is blasé and apparently well informed about sex, cynical about business and politics, and seems at the age of ten to have passed through all the possible stages of adult disillusionment. He calls his father "Homer" (though Marge Simpson is still "Mom"), uses either "Eat my shorts" or a full moon as all-purpose put-downs, and thinks no social taboo inviolable. His heroes are Krusty the Klown, a raspy-voiced, chain-smoking show-biz cynic, and Itchy and Scratchy, a sadistic cartoon mouse and masochistic cat. The Fox TV network promotes the Simpsons as "America's Favorite Dysfunctional Family," presided over by obese, beer-swilling, infantile Homer. Springfield, their home town, amalgamates everything below par and above the threshold of disgust in contemporary America, from its pseudo-professional local TV news program and malfunctioning nuclear power plant to its venal politicians, dim-witted fundamentalists, shiftless cops, and secondhand monorail.

The Simpsons started as an alternative-press cartoon, became a television series in 1989, and has since begotten a sequence of ever vulgarer television cartoon shows, each self-consciously outdoing its immediate predecessors in the violation of decorum: *Ren and Stimpy, Beavis and Butt-head,* most recently the moon-faced and sewer-mouthed children of *South Park.* But the real innovation of the televised Simpsons, and the one most interesting to a study of their manners, is the ground bass of decency that sounds against their superficial vulgarity. Bart, for all his rowdiness, is as pure if not so fine spun as his exemplary sister Lisa. His language might have shocked the Katzenjammer Kids, but he is far less malicious; at times, in fact, he behaves like a Rousseauesque child of classic vulnerability seeking dignity in a world of adult sleaze. In one episode, "Crêpes of Wrath," the family participates in a student exchange, Marge and Homer heedlessly taking in an Albanian child spy while feckless Bart ends up in virtual slavery in a French vineyard, eating raw turnips and replacing an overworked donkey named Maurice.

A fresh coat of polish in *The Simpsons* is often the clue to underlying rottenness. Which, of course, is an insight that wouldn't have surprised William d'Alton Mann. New to Bart Simpson and the 1990s is a fusion—indeed a *con*fusion—of the sinful infant barbarian of Christian orthodoxy with the glorious innocent of post-Enlightenment idealism. A history of veering between these poles (given the contradictory and unpredictable behavior of children and the irresolution of adults) is to be expected. But contemporary Americans seem to have blended them.

Advice from the Experts: Rules, the Rod, or Ritalin?

Hence the bewilderment experienced by any parent who, faced with a behavior crisis, visits the child-care section at the bookstore. Spock, of course, still figures prominently, with his levelheaded view that children are usually neither hardened brutes nor fragile blossoms, and that parents can normally trust their instincts in training them. But there are hundreds of competing authorities, from pediatricians to psychologists to clergy to parents, whose sole qualification is their experience. Religious and cultural conservatives see childhood misbehavior as a reversion, to be corrected by a kind but more or less forceful laying down of laws. Clinically trained experts often regard rudeness as a symptom crying for treatment, counterculture sympathizers as a natural spontaneity to be tolerated if not celebrated.

There are purely practical offerings, like Carol Wallace's evocatively titled *Elbows Off the Table, Napkin in the Lap, No Video Games During Dinner: The Modern Guide to Teaching Children Good Manners*.[32] And a small industry dedicates itself to face-to-face instruction in etiquette and related graces. The National League of Junior Cotillions, based in Charlotte, North Carolina, sponsors a SWAT team of 120 instructors who fan out, mainly across the South, to offer classes to children on table manners, the art of proper introductions, and, for some reason, the cha-cha and the waltz: a typical nine-month course costs $225.[33] Judith Ré, of Fairfield, Connecticut's, Academie for Instruction in the Social Graces, offers a similar service, at $245 for a one-day crash course.[34]

Recurrent and predictable themes often divide the experts into two roughly defined camps, maintaining either that manners training is a casual and purely pragmatic affair or a deeply moral one. Kathryn Murray, the distaff pillar of the Arthur Murray dancing school empire, wrote a guide in 1961—*Kathryn Murray's Tips for Teenagers*—and she tapped a vein of practicality reminiscent of Lord Chesterfield (insofar as one equates practicality with pleasing a date and landing a spouse): "Though this may surprise boys who have never thought about it most girls notice table manners. . . . Girls take a dim view of a boy who slouches on his elbows, grips his fork like a shovel, or eats untidily."[35]

Viola Tree, Lord Northcliffe's etiquette columnist, blended both themes with panache in a list of "Things to Enforce" on children in the home, which added up to a laconic three:

(a) *Saying prayers* of some sort. In my opinion, the Lord's Prayer is better than their own funny little prayers.

(b) *Sitting up* (holding oneself straight).

(c) *Folding up clothes.*[36]

Tree was a product of Bloomsbury in the 1930s, yet her insistence on morality inculcated with a light and uncensorious touch was a note by no means absent in the history of American child-rearing literature. Enos Hitchcock (1744–1803), a Congregationalist minister who led churches in Massachusetts and Rhode Island, served as an army chaplain during the Revolutionary War, and acted as preacher to George Washington,[37] also wrote extensively on children. His magnum opus, issued in 1790, bore a marathon title: *Memoirs of the Bloomsgrove Family, In a Series of Letters to a Respectable Citizen of Philadelphia, Containing Sentiments on a Mode of Domestic Education, Suited to the Present State of Society, Government, and Manners, in the United States of America, and on the Dignity and Importance of the Female Character, Interspersed with a Variety of Interesting Anecdotes.* Hitchcock, despite his denomination, his New England roots, and his era, was no Puritan disciplinarian; rather, he endorsed the child-friendly sentiments brought into new fashion by Locke and Rousseau. But he was also a realist. "Every man, to whom the care of children is committed, is not a Rousseau, nor is every child an Emilius or a Sophia: neither are we aerial beings, that we should subsist on sentimental diet. . . . We must take children as they are, endued with a variety of humors, dispositions, and propensities; and endeavor to make them what we wish them to be."[38] Though Hitchcock's test case children bore resonant Augustan names—Rozella and Osander Bloomsgrove—they sometimes failed to behave in accordance with these uppity sobriquets.

> It is not uncommon in a child, after caressing its favorite puppy, to kick and beat it; or after stroking a sparrow, to pull off its head. I have seen a little girl, after spending hours in dressing her doll, throw it out of the window in a sudden fit. . . . There is in children a curiosity to see animals slain, and a pleasure in triumphing over their agonies, which has a most dangerous tendency upon the fine feelings of human nature.[39]

Hitchcock's prescriptions for easing children out of such behavior tend to be mild, in a prescient foreshadowing of twentieth-century ideas about proper discipline:

> To cross children, in things perfectly indifferent, has the appearance of capriciousness, and tend[s] to chafe and sour their minds. Restraints, where they are indispensable, should be so laid, as rather to call off the mind from the object, than to prohibit enjoyment. To maintain that entire control over the appetites of children, which is the parent's prerogative, so as not to induce dissimulation on the one hand, nor disaffection on the other, is a critical point. When the parent, or the preceptor, becomes a tyrant, and the child is a slave, there is an end of all education.[40]

This delicate balance between a powerful desire to improve the child, and a healthy fear of tyrannizing it in the process, recurs in the literature of twentieth-century American child rearing. William E. Blatz and Helen Bott, in a 1930 offering, *The Management of Young Children*, advise just such a tactful approach: "It may be assumed that we all want our children to be courteous and considerate of others; the difference is one of procedure rather than of ultimate results. . . . Do we make a truly polite child by making him acutely conscious of social forms, or does he absorb politeness by living in an atmosphere of consideration?"[41] The latter, they opine: "Rudeness should be met by courtesy on the part of the adult rather than by rude rebuffs or reproofs."[42]

In contemporary child rearing, where interventions are at least as likely to come from the medical as the religious establishment, the more skeptical authorities sometimes warn against too readily clinicalizing behavior problems. Stanley Turecki and Leslie Tonner's *The Difficult Child* (1985) is a noteworthy example of this attitude. Although Turecki is a practicing child psychiatrist, he resists medicalizing every act of insurrection as a symptom of some syndrome like hyperactivity. Rather, he believes much if not most childhood misbehavior is normal, and that assessing it should only rarely lead to a formal psychiatric or medical diagnosis. The "easy" child, in Turecki's system, is relatively inactive, adaptable, regular of habit, and doesn't distract easily; while the "difficult" child is contradictory, withdrawn, intense, negative, distractible, highly active, a trial to everyone and a cross of red-hot iron to its parents. But none of this necessarily means the child has crossed the line either into reprobation or treatable pathology.

Turecki illustrates in a chapter called "A Day in the Life of a Difficult Child." Adam, the composite three-year-old featured, is an emblem of the uncouth mid-American brat at his worst. The only television programs he consents to watch are blaring hyperkinetic MTV videos. To wash and dress him requires main force. He beats his nursery school classmates, indulges in a howling tantrum at the grocery store, defaces the wallpaper with a marking pen, spits his dinner pizza onto the table, assaults his father, and finally tops off the day with a spectacular bath- and bedtime blitzkrieg.[43] Trying though Adam is, Turecki recommends neither medication nor disciplinary intervention, locating him rather at the troublesome end of a normal behavioral continuum between "easy" and "difficult." A good portion of Turecki's book is devoted to strategies for coping with such difficult children—practical advice for moderating behavior and keeping a grip on one's own temper. Presenting Adam as normal rather than vicious or psychotic has its appeal: it defuses tension and discharges the frustrated parent's anger and anguish.

Linda and Richard Eyre advance a very different, more ethically charged approach. A husband-and-wife team with nine children, they have written a number of widely read books like *Teaching Your Children Values*, *Teaching Children Responsibility*, and *Teaching Children Sensitivity*, which advocate—as the titles suggest—a need to indoctrinate offspring, albeit tactfully. They spare the reader hair-raising accounts of antisocial behavior, and instead offer instructional tips about how to reform it. Train toddlers to share by using a kitchen timer to signal trade-off time for playthings. Praise a child lavishly whenever she seems willing to share. Encourage her to sacrifice a favorite toy to an underprivileged child at Christmas. Stimulate empathy by showing preschoolers pictures of people in different situations and asking them to imagine how it would feel to be living the picture.[44] The Eyres aren't dogmatic as to whether selfishness rises from original sin, innate animal cruelty, or just from chance. But they are nevertheless emphatic that parents have a duty to coax children out of such behavior.

Over his long career as a guru for parents, Banjamin Spock captured and orchestrated all these nuances of concern, uneasiness, and equanimity. He has a less than fully deserved reputation for advocating permissiveness, and has sometimes been blamed for the perceived triumph of mannerlessness in the baby boom and Generation X. But his classic *Common Sense Book of Baby and Child Care*, and its successive revisions (the most recent in collaboration with Michael Rothenberg in 1992), reveal this as an exaggeration. Spock's advice, constant throughout the publishing history of his book, has been a reassuring and pragmatic "trust yourself" to the parent, reflecting an assumption that the parent-child relationship, apart from the occasional crisis, tends to regulate itself as long as the adult uses good sense.[45]

In his first, dawn of the baby boom edition, Spock emphasized the normality of misbehavior as a natural feature of child development. The two-year-old who grabs toys from playmates is simply too young to empathize with others; the three-year-old's suddenly acquired vocabulary of bathroom insult is a universal phase. Spock, seconding authorities from Hitchcock to Blatz and Bott, thinks one should ease the child nonchalantly out of such behavior.

> I'd let a child have a little fun with his bad words, provided they aren't too awful, perhaps even grinning a little to show him that I had my wicked side, too, and then change the subject. Then if it didn't wear off, or if he came to words that would certainly offend the neighbors, I'd tell him in a matter-of-fact way that lots of people don't like to hear those words at all and that I don't like to hear them all day long.[46]

Likewise, the toddler who pretends to kill people with a toy gun probably knows it's wrong to harm anyone in earnest; the violence is playful, a way to dissipate excess energy, and no cause for alarm. Implicit in such advice is the faith that between them, the child's nature and the normal human social environment tend to civilize his or her personality; only unusual cases require intervention, and that, Spock intimates, should take the form of a consultation with a teacher or psychiatrist rather than punishment.[47]

Yet Spock's ideas—among them his thoughts on rudeness and good manners—evolved over the decades. The Vietnam War, Spock's vociferous opposition to it, and the fraying of public comity it both reflected and worsened, seem to have had their effect. In recent editions, he has urged parents wherever possible to guide their children away from expressions of anger and violence, even where these appear natural or harmless. In a considerably expanded section on social aggression, he cites the Kennedy assassination and the many reports of youngsters who cheered when they first heard of it. He denounces the nation's history of (and its fascination with) violence. And he castigates crude and brawling TV—particularly the Three Stooges shorts that formed a staple of commercial children's television in the fifties and sixties (one wonders what he would have thought of Kenny, the dirt-poor *South Park* child who is horribly mutilated and killed in every episode).[48]

This suggests a quiet shift from optimism to doubt, if not frank angst, and mirrors a wider American anxiety. Consider the recurrent worry about shielding children from shocking stimuli, powerfully exemplified by the recent debate over how best to protect them from Internet obscenity. Are we disturbed because we see children as innocents, who might be destroyed by exposure to such material, or as powder kegs, brimful of latent urges and obscene appetites to be ignited at a spark? Are we worried about children because we think them fragile saints or smoldering savages?

Both, the answer seems to be. The Academie for Instruction in the Social Graces is no novelty; every major etiquette writer of the twentieth century has at one time or another addressed childhood manners, in open acknowledgment that the subject requires special attention. Emily Post wrote *Children Are People* in 1940; most recently there was *Letitia Baldrige's More Than Manners! Raising Today's Kids to Have Kind Manners and Good Hearts*. Judith Martin's *Miss Manners' Guide to Rearing Perfect Children*, first published in 1979, became a best-seller. To one degree or another, they all evince an ambiguity that Martin captures with characteristic tartness in her introduction. On the one hand, she acknowledges the belief that rudeness is rampant and on the ascendant.[49] Yet she denies with equal firmness that an urge toward boorishness is hardwired into the child's mind. On the contrary.

> Miss Manners has also observed that when children are truly allowed to express their preferences, uninfluenced by the dreary adult expectation that they must all be artistic and orig-

inal little noble savages, they come out resoundingly in favor of rigid traditionalism. The devotion to ritual exhibited by the average toddler in regard to his bedtime routine would make a nineteenth-century English butler look like a free spirit.[50]

Dick and Jane took their bland refinement into oblivion when the series of readers they starred in began to disappear from schools. But Barney arrived in their stead, oozing a harmlessness even they might have found cloying. *Slovenly Peter* ceased to be a staple of American children's literature, but Bart Simpson and *South Park* held the banner of calculated grossness aloft. And even PG-rated movies now feature language and behavior that would have reduced the Hays office to apoplexy: Disney's 1997 *Mr. Magoo*, whose broad humor seems aimed principally at six- to eight-year-olds, makes casual jokes of a peeing bulldog and miscellaneous groin-kickings.

The moral nature of the child in him- or herself might be debatable. Indeed, the cultural historians might conceivably be right: the nature of the child may not even exist, except as an endlessly evolving collective illusion. But really we need look no further than ourselves for the cause of adult confusion over manners and the inculcation thereof. For we ourselves haven't finally decided whether civility is true liberation or genteel slavery.

chapter nine

Co-Ed Naked Neo-Victorianism: Manners and Sex in the Nineties

In 1996, *The New York Times* announced that, en masse, American high school students had stopped taking showers after gym class,[1] a stand against public nakedness that they had begun to view as a right. In support, the American Civil Liberties Union (ACLU) threatened a lawsuit against a Pennsylvania school district that had instituted a mandatory shower policy, forcing the school bureaucracy to back off. Some schools even considered closing down their shower rooms, which had rusted into almost complete disuse, not from adolescent rebellion against hygiene, but from a strangely anachronistic revival of old-fashioned shame. "Standing around together naked?" one student incredulously asked. "Oh, no, man—people would feel really uncomfortable about that."[2] This uneasiness, according to the article, was not confined to the hinterlands or to students from fundamentalist backgrounds: it stretched uniformly across geographic and demographic divides.

Odder yet, though, this modesty epidemic halted abruptly at the locker-room door. For if, in the mid-nineties, the nation's high school shower rooms had gone curiously dark and chaste, its class-rooms were deep in raunch: "Coed Naked" T-shirts had become a widespread fad by 1993. When a student showed up at South Had-ley High in western Massachusetts wearing a shirt that read, "Coed Naked Band: Do It to the Rhythm," the school sent him home and provoked more ACLU litigation, this time in support of free speech. The case ended with the Massachusetts Supreme Judicial Court rul-ing that schools were not entitled to ban language they deemed inappropriate or vulgar.

Which is the dominant trend, prudishness or prurience? The truth about sex is almost proverbially hard to ferret out: what people tell interviewers about their sexual behavior has notoriously little in common with what they actually do. As Edward O. Laumann and his collaborators found in their monumental 1994 study, *The Social Organization of Sexuality*, Alfred Kinsey was often deluded when he thought he had discovered some long-hidden facts—like the fre-quency of homosexuality—in his famed 1950s studies.[3] Yet among adolescents, at least, reliable statistics seem to indicate a long-term trend toward more and more sex, even if attitudes toward it are conflict ridden. According to the Alan Guttmacher Institute, in the 1970s 35 percent of young women and 55 percent of young men reported having sex by the time they turned eighteen. But by 1994 these numbers had skyrocketed, with 56 percent of the girls and 73 percent of the boys admitting to sexual activity. Teenage pregnan-cies occur in the United States at nine times the rate per capita in the Netherlands or in Japan; more than three quarters of teen-aged American mothers are unwed.[4] In 1950, 4 percent of all births were to unmarried women. This rose to 5.3 percent in 1960, 10.7 percent in 1980, 26.6 percent in 1990, and 30.1 percent in 1992.[5]

Culturally, on the other hand, the signals have been mixed, at least since the onset of AIDS in the 1980s, with strange hybrids of libertinism and neo-Puritanism proliferating. Explicit sex has be-come a startlingly offhand presence in popular television entertain-ment like *Beverly Hills 90210* and *Dawson's Creek*. Yet many real-life venues have seen a marked narrowing of tolerance. "Workplace sex harassment" was a term unheard of until the mid-1970s. But by the eighties, owing to a string of landmark court rulings, it became a universal fact of the modern office, with harassment hard-liners arguing that a mere request for a date from a boss to a subordinate constitutes sexual harassment. In a 1998 decision, the Supreme Court ruled that such cases could involve members of the same sex, even where the offense seemed rude rather than truly predatory. In the incident in question, a worker at an all-male offshore oil rig complained of what seemed to amount only to tasteless horseplay from a hostile boss and coworkers—and won.

The stiff-necked British bourgeoisie of the nineteenth century, Steven Marcus famously argued in his classic book *The Other Victorians* (1966), were guarded in the public discussion of sex, enthusiastic in practicing it. By the 1970s, in a decade epitomized by the success of Erica Jong's *Fear of Flying* (1973) and wistfully commemorated by the successful movie *Boogie Nights* (1997), talk about sex became as frank as sex itself was frequent. But in the nineties Americans appear to have come down with a national case of multiple personality disorder on this subject, slavering one moment, bristling with outraged modesty the next. A 1996 survey of sex among college students, conducted by Random House and *Details* magazine, reflected the dither: asked, for instance, about the ubiquitousness of sex in contemporary popular culture, 39 percent of the responding students thought it was a turn-on; 40 percent thought it was exploitative.[6]

It might, of course, be argued that such contrasting signals reflect not mass schizophrenia but a simple pitched battle between advocates of free sex and guardians of morals, liberationists and moral authoritarians. There are, surely, purists of both stripes, adamant in their convictions and eager to demolish each other; but the same people often express a peculiar mixing of contrary sentiments, as if beset by competing surges of lust and disgust at the same time. Marabel Morgan's enduringly popular "Total Woman" books, in circulation since the 1970s, illustrate the disconnect in one way, being conservative and deeply Christian in outlook, yet also insistent that a good Christian wife should be a conjugal sex bomb. "Sex," she wrote in *The Total Woman*, "is for the marriage relationship only, but within those bounds, anything goes. Sex is as clean and pure as eating cottage cheese."[7]

Then there are the melodramas enacted on a current syndicated hit, the *Jerry Springer Show*—a spectacle so crude that conservative critic William Bennett and liberal Connecticut senator Joseph Lieberman concurred in urging the National Association of Broadcasters to take it off the air.[8] Springer's studio audiences careen from roars of approval to jeers, raucous laughter, and boos when confronted with themes like "Tell Her It's Over" (in which current girlfriends advise their superseded predecessors to get lost).[9] In that installment—as always on Springer—the adversaries spend their moment of notoriety spewing bleeped-out obscenities and ritually pounding their adversaries as the audience eggs them on. The new girlfriend, Heather, calls the cast-off Ellen a crackhead and a few other deleted epithets, then leaps out of her seat to administer some rehearsed-looking whacks by way of punctuation. J. D. (the lackwit boyfriend over whom they are quarreling) appears, admits he has recently finished a prison term for "simple assault," and proposes to Heather onstage, as Ellen squirms in disgust. During all this the audience cheers, boos, groans, claps, periodically emits a long "*Whooooooo!*" which seems to signify that the sexual revelations are becoming intriguingly lubricious, or chants: "JER-EE! JER-EE! JER-EE!" in approval of one of the comments Springer throws out from the sidelines.

The studio audience is plainly energized by the unhinged goings-on, but its underlying attitude, beneath an overexcited buzz, seems impossible to plumb. At times it appears to evince noisy contempt for the low behavior of the guest-combatants; at others it appears to be applauding their salutary lack of shame. Quick to moral judgment, it sometimes executes hairpin turns in loyalty, booing a speaker it had cheered a moment before. Sometimes it seems to be taking misanthropic delight in the sheer disgustingness of the display, at others laughing the antics off as harmless human comedy. And if onlookers seem strangely unable to decide whether to be repelled, sympathetic, or merely titillated, Springer, though on record as sympathetic to the trailer-park lives of typical guests, is more often than not snide in his comments.

A glossier exploration of sex manners, and another television hit, in this case aimed at adolescents, is the Warner Network's *Dawson's Creek*. Appropriately to its target audience, it brims with detailed sexual references, nervously knowing discussions of adultery, homosexuality, and adult-teen affairs: familiar adolescent obsessions, surprising only in having made it intact onto network television. But the more revealing curiosity of the series is the essentially chaste old-fashionedness of the hero, Dawson. In one episode he displays shock, disgust, and censoriousness when he learns his mother is having an affair. The effect is no doubt calculated, with Dawson's intermittent but eloquent pleas for restraint and decorum offsetting the show's otherwise uninterrupted leering salaciousness. But the drama of approach-avoidance is unmistakable, and it has plainly struck a chord with viewers.

Perhaps the defining recent example of our current neurasthenic strangeness on this subject was the Bill Clinton sex scandal. Semen-stained dresses and oral sex became common topics of discussion on television news programs; parents and schools had somehow to cope with the aroused curiosity of children on the subject. Revulsion, bemused tolerance, and prurience seemed to fuse, with the public clamoring for gossip but reacting with revulsion when it surfaced, and pundits alternately flagellating the press for pudor, congratulating it for dogged candor, praising us Americans for our newfound maturity, or berating us for our nosiness, Puritanism, apathy, or all three.

This odd battle between panic and celebration, whatever it may portend, is being played out in a Punch-and-Judy-like theater of crudity in which conflicting emotions find an outlet in knockdown slapstick rather than reasoned discussion. Yet confusion about sex seems natural enough, given the passions it arouses: the problems are ancient—indeed, they may be prehistoric, even prehuman.

Six-Legged Sex and Beyond: The Biology of Courtship Manners

Sex is the only domain of human relations whose peculiarities we can plausibly trace back (thus far at least) to biology. Genes and hormones plainly generate the urges that ultimately flower in courtship and mating. Further, we share some social features of our courtship behavior with other, more easily studied organisms. Even bacteria copulate, in a maneuver that allows them to exchange useful genes. Any style of mating requires a series of moves that make coitus possible; in other life forms, these are likely to be both distinctive and unvarying from individual to individual—a fact that has enabled scientists to find biological origins for behavior that often resembles human manners and customs. The common fruit fly, *Drosophila melanogaster*, lends itself particularly well to study, and research into its courtship and mating habits has yielded some striking results.

The fruit fly's sexual repertory is limited but not devoid of interest for humans. Normal males and females work up to copulation through fairly elaborate rituals of courtship. After noticing a female, a male first orients his body toward her, and taps her abdomen with his forelegs; often he extends one wing and vibrates it, producing a distinctive "love song," which varies significantly from one fruit-fly species to another. The female may flick her wings—a mild and provisional rejection. If the male persists and the female cooperates, the courtship will proceed, with the male first licking the female's genitalia and then bending his abdomen into the configuration necessary for copulation.[10] Some of this behavior has been traced directly to specific genes: when mutations occur, the flies' behavior changes—generally for the worse, in the sense that many such mutations disrupt the mating process. Courtship songs, for example, can be changed by certain gene mutations.[11] Others abort the ceremony by causing females, normally receptive to approach, to dart erratically around the observation chamber, even administer a kick to pursuers. Genetically dysfunctional males don't bend their abdomens normally, and thus funk a move both socially and physically necessary for successful copulation.[12]

In higher animals, the genetic basis of mating rituals has not been characterized in quite so much detail, but biology is surely behind some if not all of them. Nor are all such rituals merely functional. Chimpanzees, for example, utter *cris de joies* as they mate, with the males panting softly and the females shrieking aloud. Females sometimes seem to scream more often when copulating with large and high-ranking males.[13] This behavior might, of course, have some yet to be discovered practical effect on mating, but it may also be analogous to a human custom: something done simply as a habit, a confirmation of the species' collective identity. With humans, we often attribute such behavior wholly to ethics, education, or the play of free will—motives that seem above biological causation. Scientists hesitate to draw glib parallels between animals and humans, but their work strongly suggests that there are real links. In the lower animals, what looks to us very much like rudeness or politeness in courtship clearly lies in the genes. Are we likely to be different?

Jane Goodall's extended and exhaustive field observation of chimpanzees, conducted since 1960 at Gombe, near Lake Tanganyika in Tanzania, suggests that indeed we aren't. Though their mating is far more dependent on the female menstrual cycle than is the case with humans,[14] chimpanzees almost always preface copulation with a courtship ritual. A male signals interest in a female by the unambiguous (and probably involuntary) means of an erection, but adds a series of prefatory gestures. He stares at the female, extends both arms toward her, rests one hand on a branch, shakes it, swaggers about on two feet, rocks from side to side, or pounds the earth with his knuckles. Significantly, Goodall notes, all of these gestures (except for the erection) are also signs of aggression.[15] Yet courtship for chimpanzees is rarely hostile. Males may use the iconography of hostility to indicate interest; but females, who usually initiate copulation, decide. Adolescent females can be extremely aggressive in (apparently) demanding sex, even from unerect and apparently uninterested males. Exclusive pair bonds are not the rule, but do form: as a female passes through her menstrual cycle, a high-ranking male may drive others away and join her in what Goodall calls a consortship, wandering off toward the edge of the group's normal range and remaining with her as long as three or four months.[16]

Chimps thus echo the customs of human mating in several ways. But most suggestive for the student of manners is the remarkable fact that in chimpanzees a single set of gestures serves both to initiate the amicable bonding of males and females and to threaten aggression. Human wedding customs, as we've seen, often seem to share this paradox, mixing romance with grossness and sometimes even ritualized violence. Something about sex seems to demand equal measures of interdependent rudeness and civility. Without some unseemly aggression, perhaps, sex would never happen; with too much, it becomes indistinguishable from assault. And uneasy though this makes us, it may—along with much else that troubles us in human social behavior—trace ultimately to the inexorable microbiology of our cells.

Could this lie behind the incomprehensible mélange of reactions in Jerry Springer's hyperkinetic audiences?

From Dr. Edith to Mrs. Wilcox: Mating Manners and Sexual Hygiene

Less speculatively, the natural kinship between sex and biology gave rise to a historical curiosity with important cultural implications: an attempted takeover of human courtship manners by doctors. This began in the nineteenth century, as the American medical profession embarked on a concerted effort to improve a formerly dubious reputation and thereby increase its wealth and social influence. It was natural enough, of course, for the profession to exploit breakthroughs in the biology of disease as a pretext for pronouncements on sexual mores, since an important class of illnesses was (and is) sexually transmitted. Less natural and logical, but apparently as tempting, was an impulse to make the biological realities of sex a pretext for pronouncements on social behavior and even on morals. The urge gave rise, in the late nineteenth and early twentieth centuries, to one of the daffier instances of American gullibility before the claims of self-defined expertise, the sexual hygiene movement. Its influence has much abated, but it contributed to the formation of American attitudes toward sexuality, and can help to explain some of the contradictions in our current attitudes toward the subject.

In *Intimate Matters: A History of Sexuality in America* (1988), John D'Emilio and Estelle B. Freedman trace the first stirrings of this movement as far back as the 1830s, in popular and much-reprinted books like William Alcott's *Young Man's Guide* (1833), Russell Trall's *Sexual Psychology* (1866), and Alice Stockham's *Tokology: A Book for Every Woman* (1883), and in the work of health reformers like Sylvester Graham (1794–1851) and John Harvey Kellogg (1852–1943). After the 1847 founding of the American Medical Association, prominent medical figures soon began offering themselves as arbiters of human sexuality, particularly as it pertained to women. Influential physicians like Horatio Storer (1830–1922), a passionate opponent of abortion, reduced every significant trait of female behavior to physiology (Storer wrote that woman is "what she is in health, in character, in her charms, alike of body, mind and soul because of her womb alone").[17] For the doctors, at least, such insights seemed empirical rather than subjective; thus they translated easily into guidance for the chastely married female, and authoritarian controls over sexual outlaws, like prostitutes.

Feminist historians have attacked this presumptuous seizure by male physicians, using science as a pretext, of female bodies, minds, and souls. The arrogance of this enterprise was very real, but not exclusively male: by the twentieth century, men were not the only advocates of sexual hygiene, nor were they always the most conservative. The movement throve and women became prominent in it. No one exemplified this better than Edith Belle Lowry, M.D. (1878–1945), who wrote, in 1911 and 1912, a series of sex and health guides for adolescents and adults. Lowry melded unfazeable medical frankness with a narrow moralism the most eagle-eyed small-town gossip couldn't improve upon. One of her most evocative titles— *False Modesty That Protects Vice by Ignorance* (1912)—suggests the cast of her thought; the others—*Confidence: Talks with a Young Girl* (1911); *Truths: Talks with a Boy* (1911); *Herself: Talks with Women* (1912) and *Himself: Talks with Men* (1912)—convey the extent of the audience with whom she was eager to share it.

Lowry began her career as a schoolteacher. Graduating from the Winona, Minnesota, State Normal School in 1898, she spent the next six years in the Minnesota and Utah public schools. Then, in a career turn, she switched to medicine, completing her nurse's training in 1905, and gaining an M.D. from the Bennett College of Medicine and Surgery in Chicago in 1907.[18] In 1911, she married Richard J. Lambert, M.D., and began the series of books that brought her national prominence. In later life she and Lambert set up a joint practice in St. Charles, Illinois; she went on to serve in the U.S. Public Health Service as a director of field investigations in child hygiene in the South in the early twenties.

Lowry's advice books illustrate with unparalleled clarity a general feature of the sexual hygiene movement: a clarion call for frankness about sexual matters (and an impatient dismissal of shame and false modesty) combined with an extreme censoriousness, and a repeated insistence—on "scientific" principles—that monogamous and exclusive marriage is the only proper and desirable outlet for sexual desire. At times Lowry and her compatriots in the movement seem determined to yank the initiative in prescribing proper sexual mores away from the clergy, as if to suggest that foggy and subjective religious imperatives had been definitively replaced by the clinical clarity and objectivity of the laboratory. In the preface to *Himself: Talks with Men Concerning Themselves,* Lowry (writing in collaboration with her husband) announced that her sole aim was to impart "things concerning the body that should be known by every adult male without any attempt to dictate."[19] But the book itself is sexually conservative, not to say reactionary, and thoroughly dictatorial to boot.

The chapter on masturbation—titled "Self-Abuse"—begins with a show of objectivity. "Some animals, including monkeys and goats," Lowry and Lambert remark, "have the same habit."[20] But the aura of dispassion quickly evaporates. "Continued masturbation," they announce, "is capable of producing the most serious of results, such as insanity, idiocy, impotency, and sterility."[21] And at the very least it generates distinctive and undesirable mannerisms, for which they supply a short manual of detection:

> Children who have acquired the habit of self-abuse usually sleep badly, become thin and haggard-looking, peevish, nervous and excitable. Some even have convulsions. Older boys who are masturbators usually get a sallow look and have a hang-dog expression. . . . Adult masturbators may show no signs otherwise than that they usually are cowardly and mean-spirited. They frequently are sexual perverts or old rounders.[22]

Himself offers practical chapters on topics like constipation and sleeplessness, but returns repeatedly to sexual behavior, offering a mix of dubious science and Grundyism. Unambiguous though they are about the impropriety of sex outside marriage, their rationale is health rather than morality: "Fornication always is irregular, often excessive, hence is not conducive to health. Marriage only allows natural, unstimulated sexual desires and accomplishes that which is necessary for health, sexual quietude."[23]

Predictably, Lowry and Lambert were enthusiastic eugenicists, asserting that apart from being appropriate only in marriage, sex was also only for the genetically lucky. One chapter, "Shall the Unfit Marry?", approvingly cites an Indiana law forbidding marriage to imbeciles, epileptics, the feebleminded, males who have lived in a county asylum or home for the indigent, even to carriers of any transmissible disease.[24]

On the relations between men and women, Lowry and Lambert were progressive in decrying the double standard. But their remedy was to grant women equal rights not to sex but to vigilantism, raising them to parity with the physicians and other moral patriarchs. "Women of the past," they argue, "have been too inert, too ready to condone the sins of the other sex and too quick to condemn their own sisters."[25] When, no longer in collaboration with Lambert, Lowry addressed females in guides like *Preparing for Womanhood* (1918), she asserted not just female equality but dominance in the responsibility of maintaining the health of the gene pool.

> You cannot be too particular in the selection of a mate. Before you become very interested in any young man, investigate his family a little. . . . You certainly do not want to marry into a family prone to insanity or feeblemindedness. Remember the children of drunken fathers often are degenerates, therefore be certain your future husband is not in this class. If the family is inclined to be shiftless and ne'er-do-well, they will stand considerable investigation; for these shiftless families often owe their condition to a lack of mental ability to be otherwise.[26]

In the 1920s and 1930s, the National Health Council published a series of twenty pamphlets on health issues of general interest, with titles like *Staying Young Beyond Your Years, Taking Care of Your*

Heart, and *The Healthy Child*. In the spirit of Edith Lowry, the sex manual in this series, *Love and Marriage: Foundations of Social Health*, treated its subject as a branch of science: its author, Thomas Walton Galloway, though not a physician, was a professor of zoology at Beloit College, and shared the progressive tendency to deduce rockbound traditional morals from the truths of biology. "The writer of this book," as Galloway put it, "believes that there are the strongest scientific grounds for the following propositions," the linchpin among which was "that monogamous marriage, and the home and family life which may grow out of it, are not only the most beneficent of our social institutions, but are at the same time the most successful."[27]

Humans, Galloway argued, shared with lower animals an appetite for sex, but combined it with higher impulses. "The individual may be so conscious of emotional and esthetic elements, such as beauty, fair-dealing, and love; of social elements, such as consideration, sense of comradeship, and hope of happy family life later; of ethical elements, such as a sense of honor and respect for others; and of moral and religious elements, such as right and duty and obligation, as to deny himself immediate satisfaction."[28] These higher faculties, though every bit as much a product of evolution as hormones and gonads, lead humans into slow and careful courtship, and draw them toward the exclusivity of monogamous marriage; the pamphlet, while arguing that such traits are natural among humans, is full of advice about how to supplement nature by indoctrinating children in them at every stage of development.

The mixture of frankness and prudery about sex, then, is no novelty of the nineties; whether biologically programmed or not, it has been a persistent fixture since early in the twentieth century. The distinctive note of the 1970s, 1980s, and 1990s is less an increased openness than a decreased reliance on euphemism, a gradual pulling down of barriers between street language and the formalities traditionally demanded in public discourse. Sexual frankness took a different shape early in the century. Though fairly pervasive, it looks quaint and hesitant to our jaded eyes because, while it didn't shrink from sex, it employed a vocabulary of indirection and allusion, like Lowry's. Blunt Anglo-Saxonisms were rare; delicate though unambiguous Latinate circumlocutions predominated. Then-new media like glossy magazines, films, and broadcasting were cautious with sex, but it sold; the taboos had been broken. When Edward Bok published his series of articles on venereal disease in the *Ladies' Home Journal* in 1906, he was being prescient as well as brave. He lost seventy-five thousand subscribers in the immediate wake of their appearance,[29] but the setback was temporary; in the long run the series gained credibility, authority, and new readers for the magazine. By the twenties, most women's magazines were confronting sex, and a new theme had begun to emerge. If it could be spoken of without embarrassment, people could also admit they liked it. Gradually, the discussion of courtship manners began to shift from conventions that controlled sex to protocols for enjoying it.

Between 1922 and 1928, *McCall's* magazine featured Winona Wilcox, an adviser for women. Her column kept changing its title ("Mrs. Wilcox's Answers to Women" was its name in 1924), but returned insistently to sex, mixing unashamed (and scientifically backed) advice about how to make it successful, with an unyielding assertion that the only rightful place for it was monogamous marriage: "Today's wife is a pal, a good sport or business partner. She walks hand-in-hand and side by side with her mate. From her new vantage of equal sex rights, a girl can see, as soon as her man does, an approaching free-booter in love; also she can distinguish the devious and flowery alleys diverging from the straight and narrow road of monogamy."[30] But that did not mean there was no art to sex. For Wilcox, sexual gratification was both natural and a right, for the female as well as the male. One 1924 column bore the headline "New Science May Supply Lack of Sex Attraction," in response (Wilcox said) to a flood of letters from women bemoaning their lack of chemistry with males. "The big trouble," Wilcox wrote of one of such reader, "lies deep within herself—but not entirely in the subconscious mind. Rather, some inadequate functioning of the ductless glands may be the secret of her wretchedness."[31] If so, she suggests, a good endocrinologist may prove a better resource than a psychoanalyst.

Insistent as the hygienists had been that the science of sex is a science of unswerving morals, there was something unsustainable about their position over the long term. One can't insist upon sex as a purely functional fact and yet at the same time accord it the dignity of ethics and religion. The near-constant trend in twentieth-century culture has been to demote it from a taboo-laden institution to a discretionary personal prerogative (albeit one with powerful consequences for health, the emotions, and human relations). In insisting on honesty about sex, figures like Edith Lowry were equally at pains to insist that openness would not lead to licentiousness; *au contraire*. But having introduced sexuality into matter-of-fact discussion, they had effectively delivered it into other, far less fastidious, hands.

The Dawn of the Date

From the 1920s through the 1960s, the transformation of sexuality from the ceremonial to the customary accelerated apace. In the mid-1800s, a "date," in colloquial American parlance, seems mainly to have meant an assignation with a prostitute.[32] The model middle-class courtship, at least in the larger cities, consisted at the close of the nineteenth century of "calling": a young man presented his visiting card at the home of the girl he admired, and, if admitted, spent a carefully regulated amount of time visiting with her under the eagle eye of her mother or some other designated chaperon. If the relationship blossomed and the girl's family approved, the couple might gradually be permitted unsupervised visits, but their romance remained firmly within the domestic ambit. In *Hands and Hearts* (1984), a history of American courtship, Ellen K. Rothman designates the sharing of confidences as perhaps the definitive bonding experience between such young men and women.[33] They bared their hearts in letters or in the drawing room or on the front porch, but bared nothing else: they were supposed to diffuse sexual energy into speech and emotion, and to approach marriage slowly and ceremoniously, in the home and family context.

But the twentieth century fatefully changed the milieu in which adolescents and young adults socialized. More and more young people were staying in coeducational schools ever later into adolescence, and though educators often tried to discourage or at least to restrain boy-girl interactions, they failed: by the twenties, dating had become the dominant social institution of courtship, and it increasingly became a thing regulated by youth for youth, free of adult control.[34] Mobility, of course, was also a destabilizing factor: streetcars and automobiles drew couples away from the living room, off the porch, and out to an enticing new range of entertainments—dance halls and movie houses were the magnets that most concerned adults worried about the social and sexual stability of adolescents. Telephones allowed couples to converse—and make plans—in hard-to-monitor ways. Dancing, traditionally a community activity that brought children, the young, the middle-aged, and the elderly together, now became primarily an activity of adolescents and young adults, carried on in commercial venues, and in forms more frankly evocative of sex. Then there were the movies. They virtually eliminated conversation; social psychologists like the Iowans who hooked up impressionable children to measuring equipment and tried to gauge their responses to provocative movie scenes were worried about the corrupting power of images, but they might have been more anxious over the social effect of seating boys and girls side by side and then turning out the lights.

And if the rise of dating marked a shift in generational power, it also accommodated a gradual and subtle sea change in relations between the genders. Again, at least since the mid-nineteenth century, a set of social conventions had grown up governing proper roles for girls and boys as they approached sexual maturity. At first glance these conventions look like simple old-fashioned sexism, and they were concisely stated (and also criticized) by Alice Stockham in the 1887 edition of her hugely popular *Tokology: A Book for Every Woman*: "We teach the girl *repression*, the boy *expression*, not simply by word and book, but the lessons are graven into their very being by all the traditions, prejudices, and customs of society."[35]

For her time, Stockham took the advanced position that the supposed sexual aggressiveness of males besieging the fortress of female self-control was a cultural imposition rather than a biological fact; but many of her predecessors, contemporaries, and successors nonetheless insisted that the God-given (and biologically natural) female role in courtship was to apply reins to male ardor. Yet this convention was double-edged—moralistic in appearance but potentially subversive. For if on the one hand it saddled women with an obligation to guard purity, it also gave them a new hold over the conduct of sex: the duty of restraint, after all, entails the power to cast it off at one's discretion. And that, in the early decades of the twentieth century, is exactly what teen-aged and young adult females began to do. Columnists like Winona Wilcox continued to advise their younger readers to avoid stimulating each other sexually; social hygienists like Galloway insisted with undiminished rigor on the morality (and the health) of monogamous marriage. But a culture of sexual license, visible at the beginning of the century only in ghettoes of bohemianism like Greenwich Village,[36] became a mid-American fait accompli by the late twenties.

The most obvious signs of the change were two timeless practices that, beginning in the twenties, acquired new names and became the central conventions of dating, though guardians of conduct disapproved of them: necking and petting. As Beth Bailey describes them in *From Front Porch to Back Seat: Courtship in Twentieth-Century America* (1988), their meanings were precise, though rarely articulated: necking denoted any caress above the neck and petting anything below it, up to—but not including—intercourse.[37] Necking and petting, Bailey says, had become standard dating practices by the 1920s, and by the 1950s were countenanced even by dating guides from major publishers. Beyond becoming more sexed as time went on, dating also became a social sport, a competitive activity dominated by money and consumer one-upsmanship. In 1937, the sociologist Willard Waller conducted a classic study of college dating, and discerned in it a system he called "the campus rating complex"[38]—in which men and women mercilessly ranked each other as desirable dates, with men scoring points for their possessions and status (cars, clothes, money, and fraternity membership) and women for their perceived popularity with males.

Whether or not they approved, etiquette authorities labored under no illusions about the realities of modern courtship. In the 1922 edition of *Etiquette*, Emily Post included a chapter on chaperons. But, as John D'Emilio and Estelle Freedman have pointed out,[39] by 1927 this had morphed into "The Vanishing Chaperon and Other New Conventions," and by 1937 to "The Vanished Chaperon and Other Lost Conventions." By the forties, Post was insisting that insofar as a chaperon could be found at all, her role was no longer to protect the virtue of her charge, but simply to act as an adviser: what the young woman did or did not do with her date was ultimately a matter for the young woman to decide.[40]

In *Live Alone and Like It*, a popular 1936 guide for the single woman by Marjorie Hillis, one chapter (titled "Will You or Won't You?") deals with the question of love affairs, and whether or not "nice" women really have them. Hillis's answer is in the spirit of her age (or at least the more sophisticated part of it):

This is every woman's own special problem which nobody else can settle. . . . Whether or not a woman has had her Moments, if she has a grain of common sense she keeps it to herself, since if she has, most people would be shocked, and if she hasn't, the rest would be superior. . . . A Woman's Honor is no longer mentioned with bated breath and protected by her father, her brother, and the community. It is now her own affair.[41]

On the question of whether or not a woman should invite a male friend to stay overnight, Hillis counsels ignoring what the neighbors might say; the only question is whether or not she and the friend will sleep together. And that is strictly for them to decide.

The Lacy and the Racy: Sexuality in the Age of HIV

Historians tend to agree that the rates of acceleration in modern American openness about sex have varied (Rothman, for instance, sees a rapid erosion of taboos between 1910 and 1930, a more gradual change from 1930 to 1965, and a renewed burst of liberalization after that).[42] But the change was constant in direction, and whatever it meant for actual behavior—increasing out-of-wedlock sex, sex at ever younger ages, more and more open nonheterosexual sex—it marked an important watershed for the ways Americans talked about and represented the subject in public. Whatever stance a writer might take, whether in favor of restraint or against, there was a steady decline in euphemism, a constant increase in willingness to face unblushingly the anatomical mechanics of sex, an ever-shrinking list of street words forbidden to polite public discourse, and a growing tendency to treat sex as a routine part of life, comparable to every other branch of manners, and no longer set apart as a subject either sacred or unspeakable.

The change is measurable in the distance between Marjorie Hillis's naughty but allusive way in *Live Alone and Like It*, and *Honorable Intentions: The Manners of Courtship in the 80s*, a 1983 dating guide by Cheryl Merser—a book that, while far from libertine in the *Playboy* or *Penthouse* mode, represents a reference point, appearing as it did just before both AIDS and the terror of it began their inevitable migration from gay men into the population at large. For Merser, sex, while not to be treated trivially, is a matter of personal choice rather than a social or moral duty. "Sex," she writes, "even if it doesn't turn out to be forever sex, is supposed to *matter*. It's also supposed to be, among other things, fun."[43]

Merser points out—correctly—that Helen Gurley Brown's *Sex and the Single Girl* (1962), despite its reputation as a cultural watershed marking the dawn of full female equality in the sexual revolution, was nonetheless generally vague in its discussion of the mechanics of sex, devoting far more attention to how a woman creates the independent life within which discretionary sex is a real possibility rather than a fantasy: "diets, apartments, clothes, budgets and careers."[44] Merser, by contrast, offers a detailed guide to bedroom etiquette—how to inveigle a reluctant partner into using a condom (apologize for your anxiety, which soothes the date but protects you), or how to deal with male impotence ("there is simply no tactful way for the woman to mention it first," Merser notes, but neither should the man say, "This has never happened to me before").[45] Neither AIDS nor the general reawakening of cultural conservatism in the 1980s and 1990s has dammed up this flood of frankness, even slightly. *Redbook*, a mid-market women's magazine not given to attitudinal excess and firmly practical in outlook, nonetheless blazons its covers with article titles like "23 Ways to Make Him Insane with Desire" (the tips, however, are disappointingly tame, with advice like liberally decorating the bedroom in passion-priming reds).[46]

Yet the real hallmark of sexual manners in the 1980s and 1990s is not solely the eruption of locker-room words and subjects into the trade press, glossy magazines, movies, and even network television, but rather the strange cohabitation between unbridled frankness and an upsurge of panic, prudery, and calls for repression. AIDS, and before it sexually transmitted diseases like herpes and chlamydia, plainly contributed to the reaction. So, of course, did understandable revulsion against the sheer vulgarity to which boundless hedonism can lead. The public that accepted Hugh Hefner, Helen Gurley Brown, and Bob Guccione wasn't quite so ready to turn Larry Flynt into a mainstream figure. The backlash *Hustler* generated in the eighties marks an uneasy retreat from the embrace of sex unleashed. What still passes after midnight on a cable channel never quite made a full transition to the multiplex: in the early seventies an X rating was unremarkable even for prestigious films (like the initial release of John Schlesinger's classic *Midnight Cowboy* in 1969), but it has since become a publicity millstone major, mass-market studios will do almost anything to avoid.

This has made for some odd historical contrasts, with the early twentieth century looking naive by some lights, strangely unzipped by others. In 1933, the grammar school audience shown *The Feast of Ishtar* in Dysinger and Ruckmick's study may have trembled with prepubescent erotic glimmerings; but one can't imagine a jaded collection of 1990s ten-year-olds reacting to the movie with anything but derisive howls. Does that represent an advance in openness or a decline in morals? Yet—perhaps even more interestingly—it would surely be impossible in today's climate for an investigator to secure approval from an ethics panel for any study that proposed to show erotic films to a grammar school–age audience. Does this connote a new sensitivity to the vulnerabilities of children, and hence an advance in civility, or merely a millennial decline into the benighted prudery of the past?

Feminism has contributed powerfully both to liberalized sexual mores and to a renewed ethic of sexual restraint. In the late nineteenth century, as we've seen, young women emerged as semi-official regulators of sexual behavior, restraining supposed male insatiability. Viewed critically, this might look like simple gender oppression, chaining women to a strict standard of morality while entitling males to the unbridled enjoyment of horniness. Yet the same custom accorded real power to women, granting them potential access to the free exercise of sexual pleasure. A role created for them by the double standard gave them the wherewithal to overturn it, which, however tentatively, they seem to have done in the de-

cades between the thirties and the seventies. Feminists in these decades—like Brown—tended to be proponents of sexual freedom,

Later feminists, like Andrea Dworkin and Catharine MacKinnon,
have rebelled, however, reviving the older view of the woman as
chaste and beleaguered defendress against male lust. Dworkin has
argued, most strongly in her book *Intercourse* (1987), that heterosexual coition, however one labors to prettify it, is in essence (if not
technically or legally) rape. "Men," she writes, "are supposed to
slice us up the middle, leaving us in parts on the bed."[47] Some
theorists of sexual harassment have asserted that gender inequality
places women in a state of permanent and structural victimhood—
which, since it's perpetuated by virtually any courtship behavior directed toward them by males, makes any approach by a male potential if not actual harassment. This casts men inescapably as
hormone-crazed aggressors and women as perpetually besieged defenders of virtue, incapable of predation as well as guiltless of it. "Is
ordinary sexuality," Catharine MacKinnon has asked, "under conditions of gender inequality to be presumed healthy? What if inequality is built into the social conceptions . . . of masculinity and
femininity, of sexiness and heterosexual attractiveness?"[48] Mac-
Kinnon's answer is that as long as women are disadvantaged by the
normal operation of society, it seems unfair to alchemize habitual
victimization into acceptable custom, and only to reprove "extraordinary" misbehavior.

But thinking like this leads to some uncomfortable and arguably
absurd conclusions, like the following assertion that a man who believes a woman is harassing him has simply projected his own lust
onto an innocent female: "Reports by male subjects of sexual over-
tures by women co-workers not only do not constitute harassment
in any formal sense, but must also be evaluated in light of data
suggesting that men are likely to interpret relatively innocent behavior as invitations to sexual contact."[49] This may seem extreme,
yet it accurately reflects the censorious side of our contemporary
split personality on the subject of human sexual mores.

The rise of open homosexuality in the 1970s and 1980s would at first seem to embody the opposing view. Increasingly visible in the United States, widely accepted by the cultural vanguard if still anathema to reactionaries, gay sexuality might seem both to embody and to advance the idea that sex is utterly normal, a matter of personal preference, and also a topic that can, in specific physical terms, be acknowledged and discussed in public. Indeed, some figures, like Susie Bright, have been prominent in making unapologetic sex central to homosexuality; and mass market titles such as Harper Perennial's *Essential Book of Gay Manners and Etiquette* (1995)[50] have contributed to the normalization of it. Some writers, though, have decried the loss of homosexuality's outlaw status, which they perceive as crucial: gay sex, they insist, can have no real identity except as a subversive attack on orthodox sexual conventions, and sacrifices its liberating rebelliousness when it seeks or accepts the imprimatur of conventional civility.[51]

Still others—notably Andrew Sullivan, in *Virtually Normal* (1995), which makes the case for institutionalizing same-sex marriage[52]—have argued for an assimilation of gay relationships into the mainstream, a prospect that (however laudably it offers to reduce the stigma of affectional difference) takes some of the sex out of homosexuality. If sexual preference becomes interchangeable with personal preference—if, in other words, the choice of the gender of one's mate becomes a matter morally and socially indistinguishable from the individual one chooses—then homosexuality, even if its origins are biological, no longer exists as a socially distinct way of life. Homosexual traits no longer mark gays off as a group in quite the same way as race (with its visible physical dimension) or ethnicity (where customs, history, and geographical origin, less indelible, nonetheless contribute to the development of a set of shared manners). The history of homosexuality is moot: that same-sex relations are ancient is obvious, but the only thing that can be said with certainty about them is that each instance of male-male or female-female intercourse represented a personal choice by at least one of the partners. It is very unclear, until the nineteenth century at the earliest, that homosexuals thought of themselves as a cultural group with ways and mores distinctively its own. To the extent that we succeed in folding sexual preference into discretionary personal preference, we will surely lessen prejudice against it. Yet we will also destroy homosexuality as a cultural identifier, and weaken or eliminate the identity of gay people as a distinct group.

If even a minority defined by sex is unsettled about it, how can the culture at large hope to work out a settled attitude? The signs of this uneasy debate, in which we seem unable to decide whether good sexual manners depend on explicit openness or a system of implicit hints and eloquent silences, are everywhere. Consider Victoria's Secret, the lingerie chain with more than seven hundred stores and 1997 sales of more than $1.7 billion. Its pull is sexy naughtiness, yet the naughtiness is lacy, soft-edged, and open to the view of every nine-year-old at large in the mall. Consider the latest *Amy Vanderbilt Complete Book of Etiquette*, a thoroughly respectable example of its kind, which nonetheless deals with how to handle menstruation and the importance of using latex rather than animal-skin condoms.[53] And finally, of course, consider Dr. Ruth Westheimer, a figure impossible to imagine in any era other than our own, who blends the clinical authority of an Edith Belle Lowry, the raunchiness of an Erica Jong heroine, and the comforting maternalism of Peggy Wood in *I Remember Mama*. Listening to her on the radio, watching her Lifetime TV program, *The Dr. Ruth Show*, or reading her books, like *Dr. Ruth's Guide for Married Lovers* or *Dr. Ruth's Guide to Good Sex*, one perceives just how far the Zeitgeist has journeyed from the uncomplicated hedonism of *The Joy of Sex*, Alex Comfort's signature guide of the 1970s—and just how far it hasn't. Westheimer flinches at no subject, from warming up to fellatio by practicing with a Popsicle to the flavors of spermicidal gel available for use with diaphragms.[54] Her zaftig grandmotherly competence makes sex as normal, homelike, and proper-seeming as milk and oatmeal cookies.

Westheimer somehow manages to blend the extremes that otherwise war for dominance in the modern American attempt to make sex civil. We want to be free, but we long for restraint; we insist on openness yet cringe when we get it; we strain at trivial offenses and swallow camels of iniquity. Sex is, perhaps, the most dramatic but far from the only example of a systemic crisis: in our contemporary schizophrenia over how to handle the manners of sex, we see our schizophrenia about civility writ large.

epilogue

Manners for the Millennium

The turn of the millennium is, of course, a chronological artifice.
But it nonetheless marks an inviting point at which to stop and
assess the state of our social comity. And the epidemic of soul-
searching it has already inspired is itself a kind of civil exercise—a
tacit reaffirmation of the importance of social bonds that we strive
mightily and tirelessly to repair, even as they fray under our clumsy
touch.

Anyone bent on proving manners are in decline would find little
difficulty locating examples of crude thought, coarse speech, boorish
acts. I've recorded a number of diagnostic instances in these pages,
beginning with Colonel William d'Alton Mann as a patron saint of
modern rudeness, and continuing with latter-day postulants of the
sect. But I have passed over far more, from Joe McCarthy to Mar-
ilyn Manson. A certain danger attends the very act of reading out a
roll call of social transgressions and monstrosities of public loutishness. It is suspiciously easy to polemicize an instance of bad behavior
into an emblem of the decay of the times and a portent of apoca-

lypse, and the pleasure of denouncing the antisocial excesses of one's age has been a conventional and rather stale reflex for, well, ages. Jeremiads against the decline of manners began in the Middle Ages, continued in the early modern era, gained momentum in the eighteenth century (with a spate of conduct books and a powerful current of satire that, from Swift to Hogarth, scourged the moral beastliness of the age), and had become a fixture of the cultural scene by the nineteenth century. In Henry James's 1886 novel *The Bostonians*, the hero, Basil Ransom, gives vent to a diatribe against the crudenesses of the present day. "It's a feminine, a nervous, hysterical, chattering, canting age," he rages, "an age of hollow phrases and false delicacy and exaggerated solicitudes and coddled sensibilities, which, if we don't soon look out, will usher in the reign of mediocrity, of the feeblest and flattest and the most pretentious that has ever been."[1]

James does not make clear whether or not he meant readers to sympathize with this rant against political correctness *avant la lettre*. Was it an impassioned prophetic outcry, the mere attitudinizing of a reactionary young curmudgeon, or perhaps both? And the fads and fancies Ransom railed against were, ironically enough, the high-minded, straitlaced, and liberal Boston pieties of the era—including abolitionism and feminism—some of which, at least, now seem notably well-meaning and civilized ahead of their time. For when moralists descend on their contemporaries with righteous outrage, their targets sometimes appear to a detached observer more civilized than the guardians of civility. And what the victim reviles as a particularly noisome case of bad manners, the perpetrator often intends as a coup struck for elegance.

In fact, paradoxically enough, attempted and failed graciousness may well produce more in the way of gaucherie than a concerted effort to insult. Some TV is crass at the level of Jerry Springer or Jenny Jones, but more of it offends by a sugary surfeit of niceness. Advertising is a sea of feel-good molasses—spouses, parents, children, and grandchildren in states of improbable harmony, eating cornflakes or communicating via their long-distance carriers in shafts of sunlight that flood through clear windows into bright country kitchens (of course in the ironic spirit of the times, parodies of such visions have also found their way into ads). Critics might see this as cynical commercial mind control; but even so, it pays a backhanded compliment to civility by invoking (and thereby reinforcing) good manners, even if its aim in so doing is naked profit. The funeral industry may have made our typical death rites expensive and hideous, but it also seems to have helped large numbers of grief-stricken people feel dignified and comfortable in one of life's difficult crises. The lifestyle business may push tasteless advice and hawk overpriced junk, but it can offer people the raw materials for domestic community in a country where families are increasingly fragmented and distracted by the endless demands not only of work but recreation. And gentility has a way of reasserting itself even in apparently willful manifestations of grossness. *South Park*'s 1997 Christmas episode featured Mr. Hankey, the Christmas Poo: a moist animated turd, who zoomed out of the toilet and ricocheted about, leaving brown footprints and gifts to good children who had faithfully observed a high-fiber diet. Self-conscious postmodern disgustingness, surely, but with an equally strong, albeit dutifully ironic, undercurrent of conventional holiday decency: Kenny, the poor little boy who normally suffers mutilation and death in every episode, is just this once spared.

So evidence, whether for decline, renaissance, or a steady state, abounds. Which is just the difficulty—there is simply too much to sift and measure; the sums to which both our rudenesses and our acts of civility have mounted are simply too gigantic to add up. A supercomputer might crunch the numbers, but who would collect the data? Instances of manners, good and bad, are too numerous to sample and impossible to sort, so protean as to vex the analyst, frustrate the historian, and elude the scientist. Expertise, system, the methodical thoroughness of academic research, are among humankind's greatest achievements. But they are not the only arrows to our quiver. The etiquette advisers who field questions in their books and newspaper columns don't earn doctorates in the subject, because—quite rightly—everyone is qualified to contribute. America's manners are in practice far more democratic than its politics, for all the strength of the traditional link between etiquette and class. Manners depend, even more than most authority does, on the assent of those being led.

This is by no means a bad thing. It benefits us, after all, to have in place a social system that can't be traced to a single cause, reduced to a set of inflexible governing principles, or commandeered by any one powerful person or privileged group. Everyone makes manners, building or breaking them at will. Indeed, one of their hallmarks— that the experts, the people we go to for judgment on the subject, have no quantifiable expertise—is a perverse but real sign of their inherent strength. With equal participation from everyone, manners never stabilize, but cycle incessantly, worsening or disintegrating in one context, re-forming themselves in another. They may decline at the table, but improve at the gallows, deteriorate at the graveside just as they evolve panache in the on-line chat forum. Perpetually under construction and subject to negotiation they may be, yet some innate and unconscious human law seems to conserve them, even against the odds. As the Internet has already begun to demonstrate, even a social space created with conscious lawlessness quickly demonstrates a need for order and generates a rough code of manners.

The very insouciance and apparent irresponsibility with which manners can be invented, revised, or simply thrown out, are useful: a kind of serious moral playfulness, by which we exercise, free of dire consequence, the ethical faculties needed elsewhere in fateful decisions. Think of what we do with anointed role models, as exemplified in the dizzying recent history of Hillary Rodham Clinton's reputation: heralded in the 1992 campaign as a stateswoman and co-executive, an Eleanor Roosevelt for our time; then, after the debacle of medical insurance reform, vilified as an arrogant and overreaching bitch; ridiculed, in the aftermath of a widely reported attempt to channel the spirit of said Eleanor Roosevelt, as a New Age airhead; and then once again admired, à la Mrs. Warren G. Harding, for her brave and stoical support of Bill Clinton in the scandals of 1997–98. This was surely hard on Mrs. Clinton, but it served a useful civic function, allowing us to test and reexamine our collective sense of what's proper and what's not, what's admirable and what's reprehensible, what's graceful and what's gauche.

Manners *are* related to morals: thus far the conservatives, from Burke to Himmelfarb and Silber, are right. But the link is far more deceptive, sinuous, and complicated than is usually admitted by those who yearn to restore some hypothetical lost bond between civility and ethics. For that bond may really be strongest when it appears broken and weak when it seems most solid. A rebellion against good manners may herald an increased tendency to take morals seriously, as it did in Athens circa 300 BCE, when Diogenes began uttering the crass taunts that shamed the polis into reassessing its understanding of ethics. Norbert Elias, perhaps the greatest modern student of manners, demonstrated that etiquette can become more and more elaborate and developed even as popular opinion sees it decaying. And indeed the subtext of Elias's study was that just as its manners were improving in the nineteenth century, the West was sliding toward the great moral debacles of the modern era, from World War I to the Holocaust.

At the beginning of this study I disavowed any attempt to offer practical advice about manners, but I think there is nonetheless a lesson in it: beware the moralists of manners, the self-appointed defenders of civility who offer to regulate everyday behavior with the authority of lawgivers. In a world widely perceived to be rupturing at the seams and rattling on its hinges, people understandably search for stable and rock-solid values. But values are always somebody's values, and somebody else, perhaps equally worthy and wellmeaning, may hold other, very different ones.

As we weigh great questions of good and evil, searing ethical debates have to be settled into law (one hopes judiciously); violators have to be judged (one hopes mercifully); and they have to be punished (one hopes humanely). Where human life is at stake, this is surely necessary. Where property is at risk, it is less necessary, but still desirable and permissible. But where the issue is whether or not children should first-name their parents, what can be said over the corpse at a funeral, whether or not coarse practical jokes are appropriate at a wedding, or whether or not "asshole" is an acceptable word on a web site, rigidities and fiats are absurd. The urge to inflate personal options into obligations is not a moral impulse but pushiness disguised as concern, whim masquerading as expertise. Behind it, however well it may be meant, lurks the urge to control, to punish, to make ourselves part of the "good" class (what P. G. Wodehouse mockingly called the "right-thinking sort"), and to brand anyone who fails to conform as a Yahoo.

This is no less true where manners matter most: in gender and race relations. There, if anywhere, it would make sense to posit a set of absolute rules, limiting if not eliminating the fluidity we normally tolerate in manners. Yet, as Karen Grigsby Bates and Karen Elyse Hudson imply in their book *Basic Black*, the attempt to do so tends to frustrate rather than produce the desired end, breeding resentment instead of harmony, heightening tensions instead of soothing them. The politeness that results is nervous, empty, insincere. Even where the moral stakes are high, a light touch in civility is more productive of good than endless contorted agonies of conscience and loud demands for a return to a lost and surely imaginary autocratic utopia.

A certain degree of parental bossiness is necessary to manners; there have to be guidelines, there have to be customs we agree on. It is, broadly, bad to be rude and good to be polite (except when rudeness awakes our consciences or politeness hides cruelty and contempt). But when etiquette lays claim to the mantle of Mosaic lawgiving, something goes haywire, and manners, paradoxically, begin to lose their very real but perennially and rightly elusive relation to morals.

In a reflective moment toward the end of the brilliant John Kander and Fred Ebb musical, *Chicago*, Velma Kelly (a vaudeville tart who has landed in jail for slaughtering her sister, then been elbowed out of the tabloid press by the show's even more shameless heroine, Roxie Hart) sits glumly in prison with Matron Mama Morton, the warden. In an immortal duet, "Class," these unlikely but perfectly sincere champions of civility lament the state of manners to which their world has descended: ladies and gentlemen, they moan, have vanished from the earth; even children have become lawless thugs.[2]

"Class" wins the loudest applause of the evening, clearly striking a nerve with contemporary audiences, who feel sympathy for the passion with which even guttersnipes yearn for the restoration of manners. Somehow, their urgency attests to both the depth and the universality of our outcry for decency—though we rarely get a satisfying reply. Morals may—if barely—yield to the human intellect and lend themselves to order, system, and at least semi-permanent preservation. But manners are simply too protean and too democratic. And that, of course, is why everybody cares about them—including the hopelessly unclassy. The forms civility takes may please or disgust us, but it's not really endangered. In fact, it's really unkillable, rising endlessly from its own ashes, and assuming new forms we can only dimly foresee. And you can learn its ever-changing ways in the Cook County Jail as easily as in the Oak Room at the Plaza.

Both William d'Alton Mann and Emily Post would have understood perfectly.

notes

Introduction

1. *Good Housekeeping* (January 1994), p. 32.
2. Allan Bloom, *The Closing of the American Mind* (New York: Simon & Schuster, 1987), p. 175.
3. *New York Times*, July 18, 1997, p. A14.
4. This memorable sentiment was voiced by Ohio Democrat James Traficant. See *Louisville Courier-Journal*, October 11, 1992, p. 1A.
5. *Arizona Republic*, April 10, 1997.
6. Viola Tree, *Can I Help You? Your Manners—Menus—Amusements—Friends—Character—Make-Ups—Travel—Calling—Children—Love Affairs* (London: Hogarth Press, 1937), p. 15.
7. See Edward O. Wilson, *Sociobiology, the New Synthesis* (Cambridge, MA: Belknap Press, 1975), p. 257. The fable was originally cited in Paul Leyhausen, "Dominance and Territoriality as Complemented in Mammalian Social Structure," in *Behavior and Environment: The Use of Space by Animals and Men*, ed. Aristide H. Esser (New York: Plenum, 1971), p. 38.
8. Anonymous, *Manners and Tone of Good Society, or Solecisms to Be Avoided* (London, 1879), quoted in Margaret Visser, *Rituals of Dinner: The Origins, Evolution, Eccentricities, and Meaning of Table Manners* (New York: Grove Weidenfeld, 1994), p. 69.

9. Viola Klein, *English Cultures*, 2 vols. (London: Routledge & Kegan Paul, 1965), vol. 1, p. 200. Quoted in Bernice Martin, "Symbols, Codes and Cultures," in *Class*, ed. Patrick Joyce (Oxford: Oxford University Press, 1995), p. 252.

Part One

Chapter 1

1. See Nancy Tuckerman and Nancy Dunnan, *The Amy Vanderbilt Complete Book of Etiquette: Entirely Rewritten and Updated* (New York: Doubleday, 1995), p. xii.

2. See Andy Logan, *The Man Who Robbed the Robber Barons* (New York: W. W. Norton, 1965), and her two-part article, "That Was New York," in *The New Yorker*, August 14 and 21, 1965. Other sources offering information on Mann, apart from the widespread press coverage of the epic scandals of 1905 and 1906, include his entry in *Who's Who in America, 1899–1900*, his obituary in *The New York Times* (May 18, 1920, p. 11, col. 3); and Edwin Post's affectionate yet frank memoir of his mother, *Truly Emily Post* (New York: Funk & Wagnalls, 1961), pp. 143ff.

3. Edwin Post, *op. cit.*, p. 143.

4. *Town Topics*, January 7, 1915.

5. *Ibid.*, October 20, 1904.

6. *Town Topics*, quoted in Andy Logan, "That Was New York," *The New Yorker*, August 14, 1965.

7. *New York Times*, July 12, 1905, p. 1, col. 3.

8. William d'Alton Mann, *Fads and Fancies of Representative Americans at the Beginning of the Twentieth Century, Being a Portrayal of Their Tastes, Diversions and Achievements* (New York: Town Topics Publishing Co., 1905), n.p.

9. Emily Post, *Etiquette: The Blue Book of Social Usage*, 1945 edn. (New York: Funk & Wagnalls, 1947), p. 2.

10. Thomas Hobbes, *Leviathan* (1651), ed. Michael Oakeshott (Oxford: Blackwell, 1947), p. 63. Hobbes was, however, not completely consistent in denigrating manners. Compare this far less familiar quote from his *Philosophical Rudiments Concerning Government and Society* (1651): "modesty, equity, trust, humanity, mercy, (which we have demonstrated to be necessary to peace), are good manners or habits, that is, virtues. The law therefore, in the means to peace, commands also good manners, or the practice of virtue." See *The English Works of Thomas Hobbes*, ed. William Molesworth (London, 1841; rpt. 1962), vol. 2, p. 40.

11. Immanuel Kant, *Lectures on Ethics*, trans. Louis Infield (New York: Century, 1931), pp. 236–37. These sentiments perhaps need to be taken with some caution: Kant's ethics lectures, given between 1762 and 1764, survive only as notes taken by his pupil, the philosopher Johann Gottlieb Herder (1744–1803), and may not be completely accurate. See Kant, *Lectures on Ethics*, ed. Peter Heath and J. B. Schneewind (Cambridge: Cambridge University Press, 1997), p. xxv, n. 2. See also Philippa Foot, "Morality as a System of Hypothetical Imperatives," *Philosophical Review* 81 (1972), pp. 305–16, for an assertion that Kant's thinking here is somewhat self-contradictory, and for the argument that serious morals don't in fact have a dimension any more universally compelling than etiquette does.

12. Edmund Burke, "First Letter on a Regicide Peace" (1796), in Paul Langford, gen. ed., *The Writings and Speeches of Edmund Burke*, vol. IX, ed. R. B. McDowell and W. B. Todd (Oxford: Clarendon Press, 1991), p. 242.

13. Edmund Burke, "A Letter from Mr. Burke to the Sheriffs of Bristol, on the Affairs of America" (1777), in *The Works of the Right Honourable Edmund Burke*, Vol. II (London: Henry G. Bohn, 1846), p. 100.

14. Judith Martin, *Miss Manners' Guide to Rearing Perfect Children* (New York: Penguin, 1985), p. 323.

15. *Newsday*, Nassau and Suffolk edn., Tuesday, August 6, 1996, p. B13.

16. See *Arizona Republic*, July 11, 1995, p. A1.

17. Gertrude Himmelfarb, *The De-Moralization of Society: From Victorian Virtues to Modern Values* (New York: Knopf, 1995), p. 22.

18. My translation from La Rochefoucauld, *Maximes Suivies d'Extraits des Moralistes du XVIIᵉ Siècle*, ed. J.-R. Charbonnel (Paris: Larousse, 1934), p. 34.

19. Jürgen Habermas, *Communication and the Evolution of Society*, trans. Thomas McCarthy (Boston: Beacon Press, 1979), p. 88.

20. Michael Sandel, *Democracy's Discontent: America in Search of a Public Philosophy* (Cambridge, MA: Harvard/Belknap, 1996), p. 129 and n.

21. All quotations following are from *Red Book* (the magazine's title in its earlier years) (February 1922), p. 13.

22. Diogenes Laertius, *Lives of Eminent Philosophers*, VI.40, trans. R. D. Hicks (Cambridge, MA: Loeb Classical Library, 1958), vol. 2, p. 43. This anecdote may well be apocryphal, but attests to a popular association between surface oafishness and deep-down good sense.

23. *Los Angeles Times*, Ventura County edn., March 15, 1996, Metro part B, p. 1.

24. *The Cimmerian Chronicle (Zimmerische Chronik)*, supposedly composed around 1566 by Count Froben Christof von Zimmern and his secretary. See Max von Böhn, *Modes and Manners*, 4 vols., trans.

Joan Joshua (London: Harrap, 1932–35), vol. 2, p. 210.

25. See Margaret Visser, *The Rituals of Dinner: The Origins, Evolution, Eccentricities and Meaning of Table Manners* (New York: Grove Weidenfeld, 1992), pp. 10f.

26. Paul L. Hughes and James F. Larkin, eds., *Tudor Royal Proclamations* (New Haven: Yale University Press, 1969), vol. 3, p. 176.

27. See the map included in Marcel Poëte, *Une Vie de Cité Paris de sa Naissance à Nos Jours* (Paris: Picard, 1924). While this plan dates from the sixteenth century, the streetscape of the city had not changed substantially since the medieval period.

28. John Stow, *The Survey of London* (1598; London: Everyman, 1945), p. 74.

29. Emily Post, *op. cit.*, pp. xii–xiii.

30. Harriet Martineau, *Society in America* (London, 1837; rpt. New York: AMS Press, 1966), vol. III, p. 28.

31. Norbert Elias, *The Civilizing Process*, trans. Edmund Jephcott (New York: Urizen Books, 1978), vol. 2, p. 251.

32. Stuart M. Blumin, *The Emergence of the Middle Class: Social Experience in the American City, 1760–1900* (Cambridge: Cambridge University Press, 1989), p. 286.

33. August B. Hollingshead, *Elmtown's Youth: The Impact of Social Classes on Adolescents* (New York: John Wiley, 1949), pp. 101–02.

34. Max Weber, *Economy and Society*, ed. Guenther Ross and Claus Wittich, 2 vols. (Berkeley: University of California Press, 1978), excerpted in *Class*, ed. Patrick Joyce (New York: Oxford University Press, 1995), p. 36.

35. Jean Baudrillard, "The End of the Social," from *In the Shadow of the Silent Majorities, or, The End of the Social and Other Essays*, trans. Paul Foss, John Johnston, and Paul Patton, quoted in *Class*, ed. Joyce, p. 90.

36. *National Cyclopaedia of American Biography* (New York: James T. White, 1901), vol. XI, p. 491.

37. Abram C. Dayton, *Last Days of Knickerbocker Life in New York* (New York: George W. Harlan, 1889), p. 148. In early American commerce, the term "store" came to denote a large-scale enterprise, stocking a wide variety of articles, as opposed to a shop, an altogether smaller, more modest—hence lower-class—operation.

38. *Ibid.*, pp. 147–49.

39. *Ibid.*, p. 97.

40. *Ibid.*, p. 131.

41. Christine de Pizan, *A Medieval Woman's Mirror of Honor: The Treasury of the City of Ladies*, trans. Charity C. Willard, ed. Madeleine P. Cosman (New York: Persea, 1989), p. 174.

42. Elias, *op. cit.*, vol. 1, p. 55.

43. Quoted in *ibid.*, p. 90.
44. *Ibid.*, p. 58.
45. *Ibid.*, p. 68.
46. *Ibid.*, p. 164.
47. *Ibid.*, p. 120.
48. See Arthur M. Schlesinger, *Learning How to Behave: A Historical Study of American Etiquette Books* (New York: Macmillan, 1947). See also John F. Kasson, *Rudeness and Civility: Manners in Nineteenth-Century Urban America* (New York: Hill & Wang, 1990), pp. 34f.
49. Kasson, p. 13.
50. *George Washington: Writings*, selected by John Rhodehamel (New York: Library of America, 1997), p. 10.
51. See Marquis James, *The Life of Andrew Jackson* (New York: Bobbs-Merrill, 1938), pp. 494–95.
52. Charles Dickens, *Martin Chuzzlewit* (1843–44; Oxford: Oxford University Press, 1987), p. 255. This scene is of course fictional, but Dickens's 1842 diatribe *American Notes* reveals that for him at least it was a distillation of pure social fact.
53. Kasson, *op. cit.*, p. 43.

Chapter 2

1. Eleanor Dwight, *Edith Wharton: An Extraordinary Life* (New York: Abrams, 1994), p. 122.
2. Edith Wharton, *A Motor-Flight Through France* (New York: Scribners, 1908), pp. 1–2.
3. Quoted in Dwight, *Edith Wharton: An Extraordinary Life*, p. 137.
4. D. A. Richardson, *Beyond the Mississippi* (1867), quoted in George W. Pierson, *The Moving American* (New York: Knopf, 1973), p. 5.
5. J. Hector St. John de Crèvecoeur, *Letters from an American Farmer* (New York: Dutton, 1957), p. 48.
6. In 1914 Germany's total accumulation of national wealth was the largest in Europe, but the United Kingdom led Germany in wealth per capita. See H. E. Friedlander and J. Oser, *Economic History of Modern Europe* (New York: Prentice Hall, 1953), p. 521.
7. Theo Barker and Dorian Grehold, *The Rise and Rise of Road Transport, 1700–1990* (London: Macmillan, Studies in Economic and Social History), p. 82.
8. *Statistical Abstract of the United States*, 1996.
9. See *Car & Travel* (January 1997), p. 4a.
10. Quoted in Howard P. Chudacoff, *Mobile Americans: Residential and Social Mobility in Omaha, 1880–1920* (New York: Oxford University Press, 1972), p. 4.

11. See George W. Pierson, *The Moving American* (New York: Knopf, 1973), p. 31.
12. Howard P. Chudacoff, *Mobile Americans: Residential and Social Mobility in Omaha, 1880–1920* (New York: Oxford University Press, 1972), p. 36.
13. *Ibid.*, p. 9.
14. Pierson, *op. cit.*, p. 90.
15. Chudacoff, *op. cit.*, p. 152.
16. Pierson, *op. cit.*, p. 150.
17. Ken Kaye and Kathleen Kernicky, "Horrors at 30,000 Feet," *Fort Lauderdale Sun-Sentinel*, February 25, 1996, p. 1E.
18. Gerhard Vowinckel, "Command or Refine? Cultural Patterns of Cognitively Organizing Emotions," *Theory, Culture and Society* (June 1987), pp. 489–514.
19. James E. Vance, Jr., *Capturing the Horizon: The Historical Geography of Transportation Since the Transportation Revolution of the Sixteenth Century* (New York: Harper & Row, 1986), pp. 7–10.
20. *Ibid.*, p. 7.
21. G. N. Georgano, ed., *A History of Transport* (London: Dent, 1972), p. 10.
22. W. T. Jackman, *Development of Transportation in Modern England* (1916; 2nd edn. 1962), pp. 109–22, cited in Theo Barker and Dorian Grehold, *The Rise and Rise of Road Transport, 1700–1990* (London: Macmillan, Studies in Economic and Social History), p. 52.
23. *Ibid.*, p. 54 (pp. 335–39 in Jackman).
24. Blaise Pascal, *Pensées* (1670; Paris: Garnier, 1964), p. 109. Yet, despite the pains of mobility, Pascal also seems to have appreciated its power over human nature. *Cf.*, "Notre nature est dans le mouvement; le repos entier est la mort" ("Our nature lies in movement; complete rest is death"), p. 108.
25. Tobias Smollett, *The Expedition of Humphry Clinker* (1771; London: Routledge, 1894), pp. 91–92.
26. Frances Trollope, *Domestic Manners of the Americans*, ed. Michael Sadleir (1832; New York: English Library, Dodd Mead, 1927), p. 101.
27. *Ibid.*, p. 83.
28. Harriet Martineau, *Society in America* (London, 1837; rpt. New York: AMS Press, 1966), vol. III, pp. 83–84.
29. Mark Twain, *Roughing It*, in *The Innocents Abroad; Roughing It* (1872; New York: Library of America, 1984), p. 546.
30. See Clifton Hood, *722 Miles: The Building of the Subways and How They Transformed New York* (Baltimore: Johns Hopkins University Press, 1993), p. 98.

31. *New York Tribune*, June 3, 1905, p. 3.
32. *New York Times*, January 7, 1915, p. 1.
33. *New York Sun*, January 7, 1915, p. 2.
34. *Ibid.*, p. 4.
35. *Ibid.*, January 10, 1915, p. 12.
36. *Town Topics*, January 14, 1915, p. 12.
37. See, for example, C. Wright Mills, "The American Business Elite: A Collective Portrait," in *Power, Politics and People: The Collected Essays of C. Wright Mills* (New York: Oxford University Press, 1962), pp. 110–39. Mills, interestingly, reports that more business leaders came from blue-collar backgrounds in the first half of the nineteenth century than in the second.
38. Editors of Vogue, *Vogue's Book of Etiquette: Present-day Customs of Social Intercourse, with the Rules for Their Correct Observance* (Garden City, NY: Doubleday, Doran, 1929), p. 4.
39. *Ibid.*, p. 2.
40. Letitia Baldrige, *Letitia Baldrige's Complete Guide to the New Manners for the '90s* (New York: Rawson, 1990), p. 3.
41. *Ibid.*, p. 167.
42. Norine Dresser, *Multicultural Manners: New Rules of Etiquette for a Changing Society* (New York: Wiley, 1996), p. 88.
43. *Ibid.*, pp. 18–19.
44. See Edwin L. Post, *Truly Emily Post* (New York: Funk & Wagnalls, 1961), p. 208.
45. Emily Post, *Etiquette: The Blue Book of Social Usage*, 1945 edn. (New York: Funk & Wagnalls, 1947), p. 280.
46. *Ibid.*, p. 331.
47. Edwin L. Post, *op. cit.*, p. 225.
48. *Ibid.*, p. 121.
49. Daniel W. Rossides, *Social Stratification: The American Class System in Comparative Perspective* (Englewood Cliffs, NJ: Prentice-Hall, 1990), p. 144.
50. *Ibid.*
51. Federica Di Castro, *Artenergie: Minimal Relieves Matter, Memory, Idea* (Milan: Charta, 1994), p. 17.
52. Fred Davis, *Fashion, Culture and Identity* (Chicago: University of Chicago Press, 1992), pp. 69–71.
53. Karal Ann Marling, *As Seen on TV: The Visual Culture of Everyday Life in the 1950s* (Cambridge, MA: Harvard University Press, 1994), p. 174.
54. Penelope Eckert, "Clothing and Geography in a Suburban High School," in Conrad Phillip Kottak, ed., *Researching American Culture: A Guide for Student Anthropologists* (Ann Arbor: University of Michigan Press, 1982), pp. 139–45.

Chapter 3

1. John Kobler, *Capone: The Life and World of Al Capone* (New York: Putnam's, 1971), pp. 189–90.
2. Quoted in Richard Gillespie, *Manufacturing Knowledge: A History of the Hawthorne Experiments* (Cambridge: Cambridge University Press, 1991), p. 2.
3. *Ibid.*, p. 155.
4. F. J. Roethlisberger and W. J. Dickson, *Management and the Worker: An Account of a Research Program Conducted by the Western Electric Company, Hawthorne Works, Chicago* (Cambridge, MA: Harvard University Press, 1947), p. 423.
5. *Ibid.*, p. 422.
6. *Ibid.*
7. *Ibid.*, p. 457.
8. Gillespie, *op. cit.*, pp. 19–20.
9. Roethlisberger and Dickson, *op. cit.*, p. 457.
10. Barbara Pachter and Marjorie Brody, *The Prentice-Hall Complete Business Etiquette Handbook* (Englewood Cliffs, NJ: Prentice Hall, 1995), pp. 92–93.
11. Thomas C. Cochran, *200 Years of American Business* (New York: Basic Books, 1977), pp. 27f.
12. *Ibid.*, p. 26.
13. Quoted in Alfred D. Chandler, Jr., "The Railroads: Pioneers in Modern Corporate Management," *Business History Review* 39 (Spring 1965), p. 29.
14. Cochran, *op. cit.*, p. 205.
15. For a full account of Taylor's life and ideas, see Robert Kanigel, *The One Best Way: Frederick Winslow Taylor and the Enigma of Efficiency* (New York: Viking, 1997).
16. Gillespie, *op. cit.*, pp. 19–20.
17. Quoted in David Lawrence, "American Business and Business Men," *Saturday Evening Post*, March 29, 1930, p. 38.
18. Quoted in Samuel Crowther, *John H. Patterson: Pioneer in Industrial Welfare* (Garden City, NY: Garden City Publishing Co., 1926), p. 111.
19. Quoted in Thomas and Marva Belden, *The Lengthening Shadow: The Life of Thomas J. Watson* (Boston: Little, Brown, 1962), p. 48.
20. Quoted in Crowther, *op. cit.*, p. 128.
*21. *Ibid.*, p. 148.
22. *About Your Company* (Armonk, NY: IBM, 1984), n.p.
23. Class Song, IBM Customer Engineering Class #576, 1930 (IBM Archives).

24. Scott Adams, *Dogbert's Top Secret Management Handbook* (New York: HarperBusiness, 1996), n.p.
25. Nella Henney, *The Book of Business Etiquette* (Garden City, NY: Doubleday, Page, 1922), pp. 5–6.
26. *Ibid.*, pp. 196–97.
27. *Ibid.*, p. 42.
28. *Ibid.*, p. 196.
29. J. George Frederick, *Standard Business Etiquette* (New York: Business Bourse, 1937), p. 9.
30. *Ibid.*, p. 31.
31. *Ibid.*, p. 33.
32. *Ibid.*, pp. 39–40.
33. See Jack Hradesky, *The Total Quality Management Handbook* (New York: McGraw-Hill, 1995), pp. 198–204.
34. Michael Hammer and James Champy, *Reengineering the Corporation: A Manifesto for Business Revolution* (New York: HarperBusiness, 1993), p. 49.
35. Michael Hammer and Steven A. Stanton, *The Reengineering Revolution: A Handbook* (New York: HarperBusiness, 1995), p. 50.
36. Hammer and Champy, *op. cit.*, pp. 177–78.
37. *Ibid.*, p. 176.
38. Hammer and Stanton, *op. cit.*, pp. 58–59.
39. Debra A. Benton, *Lions Don't Need to Roar: Using the Leadership Power of Professional Presence to Stand Out, Fit In, and Move Ahead* (New York: Warner Books, 1992), p. 87.
40. Pachter and Brody, *op. cit.*, p. 5.
41. Susan Bixler, *Professional Presence: The Total Program for Gaining That Extra Edge in Business by America's Top Corporate Image Consultant* (New York: Putnam's, 1991), p. 9.
42. *Ibid.*, see pp. 18–25.
43. *Ibid.*, pp. 76–77.
44. Letitia Baldridge, *New Complete Guide to Executive Manners* (New York: Scribners, 1993), p. 300.
45. *Ibid.*, p. 302.

Chapter 4

1. Figures on death rates are from George Thomas Kurian, *Datapedia of the United States* (Lanham, MD: Bernau Press, 1994); 1994 funeral costs are from *Statistical Abstract of the United States*, 1996; for 1995 figures, see *Wall Street Journal*, November 12, 1996, p. 1, c. 1
2. *Wall Street Journal*, February 14, 1996, and *New York Times*, June 29, 1997, sec. 4, p. 5.

3. Rana Dogar, "Here Comes the Billion Dollar Bride," *Working Woman*, vol. 22, no. 5 (May 1997), pp. 32–35.

4. *Chicago Tribune*, March 21, 1994.

5. Marcia Seligson, *The Eternal Bliss Machine: America's Way of Wedding* (New York: Morrow, 1973), p. 25.

6. Quoted in Linda Otto Lipsett, *To Love and to Cherish: Brides Remembered* (San Francisco: Quilt Digest Press, 1989), p. 47.

7. Edward Westermarck, *The History of Human Marriage*, 5th edn. (New York: Allerton Books, 1922), vol. I, pp. 27–28.

8. *Ibid.*, vol. II, p. 261.

9. Lipsett, *op. cit.*, p. 72.

10. *Ibid.*, pp. 50–54.

11. Mrs. John Sherwood, *Manners and Social Usages* (1884; rev. edn. New York: Harper & Brothers, 1905), p. 73.

12. *Ibid.*, p. 74.

13. *New York Tribune*, June 3, 1905, part V, p. 4.

14. Emily Post, *Etiquette: In Society, in Business, in Politics, and at Home* (New York: Funk & Wagnalls, 1922), p. 313.

15. *Ibid.*, pp. 317–18.

16. Seligson, *op. cit.*, pp. 6–7.

17. *Ladies' Home Journal* (June 1935).

18. Circulation figures are from *Ulrich's International Periodicals Directory*, 1996.

19. *Bride's* (Winter 1936–37), p. 13.

20. See *Bride's* (Summer 1941), p. 9.

21. See *Wall Street Journal*, February 14, 1996.

22. *Bride's* (June–July 1997), pp. 556–57.

23. Mary Roberts Rinehart, "The Second Marriage," *Ladies' Home Journal* (June 1935), p. 5.

24. See Kevin Hillstrom, ed., *Encyclopedia of American Industries* (New York: Gale Research, 1994), vol. 2, p. 984; and *New York Times*, October 13, 1996, sec. 13, p. 1, C1.

25. See, for example, Arnold van Gennep, *The Rites of Passage*, trans. Monika Vizedom and Gabrielle Caffee (1909; Chicago: University of Chicago Press, 1960), p. 146.

26. *Casket & Sunnyside* (January 1905), p. 24.

27. Quotations following are from Mrs. John Sherwood, *op. cit.*, p. 184.

28. *Casket & Sunnyside* (January 1905), p. 14.

29. Quoted in Glennys Howarth, *Last Rites: The Work of the Modern Funeral Director* (Amityville, NY: Baywood Publishing, 1996), p. 19; Howarth also notes the traditional link in Britain between undertaking and the clergy.

30. Sources: Howarth, *op. cit.*; Richard Huntington and Peter Metcalf,

Celebrations of Death: The Anthropology of Mortuary Ritual (Cambridge: Cambridge University Press, 1979).

31. *Casket & Sunnyside* (January 1905), p. 3.
32. Emily Post, *Etiquette* (New York: Funk & Wagnalls, 1945), p. 272.
33. Howarth, *op. cit.*, pp. 28f.
34. Huntington and Metcalf, *op. cit.*, p. 193.
35. See *Chicago Tribune*, May 9, 1993, Business section, p. 1.
36. *Atlanta Journal and Constitution*, June 20, 1995, p. 2D.
37. See *Wall Street Journal*, February 14, 1996.
38. *Wall Street Journal*, July 15, 1991.
39. *Chicago Tribune*, March 21, 1994, Business section, p. 1.
40. See, for example, *New York Times*, September 27, 1996, p. D1, col. 2.
41. Lois Smith Brady, *Vows: Weddings of the Nineties from the New York Times* (New York: Morrow, 1997), p. 117.
42. See *World Wastes* (May 1996), p. 138; and *Arizona Republic*, March 25, 1996.
43. "A Funeral Director Remembers," *C&S* (January–February 1985), p. 8.

Chapter 5

1. All postings were gathered from USENET's "alt.flame.niggers" board on August 7, 1997.
2. This figure is an estimate of USENET's subscriber base in 1993. See Leslie Regan Shade, "Is There Free Speech on the Internet? Censorship in the Global Information Infrastructure," in Rob Shields, ed., *Cultures of Internet: Virtual Spaces, Real Histories, Living Bodies* (Thousand Oaks, CA: Sage, 1996), pp. 11–32.
3. See www.softronics.com/peak_cam.html.
4. See the Oxford English Dictionary under "virtual" (sense 4).
5. Norman Shapiro and Robert Anderson, *Toward an Ethics and Etiquette for Electronic Mail* (Santa Monica, CA: Rand Corporation, 1985).
6. John R. Levine, Margaret Levine Young, and Arnold Reinhold, *The Internet for Dummies: Quick Reference*, 3rd edn. (Foster City, CA: IDG Books, 1996), p. 142.
7. *Ibid.*
8. See Katie Argyle, "Life After Death," in Shields, ed., *Cultures of Internet*, p. 137, for an application of carnival theory to the Internet. The controlled license of carnival has, under the influence of the Russian critic Mikhail Bakhtin, become the basis of a fashionable strain of contemporary cultural analysis.

9. Emmanuel LeRoy Ladurie, *Carnival in Romans*, trans. Mary Feeney (New York: Braziller, 1979), p. 319.

10. *Ibid.*, p. 307.

11. John Seabrook, *Deeper: My Two-Year Odyssey in Cyberspace* (New York: Simon & Schuster, 1997), p. 95.

12. *Ibid.*, p. 96.

13. Pseudonyms collected from USENET bulletin boards, August 12, 1997.

14. See Thomas Schatz, *The Genius of the System: Hollywood Filmmaking in the Studio Era* (New York: Pantheon, 1988), p. 196.

15. Carolyn Marvin, *When Old Technologies Were New: Thinking About Electric Communication in the Late Nineteenth Century* (New York: Oxford University Press, 1987), p. 64.

16. *Ibid.*, p. 18.

17. *Ibid.*, p. 70.

18. From the trade magazine *Electrical World*, quoted in *ibid.*, p. 75.

19. Emily Post, *Etiquette: The Blue Book of Social Usage*, 1945 edn. (New York: Funk & Wagnalls, 1947), p. 439.

20. Wendell S. Dysinger and Christian A. Ruckmick, *The Emotional Responses of Children to the Motion Picture Situation* (New York: Macmillan, 1933), pp. 13–15.

21. *Ibid.*, pp. 31–34.

22. Charles C. Peters, *Motion Pictures and Standards of Morality* (New York: Macmillan, 1933), pp. 177–78.

23. *Ibid.*, p. 181.

24. Quoted in Sissela Bok, *Mayhem: Violence as Public Entertainment* (Reading, MA: Addison-Wesley, 1998), p. 45. Bok accepts this policy statement as definitive, and the discussion in her book assumes that the link between image and behavior has been established.

25. Leonard Berkowitz and Edna Rawlings, "Effects of Film Violence on Inhibitions Against Subsequent Aggression," *Journal of Abnormal and Social Psychology* 66 (1963), pp. 405–12.

26. Steven F. Messner, "Television Violence and Violent Crime: An Aggregate Analysis," *Social Problems* 33 (1986), pp. 218–35.

27. Seabrook, *op. cit.*, p. 95.

28. See Levine, Young, and Reinhold, *The Internet for Dummies*, p. 24.

29. See Neil Randall, *The Soul of the Internet: Net Gods, Netizens and the Wiring of the World* (London: International Thomson Computer Press, 1997), p. 38.

30. *Ibid.*, p. xxxiii.

Part Two

Chapter 6

1. John R. Silber, "Obedience to the Unenforceable," Boston University Commencement Address, May 21, 1995, pp. 2–4.
2. *Ibid.*, p. 1.
3. John Fletcher Moulton, *"Law and Manners": An Address Given by the Rt. Hon. Lord Moulton, KCB, GBE, LLD, FRS, at the Authors' Club, London, November 4, 1912* (Wilmington, DE: Privately printed, 1923), p. 11.
4. *Ibid.*, p. 13.
5. For an exhaustive inventory and an evocative recreation, see Don Lynch, *Titanic: An Illustrated History* (New York: Hyperion, 1992).
6. G. K. Chesterton, "Limericks and Counsels of Perfection," in *All Things Considered* (New York: J. Lane, 1908), p. 158.
7. Margaret Visser, *Rituals of Dinner: The Origins, Evolution, Eccentricities and Meaning of Table Manners* (New York: Grove Weidenfeld, 1994), p. 185.
8. M. E. W. Sherwood, *The Art of Entertaining* (New York: Dodd, Mead & Co., 1893), p. 166.
9. Harriet and Vetta Goldstein, *Art in Everyday Life*, 4th edn. (New York: Macmillan, 1954), p. 1.
10. *Ibid.*
11. *Ibid.*, p. 59.
12. *Ibid.*, pp. 234–35.
13. Kathryn Kish Sklar, *Catharine Beecher: A Study in American Domesticity* (New Haven: Yale University Press, 1973), p. 263.
14. Catharine E. Beecher, *A Treatise on Domestic Economy* (Boston: Marsh, Capen, Lyon, & Webb, 1841; rpt. New York: Source Book Press, 1970), p. 103.
15. *Ibid.*, p. 120.
16. *Ibid.*, p. 128.
17. Factual information about *Godey's* cited here is from John Tebbel and Mary Ellen Zuckerman, *The Magazine in America, 1741–1990* (New York: Oxford University Press, 1991), pp. 33–36; and Theodore Peterson, *Magazines in the Twentieth Century* (Urbana: University of Illinois Press, 1964), p. 5.
18. Agnes H. Morton, *Etiquette: Good Manners for All People, Especially for Those Within the Broad Zone of the Average* (Philadelphia: Penn, 1911), pp. 58 and 61.
19. For the early history of *The Ladies' Home Journal*, see Tebbel and Zuckerman, *op. cit.*, pp. 93–95; and Salme Harju Steinberg, *Re-*

former in the Marketplace: Edward W. Bok and The Ladies' Home Journal (Baton Rouge: Louisiana State University Press, 1979), p. 2.

20. See, for example, *Ladies' Home Journal* (January 1905), pp. 24 and 26.
21. See Edward W. Bok, *The Americanization of Edward Bok* (New York: Scribners, 1922), p. 170.
22. *Ibid.*, p. 174.
23. Quoted in Steinberg, *op. cit.*, p. 55.
24. Bok, *The Americanization of Edward Bok*, p. 249.
25. *Ibid.*
26. *Ladies' Home Journal* (January 1905), p. 26.
27. *Ibid.*, p. 22.
28. *Ibid.*, p. 25.
29. See *New York Times* obituary, June 19, 1955.
30. *Ladies' Home Journal* (September 1935), p. 20.
31. See Tebbel and Zuckerman, *op. cit.*, p. 102.
32. This project, to be undertaken by Linda Robertson and Jodi Dean of Hobart & William Smith colleges, was announced in a September 15, 1997, posting in the on-line magazine *Slate*.
33. Transcribed at Kmart, 8th Street and Broadway, New York, September 25, 1997.
34. *Martha Stewart Living* (May 1996), p. 118.
35. See Jerry Oppenheimer, *Martha Stewart—Just Desserts: The Unauthorized Biography* (New York: Morrow, 1997), p. 318.
36. *Martha Stewart Living* (June 1996), p. 156.
37. *Martha Stewart Living* (September 1997), p. 216.
38. *Martha Stewart Living* (May 1996), p. 104.
39. "And the Winners Are . . . Major life changes often necessitate substantial home renovations. Tour the stunning made-over rooms that took top prize in our annual contest," *Ladies' Home Journal* (October 1997), pp. 192–95.
40. *Martha Stewart Living* (June 1996), pullout.
41. Sales figures are from www.plunkettresearch.com.
42. Emily Post, *Etiquette: The Blue Book of Social Usage*, 1945 edn. (New York: Funk & Wagnalls, 1947), p. 317.
43. See *New York Times*, April 17, 1995, p. D8.
44. *House & Garden* (July 1997), p. 81.
45. Wendy Noonan, "The Maker's Mark," *House & Garden* (September 1997), p. 172.
46. Véronique Vienne, "January 1942," *House & Garden* (September 1997), p. 152.

Chapter 7

1. See Stephan and Abigail Thernstrom, *America in Black and White: One Nation Indivisible* (New York: Simon & Schuster, 1997), pp. 233f., for a complete discussion.
2. See Karen Grigsby Bates and Karen Elyse Hudson, *Basic Black: Home Training for Modern Times* (New York: Doubleday, 1996), pp. 181 and 196–97.
3. Karen Grigsby Bates, "Excuse Me, Your Race Is Showing: We Need an Etiquette All Our Own for Those Infuriating Slights," *Washington Post*, January 26, 1997, p. C5.
4. See David K. Shipler, *A Country of Strangers: Blacks and Whites in America* (New York: Knopf, 1997), pp. 450–1.
5. Barbara Diane Miller, "The Anthropology of Sex and Gender Hierarchies," in Miller, ed., *Sex and Gender Hierarchies* (Cambridge: Cambridge University Press, 1993), p. 22.
6. Robert Hughes, *Culture of Complaint: A Passionate Look into the Ailing Heart of America* (New York: Warner Books, 1994), p. 25.
7. *Ibid.*
8. Erving Goffman, *Relations in Public: Microstudies of the Public Order* (New York: Basic Books, 1971), p. 115 and n.
9. See Maxine L. Margolis and Marigene Arnold, "Turning the Tables? Male Strippers and the Gender Hierarchy in America," in Miller, ed., *Sex and Gender Hierarchies*, pp. 337–38.
10. *Ibid.*, p. 342.
11. *Ibid.*, p. 343.
12. Carol Brooks Gardner, *Passing By: Gender and Public Harassment* (Berkeley: University of California Press, 1995), p. 4.
13. Quoted in *Ibid.*, p. 26.
14. See Mary Mitchell with John Corr, *The Complete Idiot's Guide to Etiquette* (New York: Alpha Books, 1996), pp. 268–69.
15. Gardner, *op. cit.*, p. 50.
16. See Bertram Wilbur Doyle, *The Etiquette of Race Relations in the South: A Study in Social Control* (Chicago: University of Chicago Press, 1937), p. 2.
17. *Ibid.*, p. 16.
18. *Ibid.*, p. xx.
19. See Shipler, *op. cit.*, pp. 175–77.
20. Quoted in Doyle, *op. cit.*, p. 123.
21. *Ibid.*, p. 144.
22. See Shipler, *op. cit.*, p. 452.
23. Goffman, *op. cit.*, p. 63.
24. Bates and Hudson, *op. cit.*, p. 237.
25. Margery Wilson, *The Woman You Want to Be: Margery Wilson's Com-*

plete Book of Charm, 11th printing (Philadelphia: Lippincott, 1942), pp. 203–4.

26. *Ibid.*, p. 334.
27. *Ibid.*, p. 335.
28. Lillian Eichler, *Book of Etiquette*, 2 vols. (Oyster Bay, NY: Nelson Doubleday, 1922), vol. 2, pp. 177–78.
29. *Ibid.*, p. 179.
30. Helen Frances Thompson, *Do's and Don'ts for Business Women* (New York: The Woman's Press, 1927), pp. 186–87.

Chapter 8

1. William Kessen, "The American Child and Other Inventions," *American Psychologist* 34 (October 1979), p. 815.
2. Philippe Ariès, *Centuries of Childhood: A Social History of Family Life*, trans. Robert Baldrich (New York: Vintage, 1962), pp. 261–62.
3. See Emmanuel LeRoy Ladurie, *The Beggar and the Professor: A Sixteenth Century Family Saga*, trans. Arthur Goldhammer (Chicago: University of Chicago Press, 1997), p. 339.
4. Lewis Carroll, *Alice's Adventures in Wonderland* (1865; New York: Signet Classics, 1960), p. 62.
5. William Wordsworth, "Ode: Intimations of Immortality," *Norton Anthology of English Literature*, 6th edn., vol. 2 (New York: W. W. Norton, 1993), p. 190, ll. 58–66.
6. R. K. Root, ed., *Lord Chesterfield's Letters to His Son and Others*, July 25, 1741 (London: Everyman, 1929), p. 9.
7. Jean-Jacques Rousseau, *Émile, ou de l'éducation* (1762; Paris: Garnier, 1929), livre II, p. 57 (translation mine).
8. Benjamin Spock, *The Common Sense Book of Baby and Child Care* (New York: Duell, Sloan & Pearce, 1945), p. 271.
9. Benjamin Spock and Michael B. Rothenberg, *Dr. Spock's Baby and Child Care* (New York: Pocket Books, 1992), p. 437.
10. Robert Coles, *The Moral Life of Children* (Boston: Atlantic Monthly Press, 1986), p. 98.
11. *Ibid.*, p. 35.
12. See *New York Times*, July 30, 1995, section 1, p. 16.
13. See *New York Times*, October 10, 1997, p. B3.
14. See *New York Times*, February 24, 1998, p. A12.
15. See *New York Times*, February 23, 1998, p. B3.
16. William March, *The Bad Seed*, 1954 (rpt. Hopewell, NJ: Ecco, 1997), p. 26.
17. Iona and Peter Opie, *The Lore and Language of School Children* (Oxford: Oxford University Press, 1967), p. 97.

18. Quoted in Jason Epstein, " 'Good Bunnies Always Obey': Books for American Children," *Commentary* (1963), rpt. in Sheila Egoff, G. T. Stubbs, and L. F. Ashley, eds., *Only Connect: Readings on Children's Literature* (Oxford: Oxford University Press, 1969), p. 73.
19. *Statistical Abstract of the United States 1955*, table 169, p. 143.
20. See *Dallas Morning News*, November 13, 1994, p. 10A.
21. For accounts of Lindsey and this incident in Georgia, see Elliott West, *Growing Up in Twentieth-Century America: A History and Reference Guide* (Westport, CT: Greenwood Press, 1996), p. 65.
22. See *New York Times*, April 26, 1996, p. A20.
23. Patrick Fagan and William Fitzgerald, *The Child Abuse Crisis: The Disintegration of Marriage, Family, and the American Community* (Wasington, DC: Heritage Foundation, 1997).
24. *Ibid.*
25. See *Orange County Register*, April 1, 1996.
26. See Gary Cross, *Kids' Stuff: Toys and the Changing World of American Childhood* (Cambridge, MA: Harvard University Press, 1997), p. 207.
27. Heinrich Hoffmann, *Slovenly Peter* (Cutchogue, NY: Buccaneer Press, 1991).
28. See Cross, *op. cit.*, p. 24.
29. Richard O'Brien, *The Story of American Toys: From the Puritans to the Present* (New York: Abbeville Press, 1990), p. 131.
30. See Cross, *op. cit.*, p. 179.
31. See Bill Blackbeard, ed., *R. F. Outcault's The Yellow Kid: A Centennial Celebration of the Kid Who Started the Comics* (Northampton, MA: Kitchen Sink Press, 1995), n.p.
32. Wallace's book was published by St. Martin's Press in 1996.
33. See Mark Kennedy, "Whoops! That's a Salad Fork," *Chattanooga Times*, November 18, 1997, p. B1.
34. See *Worcester* [Massachusetts] *Sunday Telegram*, January 25, 1998, p. A1; *New York Times*, November 23, 1997, sec. 1, p. 1.
35. Kathryn Murray, *Kathryn Murray's Tips for Teenagers* (New York: Putnam's, 1961), pp. 11–12.
36. Viola Tree, *Can I Help You? Your Manners—Menus—Amusements—Friends—Character—Make-Ups—Travel—Calling—Children—Love Affairs* (London: Hogarth Press, 1937), pp. 87–88.
37. See *Dictionary of American Biography*, entry on "Enos Hitchcock."
38. Enos Hitchcock, *Memoirs of the Bloomsgrove Family, In a Series of Letters to a Respectable Citizen of Philadelphia, Containing Sentiments on a Mode of Domestic Education, Suited to the Present State of Society, Government, and Manners, in the United States of America, and on the Dignity and Importance of the Female Character, Interspersed with a Variety of Interesting Anecdotes* (Boston: Thomas & Andrews, 1790), vol. I, pp. 52–53.

39. *Ibid.*, pp. 207–8.
40. *Ibid.*, p. 216.
41. William E. Blatz and Helen Bott, *The Management of Young Children* (New York: Morrow, 1930), p. 168.
42. *Ibid.*, p. 169.
43. See Stanley Turecki and Leslie Tonner, *The Difficult Child* (New York: Bantam, 1985), pp. 73–84.
44. See Linda and Richard Eyre, *Teaching Your Children Values* (New York: Fireside, 1993), pp. 187–89.
45. See Spock, *op. cit.*, pp. 3–4; Spock and Rothenberg, *op. cit.*, pp. 1–2.
46. Spock, *op. cit.*, p. 252.
47. *Ibid.*, pp. 271–72.
48. See Spock and Rothenberg, *op. cit.*, pp. 412–16.
49. Judith Martin, *Miss Manners' Guide to Rearing Perfect Children* (New York: Penguin, 1984), p. xvii.
50. *Ibid.*

Chapter 9

1. Dick Johnson, "Students Still Sweat, They Just Don't Shower," *New York Times*, April 22, 1996, p. A1.
2. *Ibid.*
3. Edward O. Laumann, John H. Gagnon, Robert T. Michael, and Stuart Michaels, *The Social Organization of Sexuality* (Chicago: University of Chicago Press, 1994), pp. 287–90.
4. All statistics from Alan Guttmacher Institute, "Facts In Brief: Teen Sex and Pregnancy," www.agi-usa.org.
5. Data are from the *Statistical Abstract of the United States*, 1980 (chart 95, p. 66) and 1996 (chart 97, p. 98).
6. Leland Elliott and Cynthia Brantley, *Sex on Campus: The Naked Truth About the Real Sex Lives of College Students* (New York: Random House, 1997), p. 12.
7. Marabel Morgan, *The Total Woman* (New York: Pocket Books, 1975), p. 141, quoted in Andrea Dworkin, *Intercourse* (New York: Free Press, 1987), p. 47.
8. See *New York Magazine*, April 20, 1998, p. 29.
9. Broadcast at 9:00 A.M., April 14, 1998, over WPIX-TV, New York, NY.
10. See Jeffrey C. Hall, "The Mating of a Fly," *Science* 264 (June 17, 1994), pp. 1702–3.
11. A. A. Peixoto and J. C. Hall, "Analysis of Temperature-Sensitive Mutants Reveals New Genes Involved in the Courtship Song of Drosophila," *Genetics* (February 1998), pp. 827–38.

12. K. D. Finley, B. J. Taylor, M. Milstein, and M. McKeown, "Dissatisfaction, a Gene Involved in Sex-Specific Behavior and Neural Development of Drosophila melanogaster," *Proceedings of the National Academy of Sciences*, February 4, 1997, pp. 914–15.

13. See Marc D. Hauser, *The Evolution of Communication* (Cambridge, MA: MIT Press, 1996), pp. 404–6.

14. See Jane Goodall, *The Chimpanzees of Gombe: Patterns of Behavior* (Cambridge, MA: Belknap Press, 1986), p. 444.

15. *Ibid.*, p. 447.

16. *Ibid.*, pp. 450–51.

17. Quoted in John D'Emilio and Estelle B. Freedman, *Intimate Matters: A History of Sexuality in America* (New York: Harper & Row, 1988), p. 146.

18. For biographical information, see *Who's Who in America 1934–35* and *Who Was Who in America 1943–50*.

19. Edith Belle Lowry and Richard J. Lambert, *Himself: Talks with Men Concerning Themselves* (Chicago: Forbes & Co., 1919), p. 7.

20. *Ibid.*, p. 60.

21. *Ibid.*, pp. 63–64.

22. *Ibid.*, pp. 64–65.

23. *Ibid.*, p. 129.

24. *Ibid.*, pp. 149–51.

25. *Ibid.*, p. 115.

26. Edith Belle Lowry, *Preparing for Womanhood* (Chicago: Forbes & Co., 1918), pp. 139–40.

27. Thomas Walton Galloway, *Love and Marriage: Foundations of Social Health*, National Health Series, ed. National Health Council (New York: Funk & Wagnalls, 1937), p. 11.

28. *Ibid.*, p. 25.

29. See D'Emilio and Freedman, *op. cit.*, p. 207.

30. Winona Wilcox, "Mrs. Wilcox's Answers to Women," *McCall's* (May 1924), p. 116.

31. Winona Wilcox, "Mrs. Wilcox's Answers to Women," *McCall's* (February 1924), p. 114.

32. See Ellen K. Rothman, *Hands and Hearts: A History of Courtship in America* (New York: Basic Books, 1984), p. 22.

33. *Ibid.*, , pp. 224–25.

34. See, for example, Rothman, *op. cit.*, pp. 289–90; and Beth L. Bailey, *From Front Porch to Back Seat: Courtship in Twentieth-Century America* (Baltimore: Johns Hopkins University Press, 1988), p. 78.

35. Alice Stockham, *Tokology: A Book for Every Woman* (Chicago, 1887), quoted in Bailey, *op. cit.*, p. 192.

36. Rothman, *op. cit.*, pp. 224–25.

37. See Bailey, *op. cit.*, p. 80.

38. Quoted in *ibid.*, p. 26.
39. See D'Emilio and Freedman, *op. cit.*, p. 258.
40. Emily Post, *Etiquette: The Blue Book of Social Usage* (New York: Funk & Wagnalls, 1945), p. 161.
41. Marjorie Hillis (Roulston), *Live Alone and Like It: A Guide for the Extra Woman*, intro. by Frank Crowninshield (New York: Sun Dial Press [Bobbs-Merrill], 1936), pp. 93–94.
42. Rothman, *op. cit.*, p. 287.
43. Cheryl Merser, *Honorable Intentions: The Manners of Courtship in the 80s* (New York: Atheneum, 1983), p. 99.
44. *Ibid.*, p. 100.
45. *Ibid.*, p. 110.
46. See *Redbook* (June 1998), p. 110.
47. Andrea Dworkin, *Intercourse* (New York: Free Press, 1987), p. 194.
48. Catharine A. MacKinnon, *Sexual Harassment of Working Women: A Case of Sex Discrimination* (New Haven: Yale University Press, 1979), p. 219.
49. Quoted from Fitzgerald and Weitzman (1990), in Michele A. Paludi and Richard B. Barickman, *Academic and Workplace Sexual Harassment: A Resource Manual* (Albany: SUNY Press, 1991), p. 21.
50. Steven Petrow and Nick Steele, *Essential Book of Gay Manners and Etiquette* (New York: Harper Perennial, 1995).
51. See, for example, Jamake Highwater, *The Mythology of Transgression: Homosexuality as Metaphor* (New York: Oxford University Press, 1997), pp. 232–33.
52. See Andrew Sullivan, *Virtually Normal: An Argument About Homosexuality* (New York: Knopf, 1995).
53. See Nancy Tuckerman and Nancy Dunnan, *The Amy Vanderbilt Complete Book of Etiquette, Entirely Rewritten and Updated* (New York: Doubleday, 1995), pp. 44–45.
54. See Ruth Westheimer, *Dr. Ruth's Guide to Good Sex* (New York: Warner Books, 1983), pp. 183–88.

Epilogue

1. Henry James, *The Bostonians* (1886), ed. Charles R. Anderson (London: Penguin, 1986), p. 327.
2. See Fred Ebb and Bob Fosse, *Chicago: A Musical Vaudeville* (New York: Samuel French, 1976), pp. 84–85.

index